Tibet

Tibet Travel Adventure Guide
by Michael Buckley
First edition: 1999

Published by:
ITMB Publishing Ltd
345 West Broadway
Vancouver, BC V5Y 1P8, Canada
tel: 604-879-3621 & fax: 604-879-4521

Printed in Canada

Text: Copyright © 1999 by Michael Buckley
Photos: Copyright © 1999 by Michael Buckley
Maps: Copyright © 1999 by ITMB Publishing Ltd
Maps & graphics: drawn by Roland Hardt
Book design: by Michael Buckley

Canadian Cataloguing in Publication Data
Buckley, Michael (date)
Tibet travel adventure guide
ISBN 1-895907-98-5
1. Tibet (China)—Guidebooks. I. Title.
DS786.B83 1999 915.1'504'59 C98-910592-X

Caveat: The information contained in guidebooks can change rapidly—even overnight. At the time of going to press, every effort has been made by the author and publisher to ensure that the information contained in this edition is as accurate and up-to-date as possible. The author and publisher do not accept any liability for incorrect information, nor any responsibility for inconvenience, loss or injury sustained by anyone as a result of the advice and information given in this guide.

Other travel adventure guides by ITMB:
Prague and the Czech Republic, ISBN 1895907926
Alaska's Inside Passage Traveller, ISBN 0942297113
Northern California, ISBN 1895907969
Mexico and Central America by Campervan, ISBN 189590787-X
Yukon, ISBN 1895907942

International Travel Maps (ITM) is North America's leading cartographic publisher of international travel reference maps, concentrating on exotic travel destinations in newly-developing travel destinations—in the Himalayas, the Indian sub-continent, Southeast Asia, Latin America, the Caribbean, Africa and the Middle East. Write, phone or fax for a catalogue of ITM titles.

TIBET
Travel Adventure Guide

Michael Buckley

ITMB Publishing ltd

Your Input

Guidebooks are like time capsules—"snapshots" taken when the data was collected. The reader should make allowances for fluctuating rules and regulations in Tibet. A guidebook is a two-way process: your input is invaluable for bringing the next edition up to date. If you notice details that have changed or are inaccurate, drop a line. Marking up maps is especially useful—feel free to photocopy maps, alter them and send them along. I believe a guidebook must do much more than present the facts: it must make sense of them. So I welcome suggestions, comments, beefs, bones of contention, insights, travel tips and travellers' tales. Writers will be acknowledged in the next edition. Drop a postcard or letter to:

Michael Buckley, author
Tibet Travel Adventure Guide
c/o ITMB Publishing Ltd
345 West Broadway
BC V5Y 1P8, Canada

Inspiration, Insights, Thanks

Fellow travellers make a big difference to a project like this: on-the-road inspiration was provided by Gary McCue and Kathy Butler, Terry and James Anstey, Kat, Rene and Kris, Thysje, Johanna, Tess, Barbara, Kozo, Pema, Jorge, Markus, Keith, Tom, John Buchanan, Rocky Dang, Shelley Guardia and all the other great people I met along the way. John Ackerly and Geoff Flack provided written input. Maps form an important component of this book: the digital maps were created by master cartographer Roland Hardt, who made electronic sense of the jumble of data provided, and assisted with graphic material for the book. Jack Joyce of ITMB oversaw the project, read over the text, and offered valuable insights; Stephen Stringall and David Sami provided technical assistance. Special thanks to Vic Marks, Rocky Ingram and John McKercher at the Typeworks for their patience.

About the Author

Michael Buckley has travelled widely in Tibet, China, Central Asia and the Himalayas, visiting many Tibetan enclaves. He is author or co-author of six books about Asian and Himalayan travel. In the course of journeys to Tibet, he has hitch-hiked overland from Chengdu to Lhasa, trekked around Mount Kailash, and mountain-biked from Lhasa to Kathmandu.

Contents

MAPS & PLANS

TIBETAN GEOGRAPHICAL TERMS

chu—river
chumi—spring
dzong—fort
gompa—monastery
kang—ice/snow
la—pass
ri—hill or peak

tang—plain/plateau
tsangpo—river
tso—lake (also *yumco*,
ringco, caka, nor)
compass points—*chang* (N),
nub (W)
shar (E), *lho* (S)

ABBREVIATIONS

ATP—Alien Travel Permit, small
    cardboard folder
CAAC—Civil Aviation Adminis-
    tration of China
CITS—China International Travel
    Service, the official govern-
    ment travel agent
CSWA—China Southwest Air-
    lines, local arm of CAAC, the
    national carrier

PAP—People's Armed Police
    (paramilitary group)
PLA—People's Liberation Army
PRC—People's Republic of China
PSB—Public Security Bureau
    (police)
TAR—Tibetan Autonomous
    Region
TTB—Tibet Tourism Bureau
WWII—World War II

STRANGE DAYS
IN TIBET

stepping into the land of snows

A visit to Tibet is a strange experience, with intense emotional highs and lows. It's weird because the real Tibet no longer exists. Since military occupation in 1950, the Chinese have systematically dismantled the Tibetan social fabric, destroyed its great monasteries, persecuted its monks and nuns—and wreaked devastating damage on Tibet's pristine environment. Any description of present-day Tibet and Tibetan culture must be framed in this context of iron-fisted Chinese occupation.

"Intense" is a word that applies to many aspects of Tibet. It applies to the amazing resilience of the Tibetan people in the face of extreme adversity. Their battle has been largely a pacifist one—suffering, enduring—a game of ultimate patience and tolerance. "Intense" captures the feel of the landscape. The intensity of colours at this elevation is extraordinary—with glacial-blue lakes, luminous-yellow fields of mustard, deep reds and browns of barren rock landscapes, and then, up on the horizon looms an ethereal Himalayan snowcap, backed by piercing blue skies. The colours practically glow: when you show photographs of these landscapes to people who haven't been there, they question the unreal colours—what kind of filter did you use?

Travel in Tibet is a guaranteed adventure, with the wildest, roughest road routes in High Asia. Here are the highest mountains and the highest trekking in the world. Tibetan Buddhist monasteries blend into the landscape, becoming navigation landmarks; imposing fortress ruins cling to sheer hilltops. Nomads herd yaks in snow-dusted pastures; pilgrims prostrate their way across the land to reach the sacred city of Lhasa. It is this combination of extraordinary landscape, extraordinary people and high adventure that makes Tibet so special.

There is only one drawback to visiting Tibet: you can easily become addicted to the place. It makes you reluctant to leave, and as you do, you're already plotting your return. A return not necessarily to Tibet itself, but to Tibetan culture. Sadly, real Tibetan culture is more likely to be found outside Tibet, in places where refugees continue their Buddhist practices, festivals and way of life in exile—in India, Nepal and Bhutan. A section of this book briefly introduces these places as well.

Tourism in Tibet

Should you go? Should you put money in Chinese coffers, thus indirectly subsidising Chinese military bills in Tibet? Most of the tourist business is in the hands of the Chinese—and some of the travel agencies are run by the military. There is the thorny question of lending legitimacy to Chinese government operations by visiting—but more important for the Tibetans is the moral support they get from visitors. Your mere presence in Tibet provides a "buffer zone" in an ugly situation between Chinese and Tibetans.

Tourists love monks. This is one of the great anomalies of tourism in Tibet: the monasteries are kept open and operating because of tourist demand to see them. Apart from Himalayan landscapes, the main tourist "attraction" in Tibet is in fact its monks and monasteries, its Buddhist rituals and sutra-chanting. The Chinese really have no difficulty with this—they simply cash in on it. Apart from making a buck out of Buddhism, the Chinese have absolutely no interest in Tibet's rich culture, its religion or its language. If you go, you line the pockets of Chinese travel agents, hoteliers and airline agents; but if you stay away, you isolate the Tibetans.

What to do? The position of the Tibetan exile leadership is to encourage tourism. When asked about this ethnical dilemma—to go or not to go—Nobel Peace Prize laureate the Dalai Lama responded *yes, go to Tibet, go and see for yourself.* He knows that any Western visitor to Tibet will learn of conditions there and of the aspirations of Tibetans—and cannot fail to be moved by the experience, and will keep the Tibetan issue alive.

In neighbouring Burma, with its appalling human rights record, fellow Nobel laureate Aung San Suu Kyi has adopted a different stance: she has advised travellers to stay away, imposing a form of economic embargo on Burma. Another Burmese phrased it this way: "We would like tourists to come and enjoy our country, but not now: the money they spend will simply water the poisonous plant."

The situation in Tibet is different: there is no organized economic embargo here as there once was against South Africa. The tourist trade in Tibet represents a fraction of the number of visitors going to China. In 1997, according to Chinese figures, 7.4 million foreigners arrived in China for various purposes, including 4.4 million Asians, 1.88 million Europeans, and 827,000 from North America. Out of that total, in 1997, perhaps only 40,000 foreigners visited Tibet (probably matched by an equal number of tourists from mainland China). While tourism is a mainstay of the economy in Tibet, in the overall picture of visits to China, it does not have a high profile. Basically, whether you go to Tibet or not comes down to a personal choice, to be weighed by each traveller.

If you can resolve the question of "Should You Go?" the next thing to consider is: "Can You Go?" The Chinese are suspicious—with good reason—of the activities of independent travellers in Tibet, and have attempted to shepherd visitors into monitored higher-paying group tours. After riots and martial law in the early 1990s, the majority of visitors to Tibet were on group tours. There are, however, ways around this, which you can uncover in this book.

Under the Surface

On the surface, to the casual tourist in Tibet, it may appear that Tibetan Buddhist culture flourishes and that freedom of religion is permitted. Monks chant in deep tones in dark assembly halls, butter-lamps are lit in monastery courtyards by shiny-eyed pilgrims, and monastic festival days such as tanka-unfurling festivals are dutifully observed. But while monks and pilgrims appear to go through the ritual motions—turning prayer wheels, making offerings in temples, and prostrating—this may be all they are doing. These manifestations are largely cosmetic: the atheist Chinese tightly control what goes on through the

Chinese Religious Affairs Bureau. This has led to a variety of "show-case Buddhism"—purely ritualistic icing for tourists.

The crux of the problem for the Chinese is that monks and nuns are the ones who have spearheaded protests against Chinese presence in Tibet and demanded the right to freedom of worship, so a gathering of monks is something that the Chinese fear. Nowhere has this been more dramatically revealed than the case of Monlam, a major festival resumed in 1986. Monlam Chenmo, the great Tibetan prayer festival, coincides with lunar new year celebrations, and takes place around February or March. Or used to. There have been no full Monlam celebrations since 1988, after a series of explosive events.

In 1986, for the first time in over 20 years, Monlam was revived in Lhasa at the request of the Chinese. Whether this was to be a spectacle for tourists, or to show the world that religious freedoms were being resumed, is not clear. Whatever the case, photography of the 1986 Monlam pops up in all kinds of Chinese sources—in photo books, in brochures bolstering the Chinese claim that there is complete religious freedom in Tibet, in video format on the Beijing-produced CD-ROM *Wonders of Tibet*. But the actual festival is no longer held with all monasteries participating.

In the 1950s, with monks coming from all over Tibet, Monlam became a focus for anti-Chinese protests. On March 10, 1959, at the tail-end of Monlam, the Lhasa Uprising took place, with monks taking up guns against the Chinese. So the end of Monlam is a particularly volatile time. In 1986, over a thousand monks from the different monasteries around Lhasa gathered for rites. Huge butter sculptures were displayed outside the Jokhang Temple at the heart of Lhasa—attracting crowds of up to 10,000 people from Lhasa and the valleys beyond.

Versions vary as to exactly what happened at the third Monlam to be staged. March 5, 1988—the last day of Monlam—turned into a riot (close on the heels of the pro-independence riots of October 1987). Apparently, when a procession was in progress around Barkor Bazaar in Lhasa, some monks chanted independence slogans. Stones were thrown at them, and they were warned to keep quiet by the Chinese. When the monks repeated the slogans, a Chinese policeman advanced, drawing his pistol. A Khampa tribesman from east Tibet stepped in to defend the monks, and was shot in the head at point-blank range. Infuriated, the monks paraded the dead man's body around the Barkor. At first the Chinese did not interfere, but by the third circuit of the Barkor, they were using batons and tear-gas—then guns. Eighteen Tibetans died that day: hundreds of Chinese troops stormed the Jokhang Temple and beat a number of monks to death with iron bars; other monks were thrown off the rooftop. Some 800 Tibetans were arrested.

The following year, Monlam was boycotted by the monks. On March 5, 1989, the most severe rioting erupted—as many as 100 Tibetans were killed, Chinese shops were burned, a state of martial law was declared, and all foreigners were ordered out of Lhasa. Martial law was not lifted in Lhasa for 13 months. By late 1991, the situation was back to normal, according to the Chinese. The place was open to tourism—business as usual, albeit with lots of permits, restrictions, checkpoints, and frequent chopping and changing of regulations.

Starting in early 1996, Chinese work-teams occupied all the monasteries and nunneries in Tibet as part of an extensive "re-education" campaign that involved signing of pledges by the monks and nuns to denounce the Dalai Lama and denounce those supporting Tibetan independence.

TIBET IN BRIEF

Reliable statistics on Tibet are very hard to come by, since facts and figures are fudged to suit whatever propaganda department is issuing them.

The Land: The Chinese and the Tibetans refer to different-sized areas when it comes to Tibet. The Tibetans refer to the much larger area of Ethnic Tibet, encompassing the entire Tibetan Plateau, and including the northeastern and eastern areas of Kham and Amdo. Ethnic Tibet or Greater Tibet covers a quarter of China's total area: ethnic Tibet is roughly 2.3 million sq.km, which is almost double the size of what is now called "Tibet" (Xizang Province) by the Chinese. In 1965, the Chinese created the Tibet Autonomous Region (TAR), having previously carving off much of Kham and Amdo and assimilating them into neighbouring Chinese provinces. Even so, the TAR is huge. With an area of 1.2 million sq. km, the TAR is roughly the size of England, France, Germany and Austria put together. The land-locked region of Tibet borders India, Nepal, Bhutan, Burma—and China. Major rivers sourced on the Tibetan Plateau are the Mekong, Yellow, Yangtse, Salween, Yarlung Tsangpo, Indus, Sutlej and Karnali. At the southern border of Tibet are the Himalayan giants of Everest, Lhotse, Makalu and Cho Oyu—the world's highest peaks.

Climate: Cool, high and dry. With an average elevation of 4600 metres, the weather in Tibet can best be described as "extreme," oscillating from searing heat to freezing cold—sometimes in the course of a single day. Climactic conditions vary with elevation and exposure. Strong winds are possible, especially in the spring. In summer there are higher temperatures, with most of Tibet's rainfall occurring during this time. Located on a high plateau, Tibet does not experience heavy monsoons like Nepal, but rainwater build-up combined with glacial meltwater can result in rampaging rivers and flooding in the fall. In winter, severe cold conditions and snowfalls can shut down high passes to traffic.

People: The main groups are Tibetan and Han Chinese. Ethnic Tibetan subgroups—differentiated by cultural, dress and linguistic variations—include the Topa (far-west Tibet), the Khampa (east Tibet), the Golok (from the northeast), and a number of minority groups closely related to Tibetans, such as the Monba and Lhoba (far southern Tibet). Any statistical data on population is dicey. In a 1996 figure, the Chinese claim the population of the TAR is 2.45 million, of which 96% is Tibetan (around 2.35 million), and 4% is Chinese (around 100,000). This does not take into account the number of roving (non-resident) Chinese businesspeople in Tibet, nor Chinese military stationed in Tibet (estimated from 200,000 to 400,000 troops)—they would be registered in other provinces of China. In Lhasa, Chinese civilians and troops clearly outnumber Tibetans. The population of Ethnic Tibet could be 4.5 to 6 million, meaning more Tibetans live outside the TAR than in it. Within Tibet, nearly all Chinese live in urban areas, while 80% of Tibetans live in rural areas—some continuing their nomad ways.

Language: Mandarin Chinese is the official language enforced. Tibetan, which is in the Tibeto-Burman language group, is spoken and written, but given a low profile in schools and very little media exposure. The literacy rate among Tibetans is very low: thought to be less than 25 percent. Many have no access to proper education facilities.

Beliefs: Tibetan Buddhism is the predominant belief, practiced by almost all Tibetans. But it's better described as "showcase Buddhism", rigidly controlled by the Chinese. Officially, the Chinese are atheist, with government and motherland as the reigning deities. The spiritual and political leader of the Tibetans is the Dalai Lama, who is vilified by the Chinese as a "separatist."

Culture: Tibetan culture is closely linked to Tibetan Buddhist beliefs—in former times the majority of literature, music, dance and drama, painting, sculpture and architecture was inspired by those beliefs. Another source of inspiration is folk, deriving from the nomad-herder culture of Tibet. Tibetan culture—ethnic stock, beliefs, customs, language, food—has little in common with Chinese culture.

Government: Communist occupation forces. China invaded Tibet in 1950: Tibet (TAR) is the largest remaining colony in the world. There is nothing even remotely autonomous about the TAR—it is ruled with an iron fist by the Chinese Communist Party.

Economy: The chief crops in Tibet are barley, wheat, millet and buckwheat; among the key industries is craft production. Before 1950, Tibet was self-sufficient in food, with barley as the staple. In the 1960s and 1970s, the Chinese ordered wheat to be planted instead of barley, banned barter, and formed communes—a disastrous policy that led to Tibet's first-ever famines. Now Beijing claims that it has to heavily subsidise the ailing economy in Tibet—but officials fail to mention several key factors. Such as how much money is drained by propping up Chinese settlers and military in Tibet, and how much of Tibet's natural resources are taken out. Half of Tibet's forests have been cut down since 1959. Tibet's mineral resources were largely untouched before 1950: the Chinese have identified reserves of gold, radium, titanium, iron, lead, bauxite and other minerals, including major deposits of uranium.

Flag: The Chinese flag shows five bright yellow stars on a deep red background. Red is the colour of revolution: the large yellow star is said to indicate the Party, while the four smaller stars represent the classes that uphold it—workers, peasants, soldiers and intellectuals. Interpretation of the star symbolism varies: another version has it that the big star is the Han majority, and the smaller stars indicate the key minorities—Tibetans, Uighurs, Mongols and Hui. The pre-1950 Tibetan flag shows two snow lions (white with turquoise manes and tails) upholding the three precious jewels of Buddhism, framed by a snow-covered mountain and a rising sun motif with red and blue rays. The flag is outlawed in Tibet: possessing one is cause for a lengthy jail sentence; displaying one in public has led to summary execution.

TOP 10 TRAVEL QUESTIONS

Can individuals visit Tibet?

Yes—if you're devious. It goes something like this: Chinese officials secretly would like all travellers to be in coddled group tours that spend lots of money; on the other hand, they're reluctant to admit that Tibet is not open, or that Tibet is a special zone in China (which in fact it is). So a compromise is reached: if individuals get together and form a small group, it's acceptable. A group of four is fine. A group of two can work. And even a group of one might pan out (on a tour, with guide). If you come in from Chengdu by plane, the group is around 10; from Kathmandu by plane, around 5 (the oldest person in the group is designated as the leader). You may be required to book a short tour (two or three days) as part of the charade. Once in Lhasa, you drop all pretence of being in a group and revert to your individual self.

When is the best time to go?

April to October is the best time. November is starting to get cold. December and January can be freezing, with heavy snow blocking high passes. Few individuals visit at this time, which means it's hard to find people to share Landcruiser rentals and restaurants may well be closed. The Kathmandu-Lhasa flight does not operate from November to March. February is Tibetan New Year and though cold, can be lively—if you can get in. April can be windy; there's a rainy season around July and August—flooding can cut roads and wash out bridges. Because Tibet is so large, climate conditions change from east to west and with the elevation.

How long do I need for a trip to Tibet?

Ten to twenty days would be good. Six weeks would be better. Two months would be ideal if you plan on going trekking. You need time to adjust to the altitude, and you should build in extra time for delays due to break-downs, road closures, overbooked flights and so on. The Western ethic of rushing around doesn't work well here.

Is a regular Chinese visa good for Tibet?

Yes. According to the Chinese, Tibet is an integral part of China, after all. When you apply for the visa, however, do not mention you want to go to Tibet. While a Chinese visa is good for Tibet, authorities there may not extend your initial visa in Lhasa without fulfilling demands like joining a tour. Therefore get the longest visa you can—two months, three months—at the point of origin. Not all Chinese embassies abroad are created equal. Some will grant you three months, others two months maximum, and still others only one month. As well as securing Chinese visas, group tour operators are issued with a separate permit on a quarto-sized sheet of paper with all members of the tour and their passport numbers listed. This is in theory a "Tibet permit" but it's not stamped in the passport.

How do I get into Tibet?

On a group tour, no problem—the operator takes care of the red tape. As an individual, it's an elaborate game. The name of the game is: Which door is open this week? The first target is Lhasa. There are three or four "doors" to try—sometimes they're open, sometimes they're not. Flights into Lhasa arrive from Kathmandu, Beijing and Chengdu, but you will be screened by China Southwest Airlines and not be allowed to board unless you have the right paperwork. Land routes snake into Lhasa from Kathmandu (Nepal) and Golmud (Qinghai). The best chance is from within mainland China itself— from Chengdu (flight) or Golmud (sleeper bus). Here Chinese travel agents will put you into a group of say, 10 aliens, for ticket purchase. The reason that Chengdu or Golmud are the best approaches is that you're already in China, and since Tibet is an integral part of China (in Chinese eyes), officials are less likely to stop you proceeding.

Once I reach Lhasa, am I free to roam around Tibet?

Not exactly. You will encounter several problems. The first is permits—although some sites in central Tibet are open without permit, many other places may require permits. The second is transport: there are few local buses and they're not in good shape. If there are not enough individual travellers in Lhasa to club together and rent Landcruisers, you may have trouble.

How much is all this going to cost?

Surprisingly, not all that much. Transportation will be your greatest cost: getting there by air can be expensive. If you have anything to do with Landcruiser groups or organised tours, the costs will rise dramatically. On their own, travellers have gotten around by local bus and on foot, and survived quite well—Tibet on $10 a day.

Will I have problems with the altitude?

Tibet is the highest region on earth—so expect some problems adjusting to the altitude. Altitude sickness is unpredictable—some travellers have no symptoms, others suffer mild cases and get over it, others become quite ill. You should be okay if you take it easy for the first few days and allow your body time to adjust to the new environment. If you get really sick, the best advice is to get right out of there by plane.

Should I hand out Dalai Lama pictures?

As of 1996, the trade in Dalai Lama pictures is banned, and there have been several incidents of tourists being detained, interrogated and searched after they were seen giving pictures to Tibetans. Of course, the gifts most appreciated by Tibetans are photos and postcards of the Dalai Lama and books by or about him. However, if a Chinese guide or the police see you giving them to a Tibetan, both you and the Tibetan could get into serious trouble. There's nothing to stop you talking about the Dalai Lama, however—if you have seen the Dalai Lama on television, or read a newspaper story about him, tell the Tibetans about it and assure them of his good health. Tibetans like to have a Dalai Lama picture to place on their home altar (if they can, under current conditions). However, that's not the only picture they put there. They'd be quite happy to place a picture of the Potala Palace or the Jokhang Temple or sacred Mount Kailash there as well. Pilgrims would be very happy to receive those pictures—and they're all street legal.

Are there any restrictions on cameras or video equipment?

No—you can bring in as many rolls of film as you want. To bring in professional video or motion-picture equipment, special clearance is required—meaning you probably won't get it without a ton of paperwork and grovelling. There is no restriction, however, on bringing hand-held camcorders and amateur video equipment—plenty of Chinese and Asians on tour in Tibet bring such gadgets. The equipment is not the problem—it's how and when you use it. A policeman might overlook it if you are in a closed or sensitive region, but making a record that can later be aired in public is a very different case. Taboo subjects include Chinese military (especially on manoeuvres and at checkpoints) and strategic locations like bridges or the airport. Tibetans do not appreciate camera flashes in temples, nor photography of sky burial rituals. Some foreigners have had their film confiscated—and even their camera equipment. At a checkpoint on the Kathmandu-Lhasa road, a bored passenger stood aside and photographed a luggage search in progress. An army officer promptly seized his camera and it was only after considerable argument that the camera was returned—minus the offending film.

TAPPING INTO TIBET

When not busy imprisoning monks or forcing them to renounce the Dalai Lama, Chinese authorities are preoccupied with building Tibet's bright socialist future. On the horizon are more plans for bigger cities, more cities, improved roads—and an expansion of tourist facilities. Among Chinese tourists, Tibet is seen as an exotic corner of the Chinese realm: Miss Tibet contests have been staged in Lhasa, and fashion magazine crews from Beijing have arrived to shoot models on location (we're talking about cameras here). So you see a picture of a Beijing model posing in semi-ethnic gear outside the Potala, or posing next to pilgrims outside the Jokhang. A Chinese chanteuse called Dadawa even dresses up in Tibetan monastic robes on the cover of her CD album, *Sister Drum* (1996), which carries a mock-Tibetan theme with songs like "Sky Burial."

What's next? Well, the Chinese haven't really yet begun to tap Tibet's tourist potential. There's a lot of scope for mountaineering, trekking, mountain-biking and other sport-touring. Eastern Tibet (Kham) has hosted activities like cliff- jumping (paragliding) and white-water rafting. Less well-advertised are hunting trips organised to parts of Qinghai province whereby Western hunters are allowed (for large sums of money) to shoot rare wildlife such as Argali bighorn sheep as trophies. Also on the boards are plans for special events like car rallies across the rooftop, motorcycle rallies, and the creation of tourist theme locations—a therapeutic hot-spring centre for health care, or a fisherman's island where tourists can learn about yak-hide boats (and cruise around in them). Perhaps the next step might be to set up a Tibetan theme park—for the time when there are no Tibetans left on the plateau.

ON THE ROAD
practical information for touring Tibet

The Chinese are very big on "the rules." Everything has stern rules: hotels have rules posted, temples have rules, restaurants may be told not to serve foreigners. Bus stations have rules posted about who can buy tickets and who can't. There are even rules restraining foreigners from riding bicycles. Trouble is, most of the time, the rules are written in Chinese—a deliberate strategy to keep foreigners in the dark. This section attempts to come to grips with rules and protocol and how to get around things like this. Some advice may appear cryptic, or doesn't quite make sense until you get there. Faced with so many rules, regulations and restrictions, you have to maintain your sense of humour. You can amuse yourself by making up your own road rules. A few unofficial laws of the land—and maxims for touring Tibet (from the author): *All loads lead to Lhasa. Lhasa is not Tibet—it's too heavily Chinese-influenced for that. If you get a chance to go to a countryside festival, go!* Another cryptic piece of advice: *When in doubt, split!*

Facilities inside Tibet are poor compared to those in neighbouring regions. Most infrastructure is concentrated in Lhasa—so you can glean more from the *Lhasa* chapter.

Hospitals: Avoid these places like the plague. You might do a lot better in a good hotel room. See the *Staying Healthy* section in this book for the gory details.

Staying in Touch: May your mail be opened, may your phone-calls be monitored, may your faxes be scanned, may your e-mail be scrambled. This is not an ancient curse—it's a reality in today's Tibet, policed by paranoid Chinese. The mailing system in Tibet is quite efficient—letters can get from Lhasa to Europe or North America within a few weeks. Poste Restante exists at the main post office in Lhasa—or you can have letters mailed care of specific hotels (a better option). Sending faxes is expensive, but still cheaper than repeating complex details over the phone (and you will be charged if you get an answering machine at the other end).

Once out of Lhasa or Shigatse, communication becomes more difficult. If planning to send postcards, buy all the stamps in Lhasa, because you may only find small-value stamps in other places—and they will cover the entire postcard. Bring your own posting materials if out of Lhasa. Although places are remote, if there's an army base around, there are probably communication towers and satellite dishes to serve the military. That means IDD phones, sometimes even in remote corners of Tibet. You can use IDD phones to call direct from Lhasa through major hotels or at the main post office. The IDD dial code is 86 (China); the Lhasa area code is 891, Shigatse 892, Tsedang 893. Lhasa phone numbers are 7-digit, with a 63-prefix; other areas of Tibet may have erratic 5, 4 or 3-digit numbers, or no phones at all. A complete IDD Lhasa phone number would look like this: 86–891–6333446 (the number of the CAAC office); while the Fruit Ho-tel in Shigatse would be 86–892–22282. Some other area codes for Chinese cities: Xining, 971; Kunming 871; Chengdu 28.

Time Zone: All China runs on Beijing time, due to the communist craze for centralised planning. The country should have five or six time zones from east to west. Even though Lhasa is thousands of kilometres to the southwest of Beijing and should be on the same time zone as Nepal (which is two and a quarter hours behind Beijing time), it runs on Beijing's clock. If you fly from Lhasa to Kathmandu, that means you actually arrive before you left! So everything is out of synch in Lhasa. Sunday is the non-working day; Saturday might be a half-day. Monday to Saturday, Chinese business hours for banks and other offices like CAAC are (in summer) 9 to 12.30 mornings, then *xiuxi* (siesta—some offices have beds in the back rooms), and open again 3 to 6.30 pm. When they say 9 am, it's actually more like 7 am in real time. Tibetans run on Tibetan time, which is like stepping back a few centuries—it's timeless. Get up when the sun comes up, and go home when the sun goes down. Beijing time is Greenwich Mean Time + 8 hours, or Pacific Standard Time + 16 hours.

Metric & Electric: Electrical supply is 220 volts, 50 hertz, with a variety of plugs: supply in Tibet is either intermittent or unreliable, with frequent blackouts. China uses the metric system of weights, measures and distances—also used in this book. To convert metres to feet, multiply by 3.28; to convert kilometres to miles, multiply by 0.62; to convert kilograms to pounds, multiply by 2.21; a litre is slightly more than a US quart. To convert Celsius to Fahrenheit, multiply by 1.8 and add 32.

MEDIA & INFORMATION

China's one-party state controls all forms of media, making independent reporting impossible. All local news media is closely monitored. In Tibet, foreign news media are not permitted entry unless reporters are considered pro-China and will toe the party line. There are a number of magazines about Tibet, printed in Beijing—the main one is *China's Tibet*. Slick colour brochures on human rights and other "hot topics" are distributed to major hotels in Chengdu and Lhasa.

The Great Electronic Leap Forward: The anarchic internet has reached Beijing, but is still light years away from the Tibetan plateau. What the fax machine was to the dissidents of the 1980s ("seek truth from fax"), the internet is to those of the new era. Surfers in Beijing can be fined if caught using the wrong websites—the crime is "splitting the motherland." There are some internet cafés in Beijing, and many more in other parts of Asia (Kathmandu, Hong Kong, Bangkok, Kuala Lumpur). These offer e-mail services—access is easier through web-based addresses. E-mail has arrived in the Holy City: there are a few places offering the service, such as Barkor Café and Pentoc Guesthouse.

Printed Matter: Anything printed outside China can be screened. However, nonpolitical books like Gary McCue's *Trekking in Tibet* have been spotted for sale at the X-Holiday Inn in Lhasa, along with *Tintin in Tibet*. "Printed matter" extends to message T-shirts:

these have caused Westerners some trouble, too, although Tintin T-shirts are acceptable—and sold in Lhasa. See the *Resources* section at the back of book for a rundown on what's available in the West and in Kathmandu, but not in Tibet itself.

Maps: The only maps available within Tibet and the PRC are the Chinese-produced ones. This is probably because of "cartographic correctness"—Chinese maps show all of Arunachal Pradesh lying in Chinese territory, much to the chagrin of India. For a listing of Western maps available, see *Resources* at the back of the book.

Radio: Tibet Radio is the official Chinese station in Lhasa, which is about all you'd want to say about it. If you bring a shortwave radio, you can pick up the BBC World Service (the Dalai Lama's favourite program—he's addicted) which broadcasts in English. Voice of America (VOA) and Radio Free Asia (RFA) are operated by the US: both broadcast in Tibetan. RFA started in late 1996 and reaches Thailand, Indochina, Indonesia and China—it espouses a free press to authoritarian governments. Apart from a Mandarin segment, there's an RFA Tibetan Service. The Chinese don't seem to like either broadcast: in mid-1998, three RFA journalists who were due to accompany Clinton on his visit to China had their visas revoked. The head of the Tibet section in Washington is Ngapo Jigme, who is one of twelve sons and daughters of Tibet's greatest turncoat, Ngapoi Ngawang Jigme. Ngapo Jigme defected in 1985 and works for the Free Tibet Campaign in Washington. Because Tibet is at such high altitude, there's excellent reception (if the signals are not jammed). Broadcasting in Tibetan is Voice of Tibet (VOT), a programme produced by Tibetan journalists stationed in India, Nepal and other countries (the target area is Tibet and neighbouring countries: VOT cannot be heard outside this range, but can be picked up in RealAudio on the website *www.vot.org*).

Television: Lhasa has its own station, Xizang TV, which is parked near the Potala; other stations or transmitters are located in Shigatse, Tsedang and Gyantse. A couple of channels broadcast in Tibetan, others in Chinese (these programs run the boring socialist gamut from pig farming in central China to ear-splitting Sichuan opera performances). Of higher interest to foreign devils is the late-night news broadcast in English on Beijing's CCTV.

Satellite TV reception is good in Tibet. In Lhasa, the mid-range and high-end hotels pick up VTV, a kind of Indian MTV. On larger satellite dishes—notably the one at the X-Holiday Inn—is CNN. Of course, the average Tibetan gets nowhere near a satellite receiver, but occasionally things work for the better. In 1996, stunned Tibetan staff at a Lhasa hotel gathered to watch a broadcast of the Larry King show where one of the guests was none other than the Dalai Lama.

Hong Kong-based StarTV programming is also available on satellite, including the Star Movie Channel (English movies), Star Sports, and a Chinese movie channel, but not BBC news. In 1994, Rupert Murdoch, chairman of the News Corporation (which owns StarTV), removed the BBC news from his satellite services to China to calm tense relations with Chinese officials who complained about a BBC profile of Mao Zedong and objected to coverage of Chinese dissidents. Although Murdoch has styled himself a foe of totalitarianism and a champion of individual liberty and free speech, in the PRC's case he decided to brush all that under the carpet—because he has extensive holdings in China and ambitious plans to expand them. In 1997, the BBC came under further fire from the PRC because it aired a program on the disappearance of the 11th Panchen Lama.

MONEY & PRICING

Two forms of readily-exchangeable money are travellers cheques and US cash. It's wise to carry some of both. Credit cards are of limited use in China and Tibet—only usable at a major hotel in Lhasa (the X-Holiday Inn takes them). Cash advances on a credit card are possible in Lhasa at the Bank of China. Changing travellers cheques or US cash is not a problem within Tibet or China. The whole idea is that you spend lots of money—otherwise Tibet wouldn't be open. So you can find Bank of China branches in Lhasa, Shigatse, Tsedang, Ali and other large Chinese towns. If not, major hotels can change travellers cheques. For travellers cheques, currencies such as Deutschmarks, English pounds and French francs are acceptable—the two most recognised are American Express and Thomas Cook. Although cash from different nations is accepted by the Bank of China, in places like hotels or on the street, US dollars are more easily negotiated. There's a very slight blackmarket in US dollars, so if banks are closed, you can always change in a shop or maybe at a hotel reception desk.

Chinese currency is *renminbi yuan* (RMB, people's money): it comes in denominations of 1, 2, 5, 10, 20, 50 and 100 yuan paper bills, and small change in the form of 100 fen to the yuan. The 10-yuan bill shows Tibet—well, the north face of Everest. Exchange rates hover around RMB8.3 for US$1 (travellers cheques—a small commission is deducted by the Bank of China; rates should be uniform across the country). The rate is slightly lower for cash: RMB8.1 for $1, with no commission charged (blackmarket maybe RMB8.2 for $1). Other relevant exchange rates: Nepal, 64 rupees to the US dollar (there's a blackmarket in US cash, higher for bigger bills); and Hong Kong SAR, HK$7.75 to the US dollar. Within Asia, you can use ATM machines to access your home bank account using your usual bank card with a 4-digit PIN number. ATM machines are common in Hong Kong, Bangkok and Singapore, but there are none in Kathmandu, and very few in China.

Paying Through The Nose

Pricing in this book is quoted in US dollars. Because pricing fluctuates and is often negotiable, variations may occur. Pricing is not a problem for restaurants and hotels in Tibet—you get used to the expected prices fairly quickly. Prices are negotiable because of the Chinese dual-pricing system (one country, two systems). The highest expenses in Tibet are for long-distance transportation—flights to and from Lhasa, and the cost of hiring Landcruisers.

Dual-pricing System: If you are from Europe, Australia or North America and have a beak-like nose, you are known as *da bizi* (big-nose) by the Chinese. Or *waiguoren* (outland person) or *yangguizi* (foreign devil—derogatory). This is a kind of separate ethnic group—in the Chinese system, Tibetans are barbarians, and foreigners are aliens. The bigger the nose, the more you pay through it. Although in theory there is no dual-pricing system in China, in practice you can pay twice, three, ten, or a hundred times more for certain services. When you buy a $6 ticket to go and see the Potala, you are paying at least ten times the going price that a Chinese or Tibetan person pays. Negotiating prices depends on what you look like, how desperate you look, and how long you're willing to argue. You can bargain for student price for some items (such as the Potala entry ticket, and even bus tickets), but this argument may only be accepted if you're a student in China, with valid ID. Chinese who live overseas (called Overseas Chinese) are often charged a rate that is above Chinese price, but lower than Western price. Usually, the seller deduces they are Overseas Chinese (or from Hong Kong) from their clothing or cameras. Westerners of Asian ethnic background who speak good Chinese can confuse Chinese sellers as they can't rank them in the pricing system.

FOOD & LODGING

Except in larger towns like Lhasa and Shigatse, be prepared for very low standards for food and lodging. It's best to bring your own supplies as back-ups: bring a Thermarest (ultra-light air mattress) and a good sleeping bag to soften the beds and to stay warm, and bring packets of soup, whatever, to compensate for lack of restaurants.

COSTS WITHIN TIBET

Pricing in this book, where given, is in US dollars. Both restaurants and hotels are arranged from low end to high end.

Hotels: These can be easily sized up—they fall into budget, mid-range or group-tour (high-end) categories. Low-end guesthouses charge $1–5 per bed in two-bed, three-bed or larger rooms. Mid-range hotels charge $10–25 for the room (whether occupied by one person, two or three). High-end (group tour) hotels charge $30 and up per room—the tariff can go to $100 and up a room for suites in Lhasa.

Restaurants: Not really a big issue in Tibet as food, if it is available, will be in cheaper teahouses or restaurants, costing around $2–4 a head for a shared meal. Restaurants in deluxe Lhasa hotels could charge $5 to $12 per dish. Occasionally, Chinese-run places might try to gouge Western customers by serving up something that looks like a banquet. Be wary of places that pile on extra dishes—ones that you never ordered—or lay on extras like face-towels and bowls of peanuts (these will appear on the bill).

Permits & Entry Fees: Entry fees for monasteries and tourist attractions (forts, palaces) are usually $1–6 a person, with the asking price for major monasteries hovering around $5 (the Potala Palace charges $6). Students can negotiate half price entry. Posted photo and video permission fees are high: at the Ramoche Temple in Lhasa, a $6 fee for photography permission is levied, and double that for a video-camera (fees for video can go much higher). At the village of Chay an entry fee of $7 per person is charged to access the Everest area to those arriving by Landcruiser. Permit fees to visit certain parts of Tibet can be high—usually one piece of paper is issued, so all names of passport holders can go on it to minimise costs. ATPs cost only a dollar (for the group) but a military permit can be $10 a person. Cultural Bureau permits for Zanda and Tsaparang can run $50 or so. The "permission" to buy a plane ticket or bus ticket into Tibet can run $50–60 a person. Fines if caught in the wrong place can run up to $60, but are negotiable.

Transportation: Bicycle hire is about $3–5 a day in Lhasa. Taxis are a few dollars to get across town. Landcruisers sometimes act as taxis: a Landcruiser from Lhasa to Gonggar Airport (a distance of almost 100 km) costs around $37. Local long-distance buses are cheap, even if you pay double as a foreigner. A run from Lhasa to Shigatse is $8 foreign price. Landcruisers run about $110 to $170 per day for the vehicle, which can take three to four passengers (if no guide, five passengers). This rate includes the driver, the guide, the vehicle and the gasoline, but nothing else. The formula is based largely on kilometres covered on the trip (gasoline consumption), terrain (wear and tear on vehicle), rest days, and so on. The guide fee is generally around $15–20 a day, so if no guide is involved, the Landcruiser rate will be lower.

Dining Out

Tibet is not noted for its culinary arts. China, however, is—ergo, find a Chinese-run restaurant if you want more variety. There's lots of variety in Lhasa—you can find Tibetan, Chinese, Indian and Nepalese cuisine. On the streets you can find fresh fruit and vegetables in abundance, and fresh bread and tangy yoghurt. Tibetans are more inclined to run teahouses with low carpeted tables, which serve tea and momos (meat dumplings) and perhaps the odd potato. Lots of atmosphere, but not a whole lot of food. Lhasa is fine for food, but once out in the countryside, it's pretty much noodles all the way. In the wilder areas, it's tsampa all the way—roasted barley-flour. Tsampa is boring but quite sustaining—you can mix it with soup or noodles (some connoisseurs add powdered milk or other substances to this Tibetan goulash). Not many travellers take to tsampa—the backpacker staple tends to be 761 army-ration biscuits.

Chinese packaged goods are not much more appetising. Olive-green army cans with stewed mandarins or pork or something equally disgusting are resold on the blackmarket. When travelling in Tibet, you should always bring along some food as a back-up, for the times when you're stuck. You can load up in Lhasa on packaged soup and so on. Some bring in freezedried food from the West. Bottled mineral water is available in Lhasa, Shigatse and larger towns in Tibet, where brands include Wahaha, and Potala Palace Mineral Water. Cheaper than bottled water is Chinese beer. Since beer goes through a fermenting process, it's safe to drink—but not advisable at altitude until you've acclimatised (beer should not be drunk if you have the runs, either). Available Chinese brands include Huanghe (Yellow River) and Lhasa Beer.

Hotels & Guesthouses

Low-end guesthouses, teahouse inns and truck-stop places generally offer a bed and not much else. These usually work out to $1–5 a bed, in dormitory-type accommodation with perhaps four beds to a room. If there's a dirt floor, a lumpy bed and a tap in the yard, you've hit rock bottom. Bedbugs can be a problem in low-end hotels. A notch up are Chinese concrete-blockhouse hotels, usually with several storeys, and possibly some internal plumbing. These places charge about $10–25 for the room, no matter if your party is single, double, or triple—so you can reduce costs by sharing. The more creature comforts you get, the higher the tariff. If you get your very own bathroom, with your own plumbing, even higher. Because of shoddy workmanship, it turns out half these gadgets fail to function, and yet you are paying for them being in the room. Some foreigners have successfully bargained down the price of a room due to absence of electricity to power the devices like the TV or the hot water. In this range are hotels designed for visiting Chinese—these may be off-limits to Westerners.

At the high end are group-tour hotels, with rooms $30–60 and up (if you have three people sharing a room, that may still only be $10 a bed). These definitely have plumbing—even hot water—and rooms with real lightbulbs and possibly satellite TV reception. Even so, the prices for the rooms are often inflated, and discounts are frequently offered to tour operators. The hotel lobby often features a dining hall, souvenir shop, bar and so on. It may even have a foreign exchange counter and a small business section able to handle faxes and IDD calls. Even if you don't stay in a high-end hotel, you can wander in and shop or use the services there: naturally, the tariff will higher than normal. There are half a dozen hotels of this standard in Lhasa; and one hotel in this class in Shigatse, Gyantse, Tsedang and Zhangmu. Another is found near Shegar. These high-end hotels may have cheap dormitories tucked away—so inquire.

Plumbing Notes: Hot showers are a rarity in low and mid-range hotels in Tibet—though they are easy to find in Lhasa. You are therefore often dependent on hot water from the large Chinese thermoses supplied at hotels, which is boiled up by solar cookers on the rooftop or with a furnace. Hotels do not automatically provide thermoses. You may have to ask—or wheedle or cajole—to get one. By using a bucket or wash-basin, you can manage basic ablutions. The hot water thermoses can also be used for making soup or tea, and if you let it cool overnight, can be carried in your own bottle as drinking water. Tibetan and Chinese toilets are of the bomb-bay door design (squat and hope). They're usually filthy. In high-end hotels, there are Western sit-down models. When Shigatse Hotel started operation, fancy imported plumbing was brought in. An overweight woman on a group tour sat on one of these brand-new pieces of porcelain—and the sit-down unit broke away from its mooring. The woman was not injured, but she was furious—she threatened to sue the manager over the poorly-installed equipment. The hotel manager promptly confiscated the passports for the group and said that they would not be returned unless he was compensated for the full value of the imported plumbing that had been destroyed. Confronted with this, the group-tour leader decided to pay up.

GEAR

Good heavy ammunition boots are the best for men, and stout ankle boots for women, and both may, if desired, be hobnailed. A pair of comfortable slippers is a great relief after the day's march is done, and should not be forgotten. Woollen socks and stockings are the best, and should be thick. To avoid chafing, boric powder should be dusted inside them before putting them on, and the toes and heels rubbed on the outside with soup. In the event of blisters developing, they should be pricked with a sterilised needle, Germoline applied, and a lint and cottonwood pad placed over them to protect them from further chafing while marching.

That paragraph comes from *Touring in Sikkim in Tibet,* a slim guidebook written in 1930 by David Macdonald, former British Trade Agent in Gyantse. Makes travel sound painful; in the 1930s, travellers rode or marched into Tibet with pack animals and an entourage of porters, carrying 30-kilogram tents, a portable bath, hurricane lanterns, stove and so on. One porter was assigned to carrying the tiffin basket, which contained crockery, cutlery and provisions for lunch. Times have changed—those 1930s travellers would have been amazed at the strong, lightweight camping gear and clothing on the market now, with the wonders of Goretex and Velcro.

Even so, on a trip to Tibet, you may end up with a lot of gear. What to take? Pepper spray for the dogs? A shovel for the propaganda? A shortwave radio? All kinds of equipment springs to mind—but can you carry it? A good idea, before you set out, is to assemble all your gear, shoulder it, and walk a dozen blocks—or better yet, hike up the nearest mountain. Carrying luggage at altitude is much more work than at sea level: the emphasis in your gear should be on strong, lightweight stuff that performs multiple functions. And you should remember that the gear you take is not the final weight: you may purchase souvenirs or books en route, adding to the burden. So you have to figure out where the weight lies, and how to reduce it without compromising on essentials like medical supplies.

High on my list would be a good pair of hiking shoes with ankle support—lightweight, strong, broken in. You rely on your feet a lot in Tibet. The next priority would be a strong flashlight that has a long battery life (and a supply of batteries). Due to erratic or non-existent electrical supply in Tibet, you constantly need a flashlight—for illuminating dark frescoes in monasteries, for finding your way around at night, for visiting the outhouse at night. Clothing for dealing with extremes of heat, cold and wind is essential. Rain and dampness are not so much of a problem—Tibet is high and extremely dry. Dust is a big problem. Silk items favoured by skiers are ideal for insulating—they're lightweight and durable. A thick pile sweater and a windproof jacket (Goretex is good) should provide protection against biting wind and cold. For more on clothing, sunglasses and protection from the elements, read the *Staying Healthy* section, which has a rundown on essential medical supplies.

If you plan to get off the track in Tibet, you need a good sleeping bag. These are bulky, but you'll find a Chinese quilt is much more bulky—though these are supplied in most guesthouses, off the track they may not be, and you can't afford to freeze or lose sleep. If a guesthouse is already warm enough, you can use a sleeping bag to cushion the bed. A sleeping bag with a down fill is recommended because it's compact, lightweight and insulates well—get one rated to sub-zero temperatures. A compact Thermarest (ultra-light air mattress) is also a good idea—in case you end up sleeping on the floor of a teahouse.

In the gadget line, an altimeter will be helpful—make sure it goes to 6000 metres. Some wristwatches have in-built altimeters, so the question is not what time, but how high.

What you bring really depends on what kind of trip you're planning. If travelling in a Landcruiser, consider that luggage space in the back is minimal if sharing with three other passengers. Obviously if you want to go trekking, you will need to be fairly self-sufficient gearwise. While supplies and food can be bought in Lhasa, these items will be heavy and clumsy. Discarded expedition gear is readily available in Kathmandu, and of high quality—but the same is not true of Lhasa. If high quality gear can be found at all in Lhasa, it will be very expensive. If you are planning to go cycling or do a lot of trekking, you might want to think about importing your own freezedried food and other supplies. Concentrate on food that can be "cooked" by adding hot water to the package and letting it sit for a few minutes. This way you can use the thermoses of hot water supplied in most hotels. While you can buy a stove in Lhasa, it will be an unwieldy kerosene stove that weighs a ton. If you want a light, compact stove that operates off any fuel source, bring it with you. The rotgut Chinese liquor sold in various parts of Tibet can power a stove.

If you're travelling by Landcruiser or truck, you may find that your backpack or main duffle bag is out of reach—buried under other baggage. Thus you need to keep a day-pack with essential items such as camera and so on with you; some day-packs have an external mesh holder for a water bottle. Within easy reach also should be food supplies if you stop for lunch: some travellers purchase a cheap vinyl bag in Lhasa to hold food supplies and things like candles—separating this from the main baggage. If staying longer in Tibet, you can use Lhasa as a base, so you could leave a duffle bag in guesthouse storage while off gallivanting around. Cargo duffles have lockable zippers on them to deflect prying fingers.

Bring all your film with you. To rephrase that: bring a lot more than you think you'll need. The price of film in Lhasa can be double that of Chengdu, and slide film can be hard to find. If you're passing through, Hong Kong is a good place to buy film or process it. The light in outdoor situations in Tibet is so intense that you can make wonderful use of fine-grained lowspeed slide film like Kodachrome 25 or Fuji Velvia 50. You will probably want a polarising filter to reduce glare. Another situation commonly encountered is exactly the opposite: a dim interior where you need a highspeed film (ISO 400 and up)—flash may be forbidden.

A couple of other notes on gear: if you don't have it, maybe your fellow travellers do. Message boards at the budget hotels in Lhasa carry ads from travellers selling sleeping bags, film, camping gear, medicines, freezedried food—or even left-over oxygen. Travellers can become fixated with their stuff and spend hours in needless aggravation over what to take. Get that part over quickly and shift your attention to more important matters like plotting your route, reading up on the areas you plan to visit, reading up on Tibetan culture and learning some Tibetan language. Knowledge is the most important thing to carry with you.

CUSTOMS & CONDUCT

Meeting Tibetans

Tibetans are a spontaneous lot—they have no trouble breaking the ice. They'll probably examine your camera, fondle your luggage or shake you down for Dalai Lama pictures. Or give you a big grin. Tibetans have great sense of humour, they're self-reliant, amazingly hardy, and have none of the shyness or coolness that the Chinese

ETHICAL GUIDELINES

The following section has been adapted from a set of ethical guidelines published by the International Campaign for Tibet. For further up-to-date information and advice, contact: The International Campaign for Tibet, 1825 K St, NW, Suite 520, Washington, D.C., 20006 (website: *www.savetibet.org*).

Respecting Customs

Tibetans are extremely religious people and appreciate foreigners respecting a few simple customs; always walk clockwise around Buddhist religious sites and within monasteries or nunneries. Take hats off, do not smoke and do not touch figures or use flash photography inside monasteries or nunneries unless it has been cleared with the monks or nuns. Do not jump queues of pilgrims within monasteries nor interrupt ceremonies. Try to be an unobtrusive visitor but feel free to show interest and ask questions. It is also important not to touch the heads or point your feet towards monks or nuns, and be careful with physical contact with them. Dress appropriately when going to any religious site—remember it is a holy place.

Sky Burial: Do not encroach on Tibetan burial rituals (known as sky or celestial burials). This unique system of disposing of the remains of the dead is a sacred and private affair—it is not proper for visitors to Tibet to intrude into a family's last rites. Some Tibetans believe photos can steal their soul. At any rate, taking pictures of people can be rude and intrusive. Put yourself in their place before you take each and every photograph.

Support Religious Freedom: Donations left on altars or donation boxes in the large monasteries will go to a committee controlled by the Chinese Communist Party, and not necessarily used for religious purposes. Donations can be made directly to individual monks and nuns or given in kind. Clothing, food, film or books are much appreciated, but don't give your dirty castoffs. Donations to smaller, out-of-the-way monasteries will be used properly, according to traditional Tibetan custom, since they are not as tightly regulated by Chinese authorities. Items such as candles, prayer flags, a bag of *tsampa* or some tea are always appreciated at remote monasteries. A wonderful way to spend some time with monastic people is to share your food. Walk the Barkor at sunrise with the Tibetans! It's a peaceful experience and allows you to be with the Tibetan people in a way that shows your support for their religious freedom.

Buy from Tibetans

If you want to support the Tibetan people, culture and their economy, buy from Tibetan shops and stalls. A large influx of Chinese immigrants in Lhasa and other Tibetan cities are now taking over the economy and putting Tibetans out of work. The Dalai Lama has called this influx possibly the greatest threat to the survival of Tibetan culture. This general rule also applies to Tibetan restaurants and tea stalls. Eat Tibetan food rather than Chinese imported foodstuffs. Inflation is also a very real problem in Tibet. You contribute to this by paying exorbitant prices to vendors, which can increase prices Tibetans must pay for goods. Don't be cheap, on the other hand. If you find a piece of finely woven cloth or a carving you like, pay a fair price for the amount of work entailed. Bargaining is a part of Tibetan life—unfortunately, being ripped off by tourists is also becoming a part of their life.

Do Not Buy Antiques: Most of Tibet's artistic treasures have already been destroyed or plundered by Chinese troops. Please leave antiques in Tibet. This goes for all family heirlooms as well as religious items. Since it is difficult to tell what is antique and what is not, a good rule of thumb to follow is that if someone tries to sell you something secretly, don't buy it. Stick to public stores and stalls. Families are often forced to sell their treasured items to put food on the table. Be creative and find other ways of helping Tibetans without taking away their culture.

Eco-Tourism

Help protect Tibet's wildlife—do not buy product made from wild animals, especially from endangered species (i.e. skins of the snow leopard and tiger, horns of Tibetan antelopes, paws of the Himalayan brown bear, or any medicinal products made from animals). If you see these items, take photographs and notify the World Wildlife Fund or the International Campaign for Tibet. This holds true for cities in Tibet, as well as Nepal, China, Hong Kong or anywhere else you come across these products.

Leave Only Footprints: The Himalayan ecosystem is a fragile one. If you go trekking use kerosene, even where wood is available. Wet trash should be buried 30 metres (100 feet) from a water source, paper burned, and cans and bottles packed up with you to a hotel or large town. Do not leave this up to your guide as environmental awareness is often low, especially among the Chinese. Plan ahead and bring food that has little packaging. Travel light and don't demand five-course meals. Bring your own food as villages rarely have surplus. If you want to bring presents for locals along the way, think carefully. Don't bring plastic baubles or contribute to begging by handing out a lot of freebies. It is much more appropriate to share time and a cup of tea with people, or play a game of jacks with the children. Tibet is becoming littered with human waste and toilet paper—bury excrement and toilet paper! Be careful where you hike as erosion and damage to fragile plants are increasingly becoming a threat to the health of the plateau and mountains.

Interacting

Try and use knowledgeable Tibetan guides. All travel companies must work through a travel operator in Lhasa. It is important to select a company which works with a Lhasa-based operator, run and staffed by Tibetans as opposed to Chinese. To quote one experienced guide, "When you go to France, you don't want a German tour guide; when you go to Tibet you don't want a Chinese one." Moreover, using Tibetan-staffed companies promotes Tibetan culture and employs Tibetans. Check and see if one of the Tibetan-run agencies is operating at the time of your visit to Tibet.

If you are on a tour with an official Chinese government guide, do not expect accurate answers to historical, religious, or political questions. Educate yourself before you leave! Read books about the history of Tibet and its people. John Avedon's *In Exile from the Land of Snows* is a classic and the Dalai Lama's autobiography *Freedom In Exile* is very informative. Reading some Chinese propaganda before you leave may help you to recognize false statements when encountered in Tibet.

Breaking Away: Almost everyone who visits Tibet says that the best part was their interaction with Tibetans. In small groups, wander the streets, follow the hillside paths or get outside of the town and visit a village. Revisit a monastery without the group or spend time in a tea stall in the market. Photos of your family and neighbourhood or Tibetan communities and celebrations abroad are great conversation pieces—don't worry

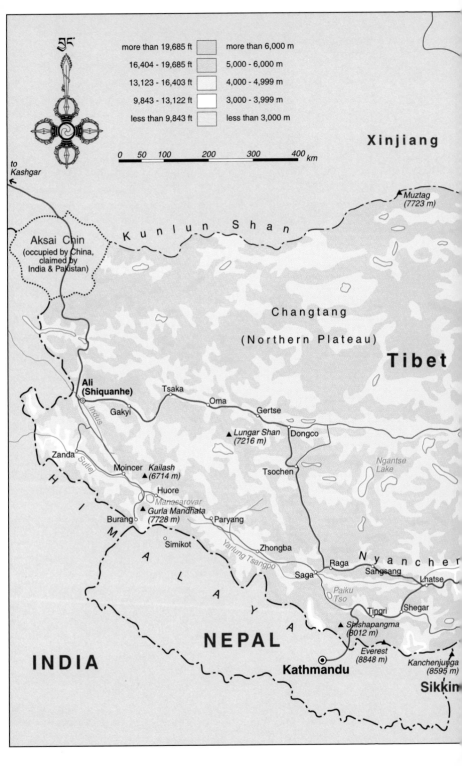

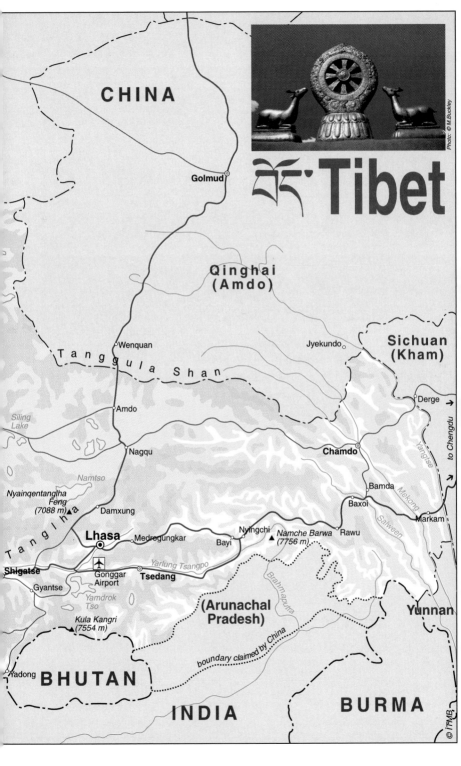

CHINA

Golmud

ཨོཾ Tibet

Photo: © M.Buckley

Qinghai
(Amdo)

Siling
Lake

Wenquan

Jyekundo

Sichuan
(Kham)

T a n g g u l a   S h a n

Amdo

Derge

to Chengdu

Namtso

Nagqu

Chamdo

Yangtse

Nyainqentanglha
Feng
(7088 m)▲a

Damxung

Bamda

Baxoi

Mekong

Markam

T a n g i h 'a

Lhasa

Medrogungkar

Bayi

Nyingchi

Namche Barwa
(7756 m)▲

Rawu

Salween

Shigatse

Gonggar
Airport

Yarlung Tsangpo

Tsedang

Gyantse

Yamdrok
Tso

Brahmaputra

Yunnan

Kula Kangri
▲(7554 m)

(Arunachal
Pradesh)

Yadong

BHUTAN

boundary claimed by China

INDIA

BURMA

© TMB

Rooftop landscapes: Yamdrok Tso / near Tingri / Yumbulagang fortress

about the language barrier. Tibetans would much rather have you attempt their own language rather than speak Chinese. Be mindful of approaching Tibetans in front of Chinese, particularly soldiers. Depending on current Chinese restrictions, Tibetans can be openly criticized or interrogated for associations with foreigners. Always be careful around dogs; they are numerous in most parts of Tibet and trained to protect their territory.

Being Critical: Don't be frightened by dire warnings that the Chinese will lock you in jail and throw away the key for your support of the Tibetans. You should however, be careful, and never endanger the Tibetans, but let the Chinese know when you disapprove of actions such as the use of monasteries for grain storage, the malevolence shown by police in and around religious sites, and unfair hiring and school enrolment practices. You can do a lot for the Tibetans and their cause, and will most probably want to after you come to know these wonderful people.

bring to bear on foreigners. They are usually direct, open and honest in their dealings. Tibetan women have a fairly high status, although they still do heavier work than the men. Outside of Lhasa, few Tibetans speak English: those that do are likely to have been educated in India. Put a Tibetan phrasebook to good use: any attempt at speaking the language is greatly appreciated. There are other ways to communicate: gestures like thumbs up and thumbs down go over well, as does singing in any language. If you're patient enough, it's only a matter of time before you are invited in for tea—or something stronger. Any kind of pictures you have are a great way of communicating. That extends to picture books on Tibet—these are engrossing to your host.

Interactions with Tibetans are not always so pleasant. Unfortunately, for a lengthy period Tibet was only open to group tours, who were in the habit of handing out pens, candy and Polaroid pictures to Tibetan kids: these same urchins may expect the similar gifts from you, and will get antsy if nothing is forthcoming. On a more serious note, when interacting with Tibetans, you have a responsibility. When it comes to an overheard political discussion, not a lot will happen to you, a foreigner—at the most, you'll be booted out of Tibet. For the Tibetan, however, it could mean interrogation and jail. An Italian tourist interviewed a monk on video about Tibetan independence, and then took the videotape to a Chinese Embassy back in Italy to protest the treatment of Tibetans. The monk in the video was traced and received a 14-year jail sentence.

Protocol

The following PSB notice appeared on the walls of budget hotels around Lhasa. The first 5 items of the notice are quoted (out of 7). Curiously, there is no mention of "Tibet" or "Tibetans"—the latter are referred to either as "Chinese citizens" or "minority nationality."

NOTICE: Ladies and Gentlemen: Welcome to Lhasa. So you may have safe and enjoyable travels, we would like you to be aware of the following government regulations. 1: Foreigners travelling to China must abide by Chinese law and must not endanger the national security of China, harm its public interests, disturb the public order, or engage in any other activities incompatible with tourist status. 2: If Chinese citizens are holding a rally or demonstration, it is strictly forbidden for foreigners to participate, follow along with, take pictures, or video film any of these activities. Foreigners are not permitted to interfere in Chinese internal affairs. 3: Foreigners are forbidden to distribute any propaganda material and join in any religious activity. 4: In accordance with regulations, foreign tourists must go through all registration formality and stay only at a designated hotel. Without prior permission, it is forbidden to travel in unopened areas, to operate individual business or privately take up an occupation. 5: It is forbidden to visit or photo the sky burial site according to the local government's regulations for the minority nationality's habits and customs. the tourist who breaks this regulation will be punished strictly.

Being Watched

Without being too paranoid about things, you should be aware that if you appear to be any kind of activist or have any connections to the Tibetan government-in-exile, your actions may be watched. You may be followed, your interaction with Tibetans noted—and your room may even be bugged. Sounds unreal? It has happened. In one case, in Beijing, a person speaking on the phone in French was asked by a Chinese wire-tapper to switch to English because he couldn't follow the conversation! In Lhasa, in 1996, a traveller wrote a political comment about Tibet in a book (for complaints) at the counter of the Bank of China: the PSB promptly tracked him down, exacted a confession, cancelled his visa, and gave him an exit visa—meaning he had three days to fly out of Lhasa, back to Kathmandu. The Chinese are not good sports when it comes to criticism.

There's no particular reason to be worried when dealing with police, army or other officials. If you are formally arrested, your embassy must usually be notified within four days. You have the right to speak to a consular officer: you can demand that a call be placed to your embassy. Incidents involving foreigners in Tibet have ranged from warnings to hotel interrogations, to confinement to a hotel for four days (Dalai Lama tapes found in baggage in Shigatse after police were tipped off), to deportation. Three tourists watching demonstrations in Lhasa in 1994 had their passports confiscated. There have also been reports of Westerners given a mild dusting-up—kicked or punched—when dealing with security officials.

In the Chinese system, if you are arrested, you are automatically guilty of something. Do not assume that innocence in a Western situation would mean you're in the clear in China. Chinese logic is different. Cast aside any notions of justice, put aside ideas of politeness and gentility, and respect. There is no innocent here: you're either guilty and you admit it—and you'll get off lightly—or you're guilty and you deny it, in which case you'll be heavily fined, deported at your expense, or otherwise punished. The arresting person would lose face if you were entirely innocent. You must leave a way out for the arresting officer—the usual method is making a written confession. There is nothing binding about these confessions—they're not legal documents. You can promise to the hilt on a confession, and then go out and break those promises the next day.

Under no circumstances should you let someone else write that confession for you (especially in Chinese!) to be signed. Insist that you write it yourself. Irksome though confessions may sound, they are really meaningless pieces of paper. Phrases that please are: "my ancestors would be ashamed of me," or "I will never even think of doing this again." In the early days of Tibet travel, a British backpacker was busy writing his confession about being in a closed area when the arresting officer noticed that he'd extended his own visa—the highest level of naughtiness conceivable. Unperturbed, the traveller continued writing his confession: "In addition to the above, I must humbly confess that I have extended my own visa, for which...."

Close encounters are usually of the PSB kind—over travel permits. As long as your papers are in order, there's nothing to worry about: if you get off the track, the legality of your travels is sometimes at the whim of the particular PSB official you are dealing with, at which point a small "fine" may be levied, going directly into his pocket. These fines are negotiable: if he asks for $100, wait until it drops to $20 or $10. Packets of foreign-brand cigarettes go down well with the Beijing Boys. Sometimes the crime is just too "serious" and the PSB won't back off. Two Germans who were caught collecting high-altitude bug specimens were fined over $300 by PSB for their illicit activities. PSB officers have amusing English-language phrasebooks for dealing with foreigners in situations like this ("Please sign your interrogation"—things like that). The military—mostly teenaged recruits—do not seem particularly concerned about foreigners, except at checkpoints.

STAYING HEALTHY

An alternate title for this section might be: Staying Alive. This material is not intended to scare you away from visiting Tibet. Rather, it is intended to make you aware of the dangers involved if you happen to get really sick, to encourage you to travel with at least one friend as a back-up in case things go wrong, and to encourage you to obtain comprehensive evacuation insurance before visiting Tibet.

Informing Yourself

The following medical matters may venture into uncharted territory, especially concerning altitude sickness. This section is a broad outline—it does not cover matters in great detail. Draw your own conclusions—and then consult other sources and experts for more thorough answers. Information on altitude sickness is hard to come by because it's not a common problem in the West. There are some books out on the subject, but these tend to get out of date as knowledge evolves. It's best to contact the experts: you can consult a website operated by the Himalaya Rescue Association in Nepal (*www.nepalonline.net/hra*). The HRA uses Western volunteer doctors to deal with altitude problems involving trekkers, so they have case histories to draw conclusions from. Former volunteer Thomas Dietz, who originally designed their website, has his own website in Oregon called the High Altitude Medicine Guide (at *www.gorge.net/hamg*). For general health concerns, The Centers for Disease Control and Prevention, based in Atlanta, Georgia, maintains a website at *www.cdc.gov/travel/travel.hml* with the latest information on prevention guidelines and strategies.

Some important facts to know before you go: Tibetan and Chinese hygiene standards are atrocious, and Chinese medical facilities within Tibet are appalling. Some conclusions to draw: you have to be your own doctor in Tibet, you have to be willing to help fellow travellers in dire situations, and you have to be prepared to evacuate if the need arises, so you need good medical insurance. Prior to departure, go and visit your local health unit and get an armful of relevant shots (get Havrix and Engerix shots as long-term protection against Hepatitis A and B). You can get some shots in Kathmandu also. Talk to your doctor and arm yourself with drugs—Ciprofloxacin (for diarrhea), antibiotics (in case you get a real infection) and Diamox (to deal with altitude). Assemble a good medical kit (see below). Check out where your embassies lie in China and in the neighbouring region—note down the addresses and contact numbers. Bring a health certificate to China (it may be checked). Find out your blood group and record it on that document.

Evacuation Insurance

You are strongly advised to carry comprehensive air evacuation insurance for a trip to Tibet. Hopefully, you will never have to use it. Your best strategy if you fall really sick in Tibet is to get right out of Tibet—and China—as fast as you can, and make a beeline for somewhere with hospitals that have real doctors, like Singapore. Use regular scheduled flights to get out of Tibet if possible. Evacuation by air can cost a fortune. Check your travel insurance to ensure that it covers emergency evacuation costs, and more specifically, if it will cover evacuation by crews like AEA or SOS, both of which have clinics in Beijing with expat doctors and imported medicines. Better yet, take out direct insurance with either AEA or SOS (for addresses and contact numbers, see the Evacuation section that follows).

Himalayan Medical Kit

Failing adequate health care in Tibet, you really need to be your own doctor. There are Chinese pharmacies in Lhasa, but medication may bear Chinese instructions and may not be familiar to Western eyes. Kathmandu and Hong Kong are quite well-stocked with Western drugs and will issue medication without prescription. You can easily find drugs like Diamox in Kathmandu (check expiry dates). While you can't be a travelling drugstore, you'll need a larger-than-usual medical kit in Tibet. If travelling with a friend or a small group, divide up a medical kit to share the weight. Camping and outdoor stores in the West sell pre-packaged medical kits that you can customise to your needs (you can even find "Himalaya kits." Items like antiseptic cream and bandaids (plasters) are hard to find in Lhasa. Take along a Swiss Army knife with scissors and tweezers. You'll need your own water bottle and purifying tablets (or filter).

A medical kit may contain a ready-made package—sealed and labelled—with sterile needles and syringes. It is highly recommended you carry these in case blood samples or injections are required. Take along any prescription drugs you need, as well as back-ups of things you are dependent upon—such as glasses. Your chances of finding contact lens solution in Shigatse are zero: dust can be a major problem for contact lenses in Tibet (take along regular glasses as a back-up). Glasses or no glasses, dust can cause eye irritation—you might want to take along soothing eyedrops.

See the *Common Problems in Tibet* section (following) for ideas on arming yourself for the rigours of Tibet—you will need medications like cough lozenges, codeine and Contact C (for colds); moisturisers, lip balm, sunglasses, sunscreen and other balms will help combat the effects of sun, wind and altitude. Recommended drugs for Tibet include: Diamox to help acclimatise, Ciprofloxacin for diarrhea (also a general antibiotic), and a phial of iodine tablets for purifying water.

Travellers buy a medical kit but overlook the importance of the medical knowledge required to go with it. A pocket-sized booklet would be worth bringing along—there are several on the market, such as *The Pocket Doctor* or *Holiday Health*. If you're leaving Tibet and returning directly home, you should consider selling or donating your precious cache of medicines and other supplies to incoming travellers. Drugs like Diamox have an expiry period and will be of little use to you in the West anyway.

The Buddy System

When you go diving, you use the buddy system. You watch out for your friend underwater, which is an alien environment and a potentially dangerous one. You could draw close parallels in Tibet: high altitude is an alien environment. If someone gets altitude sickness, he or she becomes confused and disorientated, and cannot make the right decisions. Someone else has to take those decisions. Back yourself up in Tibet with at least one buddy. And be prepared to watch out for others in a Landcruiser group if someone falls sick.

Running on Empty

To keep your system ticking properly, you need proper nutrition and high fluid intake. And that's hard to achieve outside Lhasa. So carry vitamin pills and carry freezedried soups, and carry extra food supplies—dried fruit, whatever, to supplement the meagre local offerings. You should think in terms of what can be "cooked" with the hot water supplied in thermoses in hotels and truck-stops: check the cooking times on soup packets (ideally, only a few minutes in hot water). Packets of soup are the best item here—soup is easily prepared and gives the illusion of a hot meal. *Tsampa,* the Tibetan food staple, is sustaining but tasteless—it can be mixed in with soup to make it more palatable. You can get run-down without proper nutrition intake: this makes you more susceptible to coming down with other ailments.

Fluid Intake

Two essentials concerning water: making sure the water is safe to drink, and drinking enough of it. Even though Tibet is high and the water looks crystal clear, it could be contaminated by herders and livestock on higher ground. It's best to always filter water or boil it. Staying hydrated is essential in Tibet to combat dryness and the effects of altitude. Even if you have to overload your system, keep drinking your quota of water—about four litres a day. If you get a case of the runs, you'll lose a lot of body fluids, so you need to keeping drinking water to stay hydrated. You can buy bottled water in Lhasa and larger towns in Tibet—make sure the seal is intact. The water supplied in Chinese thermoses in hotels is usually reliable since it has been boiled at high temperatures. You have to wait for this to cool down, or else drink it in tea. You should take along your own water purifying devices—the simplest is an iodine cup filter. Iodine tablets can be purchased cheaply in the West. Iodine-treated water tastes horrible—but you can buy another tablet that removes that taste. Or take along Gatorade flavouring crystals to neutralise the taste. These and other electrolyte powders are sodium and potassium, which will help restore body fluid balance (one of the main ingredients in sweat is sodium).

Hygiene Hazards

Washing and cleaning activities are a low priority with Tibetans: explanations range from lack of hot water to layering themselves with dirt to protect the skin from sun. Both Tibetan and Chinese hygiene standards are shocking; toilets are disgusting. You have to be careful about the handling of food and water—do not accept the cold face-towels offered in restaurants. In restaurants, stick to well-cooked hot food (noodles are fine). Boil it, peel it—or forget it. Some travellers prefer to use their own eating utensils, bringing an aluminium mug and spoon (soup can be served in the mug).

Although hot showers are readily available in Lhasa, in the rest of Tibet you won't be so lucky. There are the occasional hot springs to soak in, but that's about it: the rivers and lakes are pretty cold. Out of Lhasa, you have to rely on the thermos of hot water supplied to your room (or ask for it). The thermos is a source of hot water for tea, or for making soup—and can also be used for bathing. A metal basin is often supplied in the room (sometimes with a special wooden stand to hold it), so you can pour water in and wash yourself in stages (hair one day, and so on). Another technique is to soak a thin towel (preferably your own) and apply it Japanese-style, as in a sushi restaurant. Thin, spongy Western sport-towels are ideal for this as you can wring them out to dry quickly.

Dire Rear

Because of low hygiene standards, it is eminently possible that you will get a case of the runs. Usually, this is not a problem—just stick to a simple diet with liquid back-up: water, clear soups, and unsweetened juices. Do not drink beer or milk, and avoid spicy or fatty foods as they can aggravate your condition. The problem should pass within a few days. In Kathmandu you can buy packets with rehydration crystals—a mixture of glucose and salt. If these are unavailable, you can make your own by adding two or three teaspoons of salt—and a similar amount of sugar—to a litre-bottle of purified water. Packets with electrolyte rehydration powders (sodium/potassium crystals) are efficacious. If problems persist, it may be a case of bacterial diarrhea—refer to *Intestinal Bugs* (following).

The Elements

Sunburn, windburn, chapped lips, lobster-face and red-eye are definite hazards in Tibet due to the (at times) ferocious effects of the sun, wind and cold. Once you get cracked lips or chapped hands, you'll find these take a long time to heal and can be very bothersome. Moisturisers are the answer: bring along hand and face cream moisturisers (these can also be purchased in Lhasa). You need a good sunblock cream (preferably containing Paba) and chapstick (also with Paba). A hat of some kind—preferably covering the ears and neck—is essential, as are high-quality sunglasses or glacier glasses that block UV rays (ideal are *dark* polarising lenses). The use of certain drugs such as the antibiotic Tetracycline can render a person more sun-sensitised, and result in bad sunburn. One of the greatest hazards in Tibet is dust. It can get into your eyes, so contact lenses are not a great idea—dust can be very irritating if it gets under them. A silk scarf or bandanna, wrapped around your nose, throat and mouth (bandito-style) will generally filter the dust out of your breathing apparatus in extreme conditions, and the same scarf can be used round your neck to keep you warm in a sudden change of temperature.

Coughs, Colds & Sore Throats

Respiratory ailments are quite common in Tibet, and can turn very nasty when combined with the effects of extreme dryness and alti-tude. Take care. These are not your normal colds—they can be persis-tent and debilitating. New (mutating) strains of flu, originating in China, can be knock-outs. The best way to avoid this syndrome is to make sure you don't undergo drastic changes of body temperature. Make sure that you have clothing that you can layer on or off, to cope with the extremes of heat and cold—sometimes occurring on the same day in Tibet. This also applies to sleeping arrangements—there's not much heating in hotels in Tibet. Bring your own medicines for coughs, colds and sore throats. Some stronger drugs (codeine compounds) can be multipurpose—for headache, pain, coughs or colds. Tuberculosis exists in Tibet: the airborne bacteria are transmit-ted through coughing, sneezing or spitting by people in an infectious stage of TB. Conditions can be very smokey in Tibetan teahouses—with a fire burning away in the middle, and no ventilation.

DANGER ZONE

Accidents

It's unknown how many foreigners have perished in Tibet due to dri-ving accidents, but there have certainly been cases of trucks and Landcruisers being totalled, and foreigners killed. There are no safety devices along precipitous mountain roads in Tibet and few warning signs. Your fate rests with your driver's road skills. Drivers range from excellent to downright dangerous. Assess the state of your driver and his judgement calls—if he's going too fast or taking un-necessary risks, tell him to slow down and get his act together. If he looks sleepy, keep him awake—or rearrange the itinerary so you stay in the nearest hotel, where he can rest up. Avoid driving at night.

You are bound to experience some pretty close calls in Tibet. One Landcruiser hit a flock of sheep—resulting in a smashed front windshield (the passengers were all right—the incensed shepherd had to be compensated, and the group continued, albeit a bit frozen with the windshield missing). Another tour group in a Landcruiser rounded a corner near a high pass and clipped an oncoming truck in a Chinese military convoy. The drivers got out to argue. Meanwhile, another truck in the same convoy came round the corner and hit the Landcruiser again. More arguments broke out. And then a third truck hit the Landcruiser—this time moving it closer to the edge of a precipice, at which point the passengers scattered. In another situation, our driver played chicken with a military convoy, doing daredevil overtakes on mountain roads with sheer drop-offs. After overtaking all the trucks, the driver called for a pit-stop—at which time all the army trucks overtook us again.

You most likely don't want to even think about this, but you have to consider what would happen if there was an accident. The biggest problem could be loss of blood. It's not known to what degree hospitals in China or Tibet screen their blood—tainted blood carries all kinds of viruses, including those for hepatitis and HIV. Then there's the question of whether your blood type will even be stocked. Blood Type O is rare. The Chinese neither have nor store Rh-negative blood for transfusions: you'd have to be evacuated to the nearest Rh-negative country.

Dogs, Curs, Mongrels, Hounds

Tibetans are fond of dogs: these hounds perform guard duties in many villages around Tibet. Dogs are believed to be reincarnates of renegade monks who didn't quite make the grade, and hence are accepted at monasteries. Some are in good shape; others are mangy and fleabitten. Sometimes dogs operate in packs around monasteries, in which case they can be benign (lazing around, or curled up in corners) or they can be extremely dangerous. Travellers have been attacked and dragged to the ground in some places, and then rescued by monks. This can lead to lacerations requiring stitches—not a pleasant thought.

If a bite from a dog punctures the skin, it can lead to a far greater problem: rabies. If bitten by a dog, clean the wound thoroughly with soap and water. The incubation period for rabies is two months, depending on where the victim is bitten. If the victim is not given rabies shots within a certain time, then the result is fatal. Dogs are known to carry rabies in Tibet: to be on the safe side, if a dog draws blood, you'd have to get a course of rabies shots (the set of 10 shots costs around $800 in the US). You can get rabies vaccine at the People's Hospital in Lhasa, and also at clinics in Kathmandu (though there may be a shortage of the vaccine). Rabies is endemic in most parts of Nepal, and rabid street dogs are a cause for concern. You can obtain pre-exposure vaccination for rabies but not many travellers bother (even if you get these shots, you still need post-bite shots, but not as many).

The best strategy here is not to get bitten in the first place. Treat all dogs with extreme caution: carry a stick, or an umbrella, or pick up a stone if a dog approaches. If a dog attacks, try and clobber it on the sensitive snout area. You might also consider squirting a waterbottle at a dog or using pepper spray.

Intestinal Bugs

If diarrhea is persistent, with blood or mucus in the stool, this indicates a more serious illness such as amoebic or bacillary dysentery. In this case, you need a stool test to identify the culprit—merely guessing and indulging in "drug cocktails" may be detrimental. Facilities to identify bugs like this are not available in Lhasa; the nearest place is a Western-run clinic in Kathmandu, Hong Kong or Bangkok. Drugs to treat intestinal bugs are readily available in these places. For bacterial diarrhea, the best treatment is to take Ciprofloxacin or Norfloxacin. More of a problem is giardia, caused by a microscopic parasite that can elude some water filters (iodine kills it). Giardia-like symptoms include stomach cramps, sulphurous burps or gas, and persistent diarrhea: it's like something is bubbling away down there. You can treat it with tinidazole (another drug is metronidazole, also known as flagyl). Hepatitis is a viral infection of the liver, primarily spread through contaminated food and water, or dirty needles. Hepatitis is chronic in Nepal—you're advised to get long-term inoculation against it (Havrix and Engerix, or Twinrix) before you leave home. Various types of intestinal worms are also prevalent in Nepal—the larvae are often present in unwashed vegetables or undercooked meat. Intestinal worms are awful to contemplate, but not of great concern since drugs like mebendazole are highly effective in killing them. Stool tests can detect the culprits.

Acute Exposure

It can get *very* cold overnight in Tibet—and if you happen to be in the back of a truck, you may get frozen solid. Silk articles, favoured by Western skiers, are especially useful for countering the cold—they're light and pack easily (balaclavas, long-johns, T-shirts, scarves, gloves). Wool and polypropylene clothing also insulates well. A woollen tuke or similar headgear will go a long way toward countering the cold. A dangerous condition, caused by rapid heat loss, is hypothermia: this is brought about physical exhaustion when cold and wet. Symptoms include uncontrolled shivering. Shelter is the most important thing here: strip off wet clothing and replace with dry. In severe cases, the person should be stripped and placed in a sleeping bag with another person to share body heat. Do not rub affected limbs.

Frostbite is the most extreme result of rapid body-heat loss. It affects the tips of the extremities first—toes, fingers and nose. In these areas the blood freezes, preventing circulation as ice crystals expand in the cells. Again it is essential to find shelter, and immerse the affected part in lukewarm water if available. Surface frostbite can be thawed with another person's body heat—do not rub the affected part. Snow blindness results when bright sun reflected off snow (or ice or water surfaces) burns the cornea of the eye. The eyes feel like there is grit in them, appear bloodshot, and eyelids may puff up and swell shut. The condition is alarming but temporary—rest and soothe the eyes with cold compresses or eyedrops, and the condition should clear up in a few days. Wearing glacier glasses with total UV block is the way to prevent this condition.

Altitude Sickness

When Sherpas say climbing is in their blood, they may mean it literally. Sherpas have a physiology adapted to the high-altitude environment—their blood has a higher red-cell count, and their lung capacity is larger. Ability to adapt to altitude is thought to be in your genes. That may mean you either have the high-altitude genes or you don't. If you do, you can adapt quickly; if you don't, it will take longer—or so the theory goes. At higher altitudes, air pressure is lower, and the air is thinner. Although it contains the same percentage of oxygen as it does at sea level, there's less oxygen delivered in each lungful of air. So you have to breathe harder, and your body has to convert to more red blood-cells to carry the oxygen through the system.

Altitude sickness is something of a mystery. It does not appear to depend on being in shape: athletes have come down with it, and it may occur in subjects who have not experienced it before. Altitude Sickness generally occurs at elevations above 2000 metres, becomes pronounced at 3500 metres, and then requires adjustment at each 400 metres of elevation gain after that.

Terrain above 5000 metres (common enough in Tibet) is a harsh, alien environment—above 6000 metres is a zone where humans were never meant to go. Like diving at depth, going to high altitudes requires special adjustments. To adapt, you have to be in tune with your body. You need to travel with someone who can monitor your condition—and back you up (get you out) if something should go wrong. Consider this: if you were to be transported in a hot-air balloon and dropped on the summit of Everest, without oxygen you would collapse within 10 minutes, and die within an hour. However, a handful of climbers have summited Everest without oxygen: by attaining a degree of acclimatisation, they have been able to achieve this. A similar analogy could be drawn with flying in from Chengdu, which is barely above sea level, to Lhasa, at 3650 metres. That's a 3500-metre gain in an hour or so. You need to rest and recover. Coming by land from Kathmandu, you rise from 1300 metres up over a 5200-metre-pass at Tong La—a gain of 4000 metres over a few days (to soften the blow, it would be worth staying a few days at Nyalam, which is 3750 metres).

The study of altitude sickness is still evolving. Recent studies suggest that altitude sickness may be due to leaky membranes—which are more permeable as you go up in elevation. It was unknown if a person could survive above 7500 metres without oxygen until 1978, when Messner and Habeler summited Everest. Actually, a hundred years earlier, in 1875, French balloonist Tissandier reached 8000 metres after a three-hour ascent and lost consciousness: the balloon descended and Tissandier survived but his two companions died. Messner was told he would come back from Everest a raving madman, or, at the very least, a brain-damaged automaton if he attempted the peak without oxygen. Messner got his timing right, got to the top, and went on to bag all the 8000-metre peaks without oxygen. Climbers like Messner, however, will admit to impaired functions at higher elevations—and to strange encounters. Messner recalls talking to his ice axe, talking to his feet, talking to an imaginary companion and having hallucinations.

Altitude Strategy

It is essential to take it easy for the first three or four days after arriving at altitude; most acclimatisation takes place within the first 10 days (it can take two or three months to fully acclimatise). When reaching altitude, most travellers experience discomfort—headaches, fatigue, nausea, vomiting, lack of appetite, swelling of the hands or feet, difficulty sleeping. This condition is usually mild and short-lived. Headaches can be treated with aspirin: if a headache persists, or intensifies—or if the person wakes up with a headache—this is a sign of real altitude sickness. The critical question is how to distinguish between mild altitude sickness and more serious cases—read on. You don't acclimatise by sitting around doing nothing—get some simple exercise like walking, and drink lots of water. Do not drink alcohol, as it contributes to dehydration. Smoking, of course, will be a major problem at altitude.

Never underestimate altitude—it can be a killer. Go slow, be careful, experiment before you go higher. The climber's maxim is "walk high, sleep low"—climbers may trek higher during the day, but retire to lower levels to sleep. The maximum rate of ascent when trekking should be about 400 metres a day. If you're acclimatised to Lhasa (3650 metres) you really need to undergo a second acclimatisation phase to handle a visit to Lake Namtso (at 4650 metres). On a brighter note, once you've acclimatised to a particular altitude, the altered blood-chemistry should stay with you for about ten days. So if you acclimatise to the 5000-metre level and then go down to 3500 metres, you should be able to go back up to 5000 metres again without ill effects, provided you do so within 10 days.

Diamox: Diamox (Acetazolamide) is a diuretic that can help alleviate the symptoms of altitude sickness. It does not prevent you getting altitude sickness, nor does it solve the problem, but it does ease your passage when, say, arriving in Lhasa by air, or when going up and over and down a pass within the same day. It may also improve the quality of sleep at altitude. Since it's a diuretic, it leads to increased urination and to dehydration, so you need to keep drinking more if you use it. Other side effects include a tingling sensation in the lips and fingertips, and the medication may give a strange taste to carbonated drinks. You don't have to follow the dosage—the normal dosage is 250mg every 12 hours, but you could take half the recommended dosage (cut the tablets in half). If a person comes down with AMS, the dosage can be increased slightly to 250mg every six hours. With no alternative drugs for altitude sickness, it might be worth carrying Diamox along. However, its use is controversial, and it's a sulphur drug, which some have allergies to. Check with your doctor.

Acute Mountain Sickness

Acute Mountain Sickness (AMS) is a general term for a whole raft of altitude-related maladies. Symptoms of AMS include gastro-intestinal turmoil (loss of appetite, nausea, vomiting), extreme fatigue or weakness, dizziness or lightheadedness, and difficulty breathing or sleeping.

A case of severe AMS may result in High-Altitude Pulmonary Edema (HAPE), when a small amount of fluid that appears in the lungs at altitude is not absorbed normally. Instead, it accumulates, obstructing the flow of oxygen and drowning the victim in his or her own fluids. Symptoms include rapid respiratory rate and rapid pulse, cough, crackles or wheezing in one or both lungs, frothy or blood-stained sputum, and severe shortness of breath. Another serious complication is High-Altitude Cerebral Edema (HACE), where the fluid problem is in the brain. A person with HACE is disoriented, has an unsteady gait and trouble using the hands, is irritable, suffers from drowsiness and nightmares, and may suffer hallucinations. Memory, judgement and perception are impaired.

To counter HAPE and HACE, mountaineering expeditions some-times tote a Gamow bag, which weighs about 8 kilograms. It is a body-enclosing bag that can be hand-pumped to replicate atmos-pheric pressure at much lower levels. Recent studies suggest that a one-hour treatment corresponds to a descent of 1500 metres: this leads to short-term improvements, but nothing lasting. Some group tour operators carry a tank of oxygen to deal with cases—but that tank may only hold 30 minutes of oxygen (Landcruiser drivers some-times carry oxygen). Drugs like Diamox are also used to counter the effects of altitude. The best solution, however, in all cases, is simply to transport the patient to a lower elevation—as fast as possible (if this means moving in the middle of the night, do so). Unfortunately, on the Tibetan plateau, descent to lower elevation is not always feasible. In serious cases, the focus is often evacuation by road to Kathmandu, or by air to either Kathmandu or Chengdu.

EVACUATION

Medical conditions are so poor in Tibet that in the case of a serious ca-sualty or a severe altitude problem, air evacuation is the only safe op-tion. However, herein lies a conundrum because the patient must be in stable condition to be transferred by air. If the patient can be brought to Gonggar Airport without too much trauma, then you can organise the evacuation yourself. If there are other complications, you may have to go through your embassy, as one of the main sources of evacuation is military aircraft, as in a jet chartered from the PLA.

Chinese Medical Facilities

Chinese hospitals are appalling in China generally, and completely primitive in Tibet. You're better off avoiding hospitals altogether and taking a good hotel room instead. I have personally seen, in Tibetan clinics, rusting antiquated equipment, and filthy wards and operat-ing theatres (and filthy doctors—sighted one doctor greeting patients wearing a blood-spattered apron and smoking a cigarette). There's a shortage of sterile equipment and supplies; the most basic facilities for diagnosis and treatment are generally absent; doctors and nurses are poorly trained. Surgical gloves may be washed and re-used—and the same with syringes. A disturbing trend in some hospitals in Tibet is to subject the patient to a cardiogram, an X-ray and a glucose drip—regardless of what illness is presented—and then charge for these services. A person suffering from altitude sickness doesn't need an X-ray.

In Lhasa, the best facilities are at the Military Hospital, but this place is not usually accessible to tourists. The People's Hospital has an emergency centre, but no mechanism for dealing with seriously injured people. An Italian NGO has been supplying equipment and training at the People's Hospital. Costs for foreigners staying at the People's Hospital in Lhasa can be very high, and payment may be expected in Chinese cash (travellers cheques will probably not be accepted, and nor will credit cards).

The nearest places in China for good medical attention are Chengdu (a hospital can run $120 a day for foreigners), Hong Kong (even more expensive), and in major cities like Beijing and Shanghai. Elsewhere in Asia, any place that has a lot of foreign embassies is good for clinics and hospitals with Western standards, often staffed by Western doctors. The best are found in Singapore and Bangkok. Clinics in Nepal are staffed by Western doctors.

Medevac Crews

Asia Emergency Assistance (AEA) is a Singapore-based organisation that will evacuate to Singapore if possible. There are branches in Asia and around the world. In Beijing, contact AEA at 14 Liangmahe S. Rd 1/F, Beijing 100600, tel. 8610–6492–9112, fax 8610–6462–9111; in Singapore, tel. 65–3382311, fax 65–33877611. International SOS Assistance is a worldwide private company with regional head offices in Singapore, Geneva and Philadelphia. In Beijing, contact SOS at Kunlun Hotel, Suite 433, 2 Xin Yuan Nan Lu, Beijing, tel. 8610–6500–3419, fax 8610–6501–6048; in Singapore, tel. 65–226–3936, fax 65–226–3937; SOS has a website also (*www.intsos.com*). Another emergency medical assistance firm is MEDEX, Regus Office 19, Beijing Lufthansa Centre, No. 50 Liangmaqiao Rd., Beijing 100016. Tel. 8610–6465–1264, fax 8610–6465–1267.

Risky Situations

The best advice that can be offered in risky medical situations in Tibet is this: when in doubt, evacuate. Get on a regular scheduled flight to

Kathmandu or Chengdu (an alternative is to take a Landcruiser down to Nepal, but this could take three days or more). When sufficiently pressured, airline authorities will bump passengers off a regular flight to Chengdu or Kathmandu to create space for an emergency case, so the idea is to get to Gonggar Airport as fast as possible.

If it's a case of altitude sickness, it's essential to get oxygen for the patient as fast as possible. The X-Holiday Inn has oxygen "pillows" (pillows with nasal tubes attached); you can also buy oxygen in a sort of aerosol can (or larger tank) in Lhasa itself at a commercial outlet just west of the Potala.

The above evacuation advice is offered because (a) medical facilities in Tibet are completely primitive; (b) there is no system of helicopter rescue in Tibet; and (c) the Chinese don't give a fig about sick or dying tourists anyway.

If you think that last statement is unfair, then allow me to present the following macabre case, the details of which have been verified by the Western tour operator. In 1987, an elderly tourist on a group tour to Tibet died of a massive heart attack in his sleep. It was just a few days into the tour; his wife (back in North America) was phoned to inform her, and was asked what should be done. She requested that her husband be cremated, and that the ashes be brought back with the tour. The cremation was promptly carried out—and the ashes were transported around in the group leader's carry bag, in a small jar-like urn with a sealed top. Some time later, the dead man's wife requested a refund for the trip from the tour operator, who duly contacted CITS in China. CITS informed the operator that the wife did not qualify for a refund, because her husband had indeed completed the tour—posthumously, in the urn. Logical Chinese thinking at its best.

Worst Case Scenarios

Several foreigners who have died in Tibet could have been saved by evacuation. In 1991 a British tourist died from altitude sickness after being admitted to the People's Hospital. Repeated requests by a Western doctor to evacuate him were overruled by the senior medical staff at the hospital, who claimed the patient would recover. An American tourist who visited the patient said that when she checked his oxygen tank, it was empty and he was gasping for air. There seemed to be no sense of emergency on the part of the nurses. The following year, a Swiss woman with a similar altitude problem was evacuated from Lhasa by a team sent to collect the patient at the insistence of the Swiss Embassy. Again, Chinese medical opinion held that her case was not serious. Due to evacuation, she survived. Moral of

TOO HIGH FOR CHOPPERS

In Nepal, a radio or phone message can be dispatched to Kathmandu and a rescue helicopter will fly out to pick up an injured trekker for a fee of $2000. In Tibet, there's simply nothing like that. As for flying a Nepalese helicopter into Tibet, there are many complications. Flying over high-altitude terrain is a great danger for helicopter pilots, and with no proper maps of the area, they would be flying by sight. Helicopters have a limited range—usually only a few hundred kilometres—before they require refuelling. The Chinese military would not be keen on the idea of a Nepalese chopper flying over Tibetan terrain for obvious reasons.

In 1996, a 73-year-old German woman on a group tour had a stroke in far western Tibet, at Zanda. There were two Land-cruisers of German tourists in her group, including a doctor who mistook her condition for a case of altitude sickness, and recommended she rest for a few days in Zanda. They left her behind with a Nepali Sherpa who spoke no German. The woman was taken to Zanda's only clinic—a tiny place for the military.

Two American travellers who went to visit the woman were shocked by what they saw: the hospital was filthy, there was human waste all over the place, and the woman was on an unsterile IV drip. They cleaned up, and changed the woman's clothing as best they could: the terrified woman was calmed by seeing Western faces; the Chinese doctor was doing his best with the limited equipment at his disposal. The Americans realised that if the woman didn't make it to Nepal, she wouldn't pull through. They managed to contact the German embassy in Kathmandu on an IDD line, and tried to arrange for a Nepalese helicopter to fly into Zanda. However, because of the German hosting of a Tibet conference in 1996, the communication lines between the German embassy and the Chinese embassy were slow. By the time a helicopter was approved to make the rescue, five days had passed—the woman's condition seriously deteriorated, and she died.

Zanda lies at 3660 metres, so it would have been feasible for a helicopter to land there, but other parts of Tibet, a pass of 5600 metres (18,370 feet) is not uncommon, and a helicopter must fly above that, so high-altitude complications would definitely arise. At altitude, the air is so thin that helicopter rotors have nothing to cut into—making landing, take-off, or even hovering manoeuvres quite dangerous. There are US-made high-alti-

Sikorsky and Boeing CH-47 choppers in Tibet, but these are solely for military use, as are military airfields scattered around Tibet.

One of the highest-altitude helicopter rescues in history was a mission carried out in 1996 on the Nepalese flanks of Everest. This was an evacuation at 6000 metres (19,700 feet) made by Nepalese pilot Madan K.C., flying a French Squirrel helicopter, to evacuate two badly frostbitten climbers. Apparently, 6000 metres is the upper limit of this kind of chopper. So delicate was this operation that the pilot had to leave his co-pilot lower down, and could only rescue one climber at a time.

the story: don't trust the opinion of unconcerned Chinese medical staff. Here are a few more cases where evacuation worked and the patient survived—barely.

Case One: A young backpacker in the rear of a truck was sleeping with his arms and elbows resting on the edge, where the tarpaulin meets the metal compartment. Somehow the truck was sideswiped by an oncoming truck—the impact smashed one arm and ripped the other right out of its socket. Quick action by fellow travellers saved his life. The missing arm was found on the highway, and the truck raced back to Lhasa—fortunately, a fellow traveller with some medical knowledge managed to stem the flow of blood on key arteries for the 12-hour ride. The backpacker was then airlifted to Chengdu and on to Europe. He lost the arm. He was very lucky—he could easily have died through blood loss. Good medical insurance covered the air and hospitalisation bills.

Case Two: In August 1997, a 56-year-old French woman who had been travelling alone was found in a coma near Nagqu, 250 km north of Lhasa. She had a fractured pelvis: her injuries were probably caused by a road accident. The woman was transported to the People's Hospital in Lhasa, but the hospital was unable to provide a ventilator for the patient—oxygen was delivered through nasal tubes. The hospital did not carry out any X-rays, nor did they provide any medical records for the patient; her belongings disappeared.

After intervention by the French Embassy, an evacuation was arranged by AEA medical personnel, operating a Lear jet from Hong Kong. AEA is an international evacuation group—a joint-venture company which is reportedly part-owned by the PLA. Dr Richard Condon, who collected the French woman from Lhasa and provided medical treatment during the flight to Hong Kong via Chengdu, said that although AEA carries out evacuations all over the world, this one was one of the most difficult he has experienced logistically. The

People's Hospital refused to release the French woman until a bill of $11,000 had been paid for an 8-day stay in the hospital, plus another $3500 paid for transporting the woman from Nagqu to Lhasa. The bill was sent to the Beijing office of the woman's insurance company, Worldwide Assistance. The money was immediately raised by the International Campaign for Tibet, where the woman had previously worked as a part-time volunteer. As soon as the money was paid, the woman in the coma was released and flown in the Lear jet to Hong Kong. From here she was evacuated to Paris, where she remained in a coma.

HITTING THE ROOF

Getting into Tibet is a two- or three-part operation. First you have to make it to a staging-point like Hong Kong, Chengdu or Kathmandu. Then you wrangle with paperwork and ticketing, run the gauntlet of Chinese officialdom into China, and strike for Lhasa. Once safely in Lhasa, you can fan out to visit other parts of Tibet. "Hitting the Roof" is an oblique reference to the way you will feel when you deal with Chinese officials. It's also what will probably happen to you when you ride in a Landcruiser in Tibet. Bouncing across the roof of the world.

RED TAPE

Visa Shopping

This may sound odd, but the best place to get a long Chinese visa is within China—in Hong Kong. Hong Kong since the handover operates as a Special Administrative Region (SAR), with the Chinese Embassy simply altering its name to PRC Visa Issuing Office. There are certain things you should be careful with when applying for a visa. Do not mention Tibet or Xinjiang as destinations. Travellers have had their visa application knocked back solely for doing this— and told they need special permission to travel to those places. Safer destinations to mention are Beijing and Shanghai. Reason for visit: tourism. Your job: do not put down Reporter, Journalist, Writer, Photographer, Missionary or Politician, as your visa will probably not be processed. These people require special permission to travel in places like Tibet—a complex procedure that may not succeed. Travel agents in Hong Kong will advise you how to fill in the application. Agents in Hong Kong that can get visas include Phoenix Services Agency,

Friendship Travel, Lee Wah Travel, and Star Tours & Travel.

The visa issued in Hong Kong may start running immediately (from the date of issue), which means you'll lose a week or so just getting to Tibet. Visas from other embassies usually start from the date of entry into China, and will give you a two or three-month leeway to get there. Embassies closer to China are the most liberal in issuing longer visas, it seems. Hong Kong is good (three-month visa or longer is possible). Hanoi is not bad (two months possible); Islamabad offers a two-month visa; the Delhi embassy may provide a two-month visa if prodded. You might try home base and see if you can wrangle a three-month visa. Explain that China is a big place and you need a long time to see it all. Visa extensions are difficult within Tibet, but easy in other parts of China.

Probably the worst place in the world to apply for a Chinese visa is Kathmandu. The situation could change, but the Chinese Embassy in Kathmandu is in the habit of only issuing visas for the length of a tour to Tibet booked through an agent in Kathmandu. You cannot apply to the embassy as an individual: you can only approach them through a travel agent. Although there's no shortage of travel agents handling the Tibet trade in Kathmandu, prices can be steep—and then you have to work out how to jump the tour, since your visa may be short. Some agents are more amenable to the idea of booking you on a short tour, but guaranteeing you a longer Chinese visa—ask around.

If you already have a Chinese visa issued elsewhere and apply for a short Tibet tour in Kathmandu, the embassy in Kathmandu will simply cancel it and reissue another visa valid for the length of the tour. Some travellers have managed to argue that they want to fly on from Lhasa to Beijing after their tour and need the extra visa time, but this is a special dispensation. See the following section about attempting the overland crossing to Lhasa from Kathmandu, using a Chinese visa not issued in Kathmandu.

Special Permits: There is no such thing as a "Tibet Permit." This has been concocted by the airlines and police. It's a piece of paper listing the group participants on a tour. It is sometimes issued *without* a visa by the Chinese Embassy in Kathmandu for those on a tour of Tibet round-trip from Kathmandu.

Timing

Rules and regulations concerning travel in Tibet chop and change as often as the weather does with El Nino. So the following sections may be out of whack: make adjustments. There are several times of year when it is difficult to impossible to get into Lhasa. Winter is an ob-

GROUP TOURING

The majority of travellers to Tibet are on group tours. The ones that aren't often end up one way or another on impromptu tours involving Landcruisers or trucks. The Chinese would prefer that all foreigners travel this way. Why? Because tours are easy to monitor and because they get a sanitised version of Tibet. Participants are carefully insulated from the Tibetans, and chaperoned by Chinese guides with a totally warped sense of history (no sense of culture). Group tour operators take care of all the logistical problems—permits, transport, food and so on—but in the process you may lose out on other dimensions. Tours to Tibet are quite costly—even the ones organised out of Kathmandu rack up the bills.

On the plus side, group tour operators seem to magically transcend all the permit obstacles. They can mount trips and treks that individuals drool over—the vanguard of what's possible. Groups cross the border from Kailash into Nepal or India; they trek into the Karta Valley east of Everest; they engage Bactrian camels to trek into K2 base camp north of Ali; they cross the Nepalese border into Tibet with their own Western truck and driver (an Exodus Expeditions truck has been permitted to drive on the route from Kathmandu to Lhasa, on to Dunhuang and Kashgar, and down to Islamabad—a six-week trip). Expeditions liaising with Tibet Mountaineering Association (TMA) or Tibet International Sports Travel (TIST) have arranged a number of firsts—taking on trekking peaks, white-water rafting, mountain-biking, hot-air ballooning and paragliding in Tibet.

vious one—there are no flights from Kathmandu and fewer from Chengdu. The Chinese may be nervous if some military bigwig or political leader is visiting—might just shut the whole thing down for a few weeks. Nothing is guaranteed in Tibet, no guidebook written in stone. Allow for changing information.

The Tibetan calendar is filled with unofficial anniversaries—security is tight at these times, with Chinese troops on alert 10 days before and after the sensitive period. You may have trouble getting into Tibet or travelling around at these times. The easiest travel months are April, June and August (however, June to August is the most heavily booked period for flights into Lhasa). Among the "hot" times are: Losar (Tibetan New Year, around February); March 5th (commemorating major protests in 1988–89; March 10th (anniversary of 1959 Lhasa uprising); May 23rd (marks the 1951 surrender to the Chinese with the 17-point agreement); July 6th (Dalai Lama's birthday); 27 September (start of 1987 riots); October 1st (1987 protest in which Tibetans were shot dead); and December 10th (international human rights day, which sparked a protest in 1988). Tibetans sometimes gather at countryside locations to picnic and throw tsampa in the air to mark special occasions.

If you get a chance to see something more formal, like a festival in the countryside, go! If you're lucky there might be a horse-racing festival in progress at Damxung or Gyantse, or a tanka-unfurling ceremony at one of the monasteries within reach of Lhasa. There used to be festivals at every full moon in Tibet, but many were abolished by Chinese authorities, nervous about large gatherings of Tibetans. The festivals that survive are based on the lunar calendar, which is complex and unpredictable (usually only announced in February, at Losar or Tibetan New Year). Ask around when you arrive in Tibet to confirm if there are likely to be any festivals in progress.

Customs & Searches

Customs and checkpoint searches in Tibet are of the hit-and-miss variety. Some are waved through, others get the third degree. If a suspicious item is found in a Landcruiser, all the baggage may be searched. Your baggage may be searched on entry to Tibet, while in Tibet, and on exit. One passenger had a souvenir prayer wheel dismantled at Lhasa Airport upon exiting—to see if any messages were being carried in it. Even if you are on a domestic flight from Chengdu to Gonggar, you may have your bags searched. Body searches are rare. Military checkpoints on the Kathmandu to Lhasa route are on the lookout for material readily purchased in Kathmandu, like Dalai Lama pictures or tapes. Some foreigners have been hauled off at a military checkpoint and questioned about books in their possession—one of these was an autobiography by the Dalai Lama. On exit, Chinese customs may be looking for "antiques," which means anything Tibetan that is older than 1959.

Alien Health Declaration

You are required to fill in a Passenger Health Declaration when flying into China or Tibet. It starts out: "Any Alien suffering from AIDS, venereal disease, leprosy, psychiatric disorder or open pulmonary tuberculosis is not allowed to enter the territory..." and goes on to solemnly ask you to declare if you are carrying any Biological Products, Blood Products, or Old Clothes. Your health certificate may be asked for, but probably won't be.

49

Route Strategies

Direction of travel becomes very important in Tibet. Getting in from Kathmandu to Lhasa is a killer (problems with permits and altitude), but exiting from Lhasa to Kathmandu is a piece of cake. Because Nepal to Tibet is an international arrival, it leads to many more visa and red-tape complications, although some travellers have beaten the system by booking on a three-day tour to Lhasa from Kathmandu, and then jumping ship. Travellers obsessed with getting to Tibet go to great lengths: having found their route stymied in Kathmandu, some travellers have flown all the way back to Hong Kong and *back* to Chengdu, and then *back* to Lhasa! If you look at the map, you can see why that route costs a small fortune as opposed to a direct Kathmandu-Lhasa flight. Occasionally Chengdu is blocked, too—and travellers have proceeded all the way up to Golmud by land, and then overland to Lhasa.

More than most places, you need to think about your route to and from Tibet because of visa complications. There's only one consulate in Lhasa—the Nepalese Consulate (you actually don't need a Nepalese visa—pick it up on arrival). That's fine, but what about going overland to Kashgar, and then exiting on the Karakoram Highway into Pakistan? The nearest place for a Pakistan visa is Beijing—and that's a long, long way to go. A similar conundrum crops up in Chengdu if you want to go overland to Hanoi—there's no Vietnamese consulate in Chengdu or Kunming (the closest one is in Nanning). There are Lao and Burmese consulates in Kunming. Visa acupuncture points for Asia include Kathmandu, Hong Kong, Singapore, Beijing, Islamabad and Delhi. Some visas are readily available upon arrival by land or air: these include the Nepalese visa, Thai visa, and Hong Kong entry visa.

AIR ROUTES

All flights into Lhasa are on Boeing 757s operated by the regional carrier China Southwest Airlines (CSWA), an arm of the national carrier CAAC. Approximate flights durations are: Lhasa to Kathmandu, 1 hour 10 minutes; Lhasa to Chengdu, 1 hour 40 minutes; Lhasa to Xian, 2.5 hours. You will not be allowed to purchase an airticket to Lhasa on CSWA in either Chengdu or Kathmandu unless you have the right paperwork (meaning you have to go through an agent in those places, who will fix you up with a "Tibet permit," which is a useless piece of paper that says you can fly on CSWA). CAAC (China

Airlines Almost Crashes) has a poor safety record: there have been several major crashes due to hijackers attempting to get to Taiwan, and others due to poor maintenance—but an impeccable record in Tibet so far.

Gonggar Airport: Pilots landing at Gonggar must be trained in aerial manoeuvres at 3700 metres. Due to air currents, most flights in or out of Tibet are scheduled as early as possible in the morning (wind can pick up significantly in the afternoon). On arrival at Gonggar your baggage may be searched (even if you are on a domestic flight). Gonggar Airport is 96 km from Lhasa. If you don't have a ride arranged from Gonggar, find out if there's a CAAC bus running into Lhasa, or else get together with others and hire a taxi. There is lodging and food in the town of Gonggar, an easy walk from the airport. For information on departing Tibet by air, see the *Lhasa* chapter.

Chengdu Gateway

Chengdu is the main air gateway to Lhasa, with year-round flights—sometimes up to five flights a day. Flight time is just over 1.5 hours. You need to book a flight about four days in advance. It is the most reliable way to go for individual travellers. A one-way ticket costs about $145, plus another $50 for a "permit" (no reduction for the round-trip ticket except that you don't pay the "permit" when exiting Tibet). That makes a total of $195—and the $6 departure tax payable at the airport in Chengdu tips the scales at $200 (domestic departure tax is $6, tax for international flights is $11). Because it mounts the most regular flights into Tibet, Chengdu is a magnet for individual travellers, who are packaged into impromptu groups of 10–15 by local agents. The coding on the air ticket is CTU-LXA (Chengdu-Lhasa). Peak months, with heavy bookings, are July and August. You can fly into Chengdu from Hong Kong, Guangzhou, Bangkok or Singapore; you can also get to Chengdu overland from Hanoi via Kunming.

You cannot buy the ticket yourself. The best thing here is to stay at the Traffic (Jiaotong) Hotel in Chengdu and go through one of the lobby travel agents resident there—the agent will supply the air ticket by putting you in an impromptu group. The fee includes the ticket, airport transfers, and "Tibet permit." The Jiaotong Hotel happens—by more than coincidence—to be where backpackers stay, sharing rooms. The hotel is sited near the Jinjiang River at 77 Linjiang Road, tel. 5551017. Smaller agents in Chengdu channel their paperwork through bigger ones: a major operator is located in the expensive Tibet Hotel, located at 10 Renmin Bei Lu. This agent, CITS Shigatse (Chengdu Office, Room 429 at the Tibet Hotel, tel. 3317339) will in-

NOT LIKE SHANGRI-LA

In December 1943, the first airplane reached Tibet—or rather, crashed in Tibet. During WWII, American pilots used to ferry strategic supplies from India to southwest China, flying over the Himalayas. Tibet did not allow overland passage of these goods through their territory: despite pressure from the British and the Chinese, the Tibetans wished to remain neutral. And so it was that Five American airmen in a B-24 bomber got blown off course at night, started running out of fuel, and circled Lhasa, believing it to be an Indian town. With no radio response from the town—and no obvious airstrip—they decided to parachute out of the plane. The startled villagers of Tsedang clothed and fed them; eventually the wide-eyed airmen were escorted to Lhasa, by now wearing fur-lined boots and fur coats.

Here, at the British Mission, the reception was quite different—they faced angry mobs of Tibetans. It transpired that the airmen had committed great sacrilege by flying over the Dalai Lama's palace. As further proof of this, Tibetan priests had long predicted that any aircraft flying over the Holy City and daring to look down on the Dalai Lama would be doomed. This is exactly what happened to the B-24: it had crashed into a mountainside near Tsedang and exploded (eventually, Tibetan villagers salvaged usable parts of the plane). The airmen never got a tour of Lhasa: they were quickly hustled out of the country for their own safety, and because Tibet wished to maintain its neutrality in the war-theatre. Ironically, the next planes to arrive were war planes, of a kind: Russian turbo-props—the standard Chinese military aircraft in the 1960s. All the airfields in Tibet are military. Gonggar Airport doubles as a military and commercial airfield.

sist that you take a tour on arrival in Lhasa—the length is negotiable. After that, you're free, but ensure that there is an expiry date on your obligations to the agency you booked with—otherwise they may "claim" you for the duration of your stay in Tibet. The flight into Lhasa crosses the snowcaps of eastern Tibet—with 757 wingtip vistas.

Other Chinese Gateways

The plane from Beijing to Lhasa is scheduled twice weekly—the plane may stop at Chengdu or Xian en route to Lhasa. Less frequent flights go to Lhasa from Chongqing (rumoured to be twice weekly) or

Xian (once a week). There are several snags involved with these flights. The first is that the flights are pretty expensive—Beijing to Lhasa is $325 one-way. It doesn't appear that you can buy the tickets over the counter like you would for other destinations in China—you probably have to go through a local travel agent. Listing of a flight on a timetable does not guarantee that the plane will actually depart. Chinese planes only fly when seat space is sufficiently filled: if not, the plane could be cancelled or delayed. Future links planned include flights from Lhasa to Kunming, Xining, Shanghai and Guangzhou.

Kathmandu Gateway

The only international flight into Lhasa is from Kathmandu. A group of five is mandatory for ticket reservations. Flights should be booked two to four weeks in advance through a travel agent. The flight costs $195 one-way—exactly the same as the Chengdu-Lhasa flight. No Nepalese aircraft fly the route—it's all on CSWA, so again the ticketing problems come up (you can't buy the ticket yourself). Ticketing problems are worse here because the agent will take your passport to the Chinese embassy, which routinely cancels Chinese visas issued elsewhere and replaces them with a visa valid for the length of the tour you've booked. Kathmandu to Lhasa flights are twice weekly in season (the flight is closed down for winter months—late October to March). Peak months, with heavy bookings, are July and August. The flight lasts 1 hour 10 minutes, and goes straight over the Himalayas—the pilot uses Everest as a navigation landmark when turning.

ROAD ROUTES

There are two semi-sanctioned road routes into Lhasa—from Golmud and from Kathmandu. The first is boring, the second poses considerable logistical problems. Exiting Tibet by either route is not a problem, but entering can be.

Golmud Route

The 1130-km journey from Golmud to Lhasa is a two-day epic that qualifies for the most boring bus-ride in Asia. The journey takes 30 to 40 hours—longer if you break down. Leaving Golmud (3200 metres), the paved road traverses stark high terrain, passing the world's highest inhabited place (Wenchuan, at 5100 metres, established by the Chinese in 1955), and shortly after, crossing 5180-metre Tangu La into the TAR. You may be able to catch a sleeper coach, which has a spacious reclining seat. Golmud, the Black Hole of China, is a town of

90,000. It is normally reached by railway (bus is possible). Travellers may have to wait in Golmud until a group of up to 20 assembles, and along comes a CITS bus. The sleeper bus fare is a whopping $145 a person one-way, which includes a $60 "Tibet permit" and a three-day tour in Lhasa (the regular Chinese fare on this route is around $20, without the tour or the permit). Luxurious Japanese sleeper buses have been sighted on this route. There are also direct Xining-Lhasa buses, but foreigners are not permitted to travel on them. There's a military checkpoint 30 km south of Golmud, and another at Nagqu. Some enterprising travellers have sneaked out past the first checkpoint, then got rides in trucks—hiding under blankets at subsequent checkpoints.

Here's the rub: from Lhasa (where you have choices on where to go) the price of a bus one-way to Golmud, big-nose price, is about $60 (no tours involved, it's true, but still…). If you're out Golmud way, you might want to look at going overland from Xining via Labrang to Chengdu—a great run through Tibetan areas. There are details in *The Tibetan World* chapter.

Kathmandu Route

By contrast, the Kathmandu to Lhasa route cuts through diverse altitude zones and draws you on past enthralling Himalayan landscape. However, this route is better tackled as an exit, for reasons of permits, choices and altitude. See the *Lhasa to Kathmandu Route* chapter for details. The first problem you will have is getting a Chinese visa. Unless you book a tour from Kathmandu, the Chinese Embassy there will not issue a visa. Some travellers have obtained Chinese visas in other places, such as Delhi or Bangkok.

With a valid Chinese visa, you might be able to cross at the Zhangmu border, and pick up a CITS Landcruiser, usually charging $100 to $150 a person to get to Lhasa (the lower figure is a two-day run with no sightseeing stops; the higher figure could be a four-day tour, with stops). Although the Chinese Embassy in Kathmandu routinely cancels Chinese visas issued elsewhere (and substitutes a new visa valid for the length of your tour), the border at Zhangmu is an entirely different authority—over which the Kathmandu embassy has no control. Zhangmu border officials may honour a Chinese visa issued elsewhere and may allow entry because there's money to be made from CITS Landcruiser rentals in Zhangmu. Take a bus from Kathmandu to Kodari for a couple of dollars, take a half-hour truck or jeep ride to Zhangmu, and then try and wrangle through to the CITS official next to the Chinese immigration post. You're not supposed to leave the trip until you get to Lhasa, but some have wandered off into the sunset in Shigatse…

Longer Overland Routes

There are various epic routes into Lhasa that traverse the plateau: you get to see half of Tibet along the way. As with the other routes mentioned, your success rate is probably higher leaving Tibet by these overland routes rather than entering.

Chengdu to Lhasa overland takes about 10 to 15 days without stops, and crosses some 15 high passes. Past Kangding, the route diverges—a northern branch going through Derge and Chamdo, and a southern route passing through Litang and Markam. Both routes join up again near Bamda, and the road continues past Namche Barwa, the highest peak in eastern Tibet, at 7756 metres. For a very long time, geographers speculated that there had to be a huge waterfall in the area close to Namche Barwa because the Yarlung Tsangpo dropped radically as it transformed into India's Brahmaputra River. There's no big waterfall, but the river stages a dramatic U-turn around Namche Barwa, cutting through one of the deepest gorges in the world. Towns along the Chengdu to Lhasa route are mostly truck-stops. Officials and truck-stop inns don't see a lot of foreigners, but if they do, they're liable to cause problems. One group in a Landcruiser, stopping at Bayi, was fined heavily for staying overnight at a non-PSB-approved hotel (PSB wanted them to stay at a very expensive approved hotel). Chengdu to Lhasa is 2400 km via Chamdo (north route) and 2080 km via Litang (south route). The route is not covered in this book, but there is some information on Kham in *The Tibetan World* chapter. In that chapter are details on a beautiful route linking Lanzhou to Chengdu.

Coming up from Kunming is a stunning route that travels through the scenic towns of Dali, Lijiang and Zhongdian before joining the route to Lhasa near Markam. Kunming to Markam is 1200 km, and it's another 1100 km from Markam to Lhasa. Kunming is a good staging-point. If you're into long overland trips, you can reach Kunming from either the Lao Cai border (connecting to Hanoi by road or rail) or the Ban Boten border (connecting through Laos to Thailand). You would have to straighten out the visa situation well in advance to cover the route. There's a Lao consulate in Kunming, but no Vietnamese one; for Thailand you get a visa on arrival at any land border.

The wildest route of all into Lhasa is the 3100-km journey from Kashgar in the far west of Xinjiang province, southward through

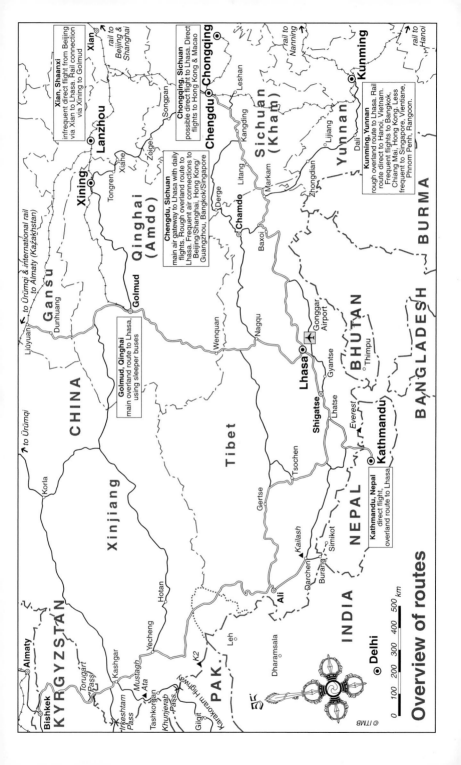

Overview of routes

Xian, Shaanxi
infrequent direct flight from Beijing via Xian to Lhasa. Rail connection via Xining to Golmud

Chongqing, Sichuan
possible direct flight to Lhasa. Direct flights to Hong Kong & Macao

Chengdu, Sichuan
main air gateway to Lhasa with daily flights. Rough overland route to Lhasa. Frequent air connections to Beijing/Shanghai, Hong Kong/ Guangzhou, Bangkok/Singapore

Kunming, Yunnan
rough overland route to Lhasa. Rail route direct to Hanoi, Vietnam. Frequent flights to Bangkok, Chiang Mai, Hong Kong. Less frequent to Singapore, Vientiane, Phnom Penh, Rangoon.

Golmud, Qinghai
main overland route to Lhasa, using sleeper buses

Kathmandu, Nepal
direct flight, overland route to Lhasa

© ITMB

Yecheng and Mazar to Ali, and then on Lhasa. The route traverses passes over 5000 metres. Travellers are frequently turned back at Yecheng on this route: permits are a problem. The old silk-route trading town of Kashgar looks like it's a long way from anywhere, but actually it's only a few days down the Karakoram Highway from Kashgar to Islamabad in Pakistan. This is one of greatest mountain road trips in High Asia, crossing the 4700-metre Khunjerab Pass. Another way of reaching Kashgar is from Bishkek (Kyrgyzstan) over the Torugart Pass.

The Jules Verne Challenge

By stringing together some of these routes, you can develop a journey on a grand scale, clocking up over 10,000 kilometres by road. In 1992, the London-based adventure tour operator Voyages Jules Verne sponsored a car rally commemorating an historic 1907 race from Paris to Peking. The 1992 rally cars left London headed for Saigon, by way of Moscow, Tashkent, Kashgar, Yarkand, Shigatse, Lhasa, Xining, Chengdu, Nanning and Hanoi. Taking a cue from this, you can set up your own Jules Verne challenge. You can overland from Saigon up through Hanoi, continuing by rail or road to Kunming and Chengdu, then go by road or air to Lhasa, continue by road to Kathmandu, and carry on overland—all the way to Istanbul. A silk route variation would be to take the same trail to Lhasa, and head north to Golmud and Dunhuang, perhaps fly from Urumqi to Kashgar, zip down the Karakoram Highway into Pakistan, and then travel overland to Istanbul. There's an international rail crossing from Urumqi to Almaty, eventually connecting all the way to Moscow.

INSIDE TIBET

All loads lead to Lhasa. Lhasa is off-limits until you get there: then it's wide open. Within Tibet you are classed as an Alien, and you require an Alien Travel Permit (ATP). Various annoying pieces of paper with fancy chops and seals dog your movements into and around Tibet—this is not like mainland China where you can virtually travel without restriction. The ATP is for cities that are supposedly not open to foreigners, but the list of what is open is top secret—and it appears that what was open a few years ago is now closed. So it goes—PSB knows the rules, but you're in the dark.

Apart from ATPs, in Lhasa other permits are issued—TTB, military, Foreign Affairs, Cultural Bureau permits—there's no end to the red tape. Foreigners are usually never shown these documents, nor allowed to keep them—they're classed as secret. In Lhasa, a guide will arrange your permits when you've booked a Landcruiser tour, and the guide will keep the permits (you could try and get a photocopy). On your own, you'll have trouble getting a permit in Lhasa: travellers have, however, obtained ATPs themselves from Shigatse PSB. Many areas of Tibet remain closed or sensitive: they could be off-limits because they are military zones.

If you are hiring a Landcruiser and guide, the best thing to do is to make it very clear to the guide that you want all the necessary permits and that if permits required are not obtained, it will be his responsibility. Hiring a Landcruiser lends legitimacy to your travels: if you're in a Landcruiser and you're not sleeping at a place overnight, who's going to know if you have a permit or not? It's more likely that PSB will catch up with you if you overnight at the hotel in a place.

Some places open without permit: sites in Central Tibet within range of Lhasa, including many monasteries like Tsurphu and Mindroling (Ganden could be sticky). Namtso Lake is open without permit. Gyantse and Shigatse should be open without permit. Places where permits have been demanded, causing problems include Samye, Tsedang, and Samding Monastery (near Nagartse).

Visa Extensions: In Lhasa, these are linked to tours—that is, only if you book a tour will you be given an extension (which will be for the length of that tour). You might be able to cut a deal elsewhere, like Shigatse. Also try under the table payments and go through an agent in Lhasa—it will cost, but you get the paperwork done.

Landcruiser & Guide

The Chinese insist that the only way you (as a foreigner) can get around Tibet is with a hired Landcruiser with a driver and guide. This works out to about $110–170 a day, which, split between 4 or 5 paying passengers, is around $25–45 per person per day. That's a fair bit of money, and most of the operators are connected to Chinese channels. In some cases, routes are monopolised by CITS Landcruisers. Landcruisers are the greatest expense you'll incur in Tibet. Many Landcruisers operate on the Lhasa to Zhangmu run (for Nepal border). You can find Landcruisers for hire in Zhangmu, and possibly in Shigatse (don't count on it). The majority of Landcruisers are hired in Lhasa—refer to the *Lhasa* transport section for more details.

One peculiar phenomenon you will have to deal with in Tibet is called "hitting the roof." This is when the Landcruiser (which has no seatbelts) hits a rut and launches those in the back seat straight into the roof. That hurts! To soften the impact, think about a wool hat or something similar. The idea of padded roofs has not caught on yet.

West Tibet: north face of Kailash / Drolma La / pilgrim truck / near Tsaparang

Horse-racing festivals: archers / nomad women dressed up / Gyantse parade

The Chinese presence: Potala / Tibet Royal Hotel / selling katas / army surplus

Temple interiors: Rampoche / murals of icons Atisha & White Tara (Tsaparang)

On Your Own

You need considerable stamina, perseverance and devious ingenuity to mount your own trips in Tibet, breaking away from the Landcruiser Syndrome. While the regular bus service is sporadic—the crates wheeze over the passes, with frequent breakdowns—you may be able to get a ride to a trailhead, where you can start trekking. Hitchhiking in Tibet means you have to pay for lifts (negotiate with the driver), and it may mean heavy fines for the driver if caught transporting a foreigner. Crazy dreamers have found ingenious ways of getting around inside Tibet. Back in the early days of independent travel in Tibet, in the 1980s, two Americans transported their kayaks up to Lake Manasarovar and started paddling the Yarlung Tsangpo—they made it part of the way. A young Englishman managed to bluff his way through the Zhangmu border with a motorcycle—and he was out by the Great Wall by the time the authorities caught up with him. Others have rented (or bought) yaks or donkeys to carry their gear, and headed off on long hikes.

If you have money coming out your ears, of course, you can arrange to realise any dream you want—through official channels. All the paperwork and aggravation might take some of the joy out of it, though. I've met several trios of motorcyclists from Europe who've been all over Tibet and Xinjiang on their imported bikes. They would not, however, divulge the cost of the entourage of vehicles accompanying them (with national guide, local guide, translators, medic...). High-paying group tours walk to the Kojinath border crossing in western Tibet, trekking in for five days from Simikot (Nepal), and are then picked by Landcruisers which take them on to Burang, and up to Kailash. That border crossing is only open to the well-heeled. A similar trek up the Indian side, crossing at Lipu Lek Pass, is also sanctioned for high-paying group tours.

Tour de Tibet

Mountain-biking is the only way to bring your own "vehicle" into Tibet (apart from the odd kayaker or motorcyclist). Mountain-bikes are ideal for the dry terrain in Tibet. You can remain independent and still cover great distances—and it's a great way to meet people and savour the land at a slower pace. However, you need a road of some sort, or a trail. Technically, you're not supposed to be cycling around Tibet at all because you've got too much freedom and authorities have no way of tracking your movements—and that's something that the PSB doesn't like. In practice, the PSB often turn a blind eye. However, try and get permits in advance for sites where you know you'll stop the night. Organised tours to Tibet by mountain-bike have been conducted by a few operators, notably one based in Kathmandu. In this case, a sag-wagon usually accompanies the group, and picks up the stragglers if they're slow on the winding passes.

Independent travellers have been able to bring their own bikes in by plane from Chengdu or Kathmandu, or by train and then bus from Golmud. The Chinese don't bat an eyelid if you try to put a bike on a train or a plane, or bring it into your hotel room: they're used to seeing bicycles in strange places. Some travellers have reported wheeling a bike to the airport check-in (no disassembly). You can also buy American mountain-bikes made in Shenzhen (Cannondales and Diamondbacks) and sold in Chengdu, Kunming, Beijing, Shanghai, Guangzhou and Hong Kong. These may take a bit of work to track down as they're primarily for export. They cost about $250–350 apiece, which is low compared to what you'd pay in the US. Taiwanese-made mountain-bikes like the Giant are good quality—but hard to find (you can buy one in Beijing). Chinese-brand mountain-bikes like the Forever are junk—they fall apart within a few weeks, (and parts like pedals may suddenly break off). You can buy one for $100 in a Lhasa department store—the bike is good for running around Lhasa—but not reliable for crossing the plateau. Nevertheless, some have bought these bikes, reinforced them, and used them to make a run to Kathmandu. The short seatpost on Chinese-made models is a problem—you might have to get it removed and a longer one substituted. If intending to cycle, bring all the (compact) supplies you need with you—Chinese pumps, for example, are monstrous steel things. It's difficult to find items like bicycle water-bottles in Lhasa. Cyclists revel in wearing a Casio wristwatch that tells not only the time but the altitude.

If you fly a bicycle into Lhasa, you should conduct acclimatisation trips around the Lhasa Valley to get used to the altitude. This particularly applies to climbing hills. There are many fine rides within a day or two of Lhasa. Some travellers indulge in hybrid travel modes—biking a bit, then putting the bike on the top of a bus. You could make it out to Tibet's wild west (Kailash region) by this method.

Although cyclists have tackled all the major routes in Tibet (including, yes, the run to Kashgar), the most popular is the Lhasa to Kathmandu route. This run has it all—high passes, Himalayan camping sites, ancient towns and temples, high winds and surly PSB officials. An interesting facet of mountain-biking is being able to race the locals on horses—they win over a short distance, but the horse quickly tires, and then you start to gain, much to the surprise of the horseman. I once raced a Tibetan on a Chinese one-speed bicycle: he was leading by a good margin until we hit a hill—and then the 18 gears left him behind, flabbergasted. Gravity is something you have to consider on the Lhasa to Kathmandu route. If you start in Lhasa, you end up with a fantastic 4500-metre drop off the plateau from Tong La. If you go the other way, you'll need a few energy bars along.

Cyclists are a peculiar breed—the talk centres around headwinds, gradients, water quality, and, in Tibet, animals. There are two animals to watch out for—yaks and dogs. Yaks are not a problem—they will bolt at the approach of a bike (mistaking it for a rival species?) but may upset the handler when they thunder off. Dogs, on the other hand, will come straight at you, fangs bared. Dogs are especially a problem when trying to sneak around checkpoints at night (which is what some cyclists attempt to do). Squirting a water-bottle at a dog may repel it; some carry fireworks, or have a pump at the ready to defend themselves.Logistically, cycling in Tibet poses major problems. The route is about a thousand kilometres from Lhasa to Kathmandu, crossing six high passes. It requires a minimum two weeks, and preferably three weeks, to complete the trip. Carrying enough food for the three-week journey would mean your bike would be too heavy. So you have to back off on the weight (carry freezedried food) and find other ways of maintaining food supply to stoke your energy level. Water alone adds considerable weight (you need four litres a day). Camping gear is essential for the run.

Some cyclists have ridden all the way up to Everest base camp. This is not a road—it's a pain in the butt, made of pebbles and glacial moraine debris. Only parts of the route are rideable. Intrepid travellers have even mounted a combination of trek and bike: Victor Chan (Tibet Handbook) and his companion arranged to have porters carry their mountain bikes over a high pass into Tibet and then proceeded to cycle along the highway. There's always the option of strapping a bike to the side of a yak for transport over difficult terrain—this has probably not been attempted because yaks don't like anything unusual (and the yak might decide to roll over on the load). Some trekking terrain is suited to biking: the jeepable road out to Lake Namtso is quite passible, and grassland areas in parts of Tibet are eminently rideable—you don't even need a road here. Bicycling in Kham and Amdo—peripheral Tibet—offers some excellent terrain with grasslands and mountain trails. A great destination is the Kunming-to-Lijiang route.

LHASA
secrets of the city

The name Lhasa is thought to derive from the Tibetan words *Lha* (Holy) and *Sa* (City). In the late 19th and early 20th centuries, Lhasa was the most reclusive city on the face of the planet—a sacred city that was as difficult a goal as Mecca to reach. Even the greatest Western explorers of the era—Nikolai Prejavalsky, Sven Hedin—failed to make it.

Now this shroud of secrecy has been ripped away...to reveal...a humdrum Chinese town. Lhasa is one large Chinatown now, with rows and rows of faceless Chinese apartment blocks and government buildings. The Tibetans are a minority in their own capital, with perhaps 60,000 Tibetans out of a population estimated at 180,000 (the real figure could be much higher—possibly 350,000). A sizeable contingent of the Chinese population is an occupation force: military, paramilitary, police or bureaucrats.

If you are disappointed with Lhasa, or feel cheated of the mystique you had expected, you won't be the first. The eccentric English traveller Thomas Manning tried to forge a route through to Peking, and by chance reached Lhasa in 1812, disguised as a Chinese physician. He found the Potala extraordinary—and the rest of the place a dump. Here's his description of Old Lhasa, one of the first "snapshots" of the Potala ever recorded by a Westerner:

> The road here, as it winds past the palace is royally broad; it is level and free from stones, and combined with the view of the lofty towering palace, which forms a majestic mountain of a building, has a magnificent effect. The roads about the palace swarmed with monks; its nooks and angles with beggars lounging and basking in the sun.... As a whole [the Potala] seemed perfect enough; but I could not comprehend its plan in detail.... If the palace exceeded my expectations, the town as far fell short of them. There is nothing striking, nothing pleasing in its appearance. The habitations are begrimed with smut and dirt; the avenues are full of dogs...

Manning not only managed to get to Lhasa, he also garnered an unprecedented audience with the seven-year-old Dalai Lama (IX), which he recorded as a moving experience. Almost a century later, in 1904, the invading English under Younghusband found their triumphal march into Lhasa impeded by piles of refuse, stagnant pools of water, open sewers, and various rabid animals foraging for putrid scraps of food. They did, however, note that the gleaming gold roofs of the Jokhang restored the balance in favour of the majestic.

Lhasa was never a big city. There was no census taken in the Lhasa of 1949 or earlier, but the population was estimated at 30,000. There were an additional 7000 monks at Sera Monastery, and 9000 monks at Drepung. This brought the figure to around 45,000—and probably double that number would be in Lhasa during festivals. Lhasa's design was based not so much on practical as sacred aspects. In the 7th century, King Songsten Gampo moved his capital from the Yarlung Valley to the site of Lhasa. Later, as the residence of the Dalai Lamas, Lhasa became the religious centre of Tibet—and the seat of government. Lhasa was (and is) dominated by the Potala Palace, the winter residence of the Dalai Lama, with his summer palace, the Norbulingka, below. Within the front walled section of the Potala was the entire Tibetan government administration, where the nobles lived—these buildings have largely disappeared. Across town, separated by meadows, was the Jokhang Temple with a market and artisan section. A third edifice was the Palace of the Regent—the man who ruled in times when the Dalai Lama was not of age.

Old Lhasa disappeared with the Chinese invasion of Tibet in 1950 and with the flight of the Dalai Lama to India in 1959. Transformation was swift: few of those Tibetans who fled in 1959 would have recognised Lhasa in 1964, when pro-Chinese writer Israel Epstein said:

> Lhasa is becoming a beautiful modern city. Not long ago, the Potala, the temples and a few mansions stood amid hovels and cesspools of medieval squalor. Now there are miles of well lit, asphalted streets and underground drains...Electricity is supplied to 90 per cent of all homes for illumination and often for cooking (ex-serfs and slaves get it free). A working people's Cultural Palace and a hall seating twelve hundred is used for meetings, plays and films; there are also two other film theatres. A State Emporium built this year, the biggest of many new shops and stores, sells everything from needles and thread to sewing machines, bicycles and transistor radios...

Picture this process accelerated over the next 30-odd years, and you get an idea of what's occurred in Lhasa. A Tibetan resident commented that Lhasa had changed more in the years 1992 to 1997 than it had over the last few hundred years. The urban area of Lhasa has rapidly expanded, with many new Chinese-built apartment buildings and offices. An industrial fringe has also cropped up, with a concrete factory and a brewery in northern Lhasa.

While technological change is a positive thing, the fact is that in Lhasa these changes have not been in the interest of the Tibetans—they're for the Chinese. The Tibetans "still preferred independence to electricity, and freedom to sewers," as Michel Peissel put it. The Chinese settlers demand electricity and street lighting, Chinese soldiers need roads—and Chinese officials need cultural palaces, and girlie bars and karaoke salons with their glitter and neon. Rows of barbershops near the Potala do a brisk business late at night. Why? Because they are fronts for prostitution—one of Lhasa's dirty secrets. Holy city or whorehouse? For Tibetan pilgrims, Lhasa remains the Holy City, but to even the casual visitor, the Chinese layering of scores of bars and karaoke salons is glaring. Not to mention the heavy Chinese military and para-military presence—with army bases ringing the city, and a network of prisons. The end result is that Lhasa has become increasingly sinicized. You see it in small details, like the statuary around the city—pairs of Chinese lions outside the entrance to the Potala, a Chinese dragon sculpture in the fountain in Potala Square, a concrete statue of Chinese mountaineers atop Everest, Chinese flags flying at strategic points, and—at night—glowing Chinese neon signs.

To make Lhasa more attractive to coastal entrepreneurs (who, according to the Chinese "go to Tibet to offer their expertise to help develop the local economy") some anomalies have popped up. Chinese office blocks are going up around the town: one of them is an 11-storey glass and steel tower on Dekyi Nub Road. For the first time in its long history, Lhasa is seeing traffic jams—caused by the importation of Chinese-built red taxis. Chinese taxi-drivers can earn up to five times as much in Lhasa as they can in other cities; other incentives for Chinese immigrants include preferential tax and loan policies. Keeping track of investments is the Tibet Stocks Business Centre, which has a satellite feed listing prices on China's stock exchanges in Shenzhen and Shanghai. Keeping Chinese residents comfortable requires improved communications—satellite reception is provided by Lhasa's Xizang TV station, constructed in the early 1990s.

Orienting Yourself

Traditionally, Tibetan pilgrims approaching the holy city embarked on three sacred circuits: the inner circuit of the Jokhang Temple (called the Nangkor), the 20-minute outer circuit of the same temple (around the Barkor), and a 90-minute circuit around Lhasa itself, called the Lingkor. The first two are eminently possible, but the Lingkor is no longer easy to follow—it has been disrupted by modern Chinese building. The description of sights that follows is based on clockwise circuits of the Nangkor, Barkor and Lingkor—that is, starting at the Jokhang Temple, and spiralling outwards around Lhasa. On the outskirts of Lhasa lie the great monastic citadels of Sera and Drepung. You have to read between the lines in Lhasa when it comes to the sacred and the secret. There's been so much upheaval in the Holy City that half the time you don't know if what you're looking at is sacred or not—whether the statuary at the Jokhang is real or not, whether the West Gate is original or reconstructed.

BARKOR AREA

There are two areas left in Lhasa where the Tibetan pulse can still be felt: at the Potala (a faint museum pulse) and Barkor Bazaar (throbbing pilgrim pulse). Other than that you're looking at Chinatown. It seems absurd to put it this way, but you really have to visit the "Tibetan Quarter"—the quarter around the Jokhang Temple and the Barkor—to catch any Tibetans in action.

The Jokhang or Tsug Lakhang (central cathedral) is Tibet's most sacred temple—the heart of Tibet—with streams of pilgrims coursing through. The temple was built in the 7th century by King Songsten Gampo when he moved his capital to Lhasa. Apart from his three Tibetan wives, the powerful Songsten Gampo had two wives offered by neighbouring nations—Nepalese Queen Tritsun and Chinese Queen Wencheng. The Jokhang was originally designed by Nepalese craftsmen to house a Buddha image brought by the Nepalese queen. Upon Songsten Gampo's death, Queen Wencheng switched the statue she had brought (the Jowo Sakyamuni) from the Ramoche Temple to the Jokhang, apparently to hide it from Chinese troops. That's why one part of the Jokhang (Chapel 13) is called the Chapel where the Jowo was Hidden. In time, the Jowo Sakyamuni statue became the chief object of veneration. The Jokhang was enlarged and embellished by subsequent rulers and Dalai Lamas. Although the building is as old as Lhasa, much of the statuary is quite new. During the Cultural Revolution, the temple was used as a military barracks and a slaughterhouse; later it was used as a hotel for Chinese officials. Much of the statuary was lost, destroyed or damaged, so it has been replaced with newer copies of originals.

Outside the Jokhang

Fronting the Jokhang are flagstones where Tibetans gather to prostrate before the temple. A bit further back are two small walled enclosures with obelisks inside. One enclosure shelters two stone obelisks with an edict in Chinese about curing smallpox—the edict, from 1794, is largely illegible because Tibetans gouged pieces out of it, supposing that the stone itself had curative properties. The second enclosure, with a tall thin obelisk, bears a bilingual inscription about a peace treaty between Tibetan king Ralpachen and Chinese emperor Wangti, concluded in 823, delineating the borders between the nations of China and Tibet. The brick enclosures around the obelisks were put up when Barkor Square was created in 1985.

Access

Exit and entry are by a side-door off the Barkor: an entry-fee is charged. It's best to visit in the mornings, from 8.30 am to noon. The Jokhang may be closed Mondays. Entering the inner sanctum of the ground floor chapels may be difficult for Tibetan pilgrims. As a tourist, you are privileged to be allowed in. Photography is allowed in certain parts of the Jokhang—if in doubt, ask first. Second floor chapels may be closed off and only accessible to monks residing at the Jokhang—you should respect this limitation. It should be all right to access the rooftop, however, and you might be able to visit the rooftop at times when the ground-floor chapels are closed.

The Rooftop

You can take a staircase near the ticket booth at the front straight up to the golden rooftop of the Jokhang, with excellent views over Lhasa rooftops and the Potala in the distance. In the summer months there is a tent teahouse up on the Jokhang rooftop, run by the monks. Visiting the rooftop seems to be a privilege reserved for tourists—both Western and Chinese—as you don't see Tibetan pilgrims up here. The rooftop is a bright, peaceful spot—a refreshing place after the dark, smoky chapels of the Jokhang interior. There are beautiful ornaments hanging from the eaves of the gilded sloping roofs—some in the shape of dragons, others in the shape of mythical birds.

Ground-Floor Icons

Walking through the dark corridors and chapels of the Jokhang, you enter another world—dim light is provided by a galaxy of butter lamps; the air is thick with the odour of yak-butter and incense; echoing through the halls is the sound of murmuring, from throngs of Tibetan pilgrims. If your timing is right, the inner sanctum may reverberate with the sound of deep, hypnotic chanting—of monks at prayer. About 100 monks live at the Jokhang, residing on the upper levels.

The world you enter seems quite complex and confusing—no point of reference, no rhyme or reason. However, that may be a matter of familiarising yourself with the icons of Tibetan Buddhism—which, admittedly, are bewildering in their scope and number. If you want to explore Tibetan temple iconography, the Jokhang has the lot—a virtual Who's Who of the Tibetan Buddhist pantheon. Using the plan of the Jokhang in this section, you can identify which images are Avalokitesvara, Sakyamuni, King Songsten Gampo and so on. The same icons pop up in many other temples in Tibet, and are referred to in other parts of this book. Only some of the ground-floor chapels are described here: the emphasis is on the icons.

Unlike most temples, the Jokhang is not identified with a particular sect. Leaders and teachers from the different sects are shown in statuary and murals. **Tsongkhapa** (Chapel 1) is the founder of the Geluk (Yellow Hat) sect. There's a finer image of him in Chapel 6,

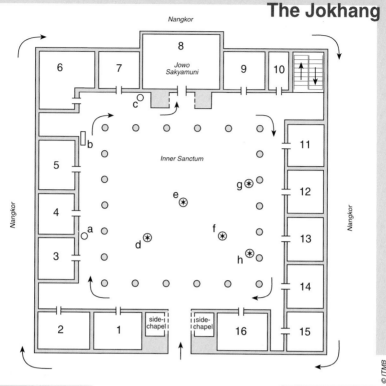

The Jokhang

Nangkor

6 7 8 *Jowo Sakyamuni* 9 10

Inner Sanctum

c

b

5

4

3

a d e f g h

11

12

13

14

2 1 side-chapel side-chapel 16 15

Nangkor *Nangkor*

© ITMB

Main Chapels
1. Tsongkhapa and his eight disciples
2. Amitabha Chapel
3. Eight Medicine Buddhas
*a. between chapels lies a statue of Milarepa
4. Avalokitesvara Chapel
5. Jampa Truze Chapel
*b. glass case with Avalokitesvara image
6. Tsongkhapa Chapel
7. Amitabha Chapel
*c. between chapels lie statues of guardian kings
8. **Jowo Sakyamuni** - the main image
9. Jampa Gonpo Chapel
10. Chenrezig Chapel
* in the SE corner is a staircase leading to upper floor (no access)
11. reconstructed chapel with rows of Buddhas
12. Jampa Chezhi--small standing Jampa image
13. Chapel where the Jowo was hidden
14. The Seven Mighty Buddhas
15. Nine Aspects of Amitayus
16. Chapel of the Dharma Kings

Inner Sanctum
d. Padmasambhava statue
e. small Avalokitesvara image
f.+g. large Maitreya statues
h. small Maitreya image

not to scale

Open courtyard with butter lamps
(former assembly area for monks)

Ground-floor Chapels
Some chapels in the Jokhang have been destroyed and reconstructed, and statuary has been defaced, replaced, restored and shifted around, so this plan may not match exactly: use it as a rough guide. Chapels may close and re-open, depending on reconstruction. With this jumble of old and new, it's debatable which statuary is original and which is copied.

Sidechapels
Entering or exiting the inner Jokhang sanctuary, you pass two sidechapels. The sidechapel to the left (north side) contains a statue of Paden Lhamo, the main protective deity of the Jokhang, as well as fierce guardian deities. To the right (south side) are three Naga deity statues, also with a protective role.

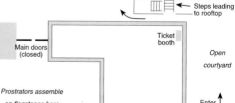

← Steps leading to rooftop

Ticket booth

Open courtyard

Main doors (closed)

Prostrators assemble on flagstones here

Enter

wearing monk's robes and a pointed yellow cap; he lived from 1357 to 1419. Between Chapel 3 and Chapel 4 is an image (statue a) of the great poet-saint **Milarepa** (1040–1123), with his hand cocked to one ear so that he can better hear the music of the spheres and the voice of teachings. The sage appears with skin a greenish hue—a case of nettle anemia (he dined solely on nettle soup for a number of years). Milarepa was a founding member of the Kagyu sect. Another historical figure seen in chapels and in larger statues at the inner sanctum is **Padmasambhava,** the 8th-century tantric Indian master who is credited with establishing Buddhism in Tibet. He is the founder of the Nyingma sect, and is shown with a stern expression and a curled moustache, wearing a folded red hat.

In the Tibetan pantheon are many Buddhas and bodhisattvas. A bodhisattva is a being on the way to becoming a Buddha, but one who has decided to delay the pursuit of nirvana and devote himself or herself to the welfare of others. The Dalai Lama is thought to be an emanation of **Avalokitesvara,** the bodhisattva of Compassion (Chenrezig in Tibetan). Often shown in a standing statue, Avalokitesvara has 11 heads (one of which is wrathful) and multiple arms, and may be encircled by a thousand hands. The many heads are said to have burst from the original head as a result of contemplating the suffering of living beings.

The figure of Avalokitesvara is found in several parts of the ground floor—in Chapel 4, outside Chapel 5 in a glass case (statue b), in Chapel 10, and right at the centre of the inner sanctum (statue e). The image in Chapel 4 has a long story behind it: some parts of the statue are original, some are copies. The image was commissioned by Songsten Gampo in the 7th century. During the Cultural Revolution, this image and others were tossed into the streets. Tibetans managed to salvage a wrathful and a peaceful aspect of the faces of Avalokitesvara—the images were smuggled out via Nepal to India. The faces were eventually made into a new image of Avalokitesvara at the Tsug Lakhang in Dharamsala.

Tara (Drolma in Tibetan) is said to be the spiritual consort of Avalokitesvara, and possesses more than 20 forms. **White Tara** is identified with Queen Wencheng and the fertile aspect of compassion, while **Green Tara** is identified with Queen Tritsun and the motherly aspect of compassion. Green Tara is the patron female saint of Tibet; she sits with her right leg extended slightly, resting on a lotus blossom. White Tara sits cross-legged upon a lotus flower—she is easily recognised by the eyes depicted in the palms of her hands: she is believed to sprung from a tear of compassion falling from the eye of

Avalokitesvara. While there is little statuary of Tara in the ground-floor chapels, her image appears in a number of murals—a Tara fresco is shown on a wall recessed at the back of Chapel 16.

Tibetans believe that the historical Buddha (Sakyamuni) is the Buddha of the present era, but only one of the many Buddhas to appear—past, present and future. The Buddha is "he who is fully awake"—an enlightened being. **Amitabha,** appearing in Chapel 2, is the Buddha of Infinite Light (Opame in Tibetan)—usually depicted in a red colour, with hands clasping an alms-bowl. The Panchen Lama is thought to be an incarnation of Amitabha. A row of eight **Medicine Buddhas** is shown in Chapel 3—these are the Buddhas of healing, and caring for the sick. **Jampa** is the Buddha of the Future—also known as Champa or the Maitreya Buddha. This Buddha is not usually shown cross-legged, but seated conventionally on a throne. The Jampa statue shown in Chapel 5 is a copy of one brought to Tibet from Nepal by Queen Tritsun. In Chapel 9 is an image of Jampa (brought in from Drepung to replace a destroyed image); this statue was once paraded around the Barkor at Monlam. In the inner sanctum are two Jampa images (statues f and g).

Centrepiece of the Jokhang is a 1.5-metre-high gilded statue of **Jowo Sakyamuni,** the Buddha of the Present, born in 543 BC in Nepal. The image was brought to Tibet by Queen Wencheng. It depicts the Sakyamuni Buddha at the age of 12: features such as long earlobes and a cranial bump are special marks of the Buddha. The highly revered statue bears an elaborate headdress and is encrusted with jewels; pilgrims crowd in to make offerings, and to walk around the statue.

Revered as deities are the early religious kings of Tibet, who converted to Buddhism. Easily identified in the ground-floor chapels is **King Songsten Gampo** (circa 608–650), the first of the great religious kings, considered to be a manifestation of Avalokitesvara. He wears a high orange or gold turban; his Chinese wife, **Queen Wencheng,** is on the viewer's right; his Nepalese wife, **Queen Tritsun,** on the viewer's left. This is the arrangement for a group (statue c) to the left of the Jowo Sakyamuni image. The three great religious kings of Tibet are found in the Chapel of the Dharma Kings (Chapel 16)—the central figure being Songsten Gampo; to the viewer's right, **Trisong Detsen** (the second religious king, who ruled 755–797); and to the viewer's left, **Tri Ralpachen** (who ruled 815–838). On the way out of the area, take a closer look at the two sidechapels by the entrance: these contain guardian deities, designed to ward off evil forces.

Barkor Bazaar is a lively combination of market-place, pilgrim circuit and ethnic melting-pot. The 20-minute hexagonal circuit, running clockwise around the Jokhang and other structures, is always busy—especially at dawn and dusk. Join the pilgrims for a few circuits—good for exercise, good for people watching.

At the front of the Jokhang, the flagstones are worn smooth—polished from many years of pilgrims performing prostrations. Two-metre-high conical incense-burners billow clouds of smoke, and the smell of juniper fills the air. Vendors—mostly Chinese making a buck off Buddhism—sell katas, prayer flags and prayer-wheels to the pilgrims. Arriving on pilgrimage from far-flung regions—such as the Kham or Golok areas—pilgrims mutter mantras as they circumambulate. You might see nomad women from eastern Tibet, their long tresses smeared in yak-butter; or an old woman leading her favourite sheep around the circuit; a proud Khampa from eastern Tibet with tassels of red yarn braided through his hair, and a dagger on his belt (not entirely decorative); or a hardy prostrator with rubber apron and padded gloves flinging himself forward on the ground—completing the circuit on his stomach.

The Barkor is a magnet for beggars seeking alms, and for pilgrims seeking funds for their return home (and to support themselves in Lhasa in the meantime). More sophisticated are sutra-chanters: for a small sum, they will recite from sacred texts. And finally, there is the bazaar itself—shops and businesses line the entire circuit. Competing with these are open-air stalls laden with souvenirs and household goods; and there are roving vendors with bags of Tibetan music cassettes or other items. Since 1987, Barkor Bazaar has assumed another role—as the focus of protesters who encircle the Barkor when demonstrating against the Chinese occupation of Tibet. This will explain the presence of police and security personnel in the area, ready to intercept any demonstrators.

Barkor Square

Officially, Barkor Square was completed in 1985 to mark the 20th year of the creation of the TAR. Unofficially, it was built to provide full military access to the troublesome Tibetan quarter and the maze of alleyways in the Barkor beyond. In the process, the Jokhang—previously hidden from view—has been exposed by a large plaza. There used to be a small square in front of the Jokhang—used as a marketplace—

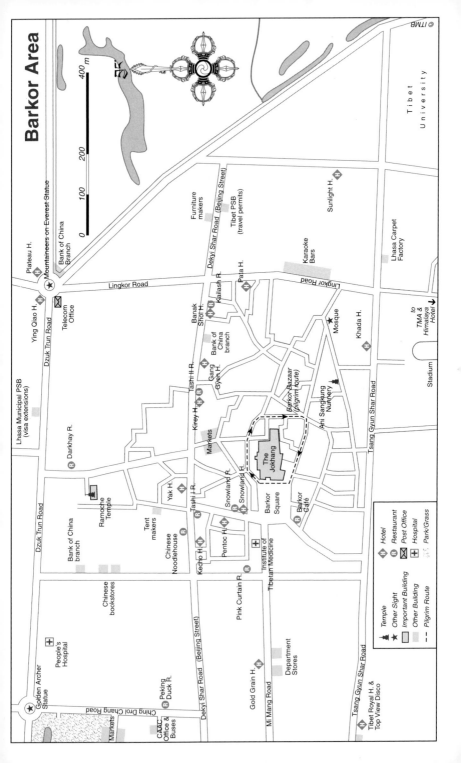

but nothing on the scale of the present plaza. This architectural approach might suit a grand European cathedral, but it is a travesty when applied to an intimate corner like the Jokhang.

Barkor Square is lined with shops and eateries—but it is also an elaborate parking lot for army trucks should trouble arise. A lot of older housing was ripped up and then replaced with mock-Tibetan-style shops, but these do not quite look the same. For one thing, the outer walls of these newer buildings are vertical—not bevelled as in old Lhasa. Old Lhasan housing is conservative in style—with an "extraordinary biblical severity…preserving for us living architectural forms of ancient civilisations", as one writer noted. Typical housing consisted of flat-roofed two- or three-storey structures made of stone or sun-baked brick. Some buildings in the Barkor area date back to the 17th century and have withstood the test of time. Like the great masons of ancient Egypt or the Inca empire, Tibetans used no nails or cement: they fitted large blocks of stone closely together and relied on gravity—which meant inward-sloping walls were constructed.

In the PRC, squares like this are used for mass shows of solidarity with the Party, but occasionally (as at Tiananmen Square in 1989) they can be used for mass demonstrations against the Party. In Barkor Square, if 20 or so Tibetans congregate, the police will break the gathering up, nervous of a repeat of the rioting that has taken place in the past.

Barkor Back Alleys

The Barkor area was proposed as a UN World Heritage site, but apparently it did not qualify because of too much destruction. The Chinese are systematically tearing down as much of the old quarter as possible on the grounds that the buildings are unstable: these same buildings are then replaced with newer ones of a similar design. Despite this, the Barkor area is a real delight for strays and alley-cats, with small markets and temples tucked away—and Tibetans playing billiards. You can explore on foot or by bicycle. Around here, you step into a timewarp, catching glimpses of what life must have been like centuries ago. Or you could try a millennium: **Ramoche Temple,** to the northern side of the Barkor, is thought to date back to the seventh century—it is older than the Jokhang. The Ramoche is Lhasa's second-largest temple and is best-viewed during prayer sessions (early morning or late afternoon) for real atmosphere. An entry fee is charged; you might be allowed to access the rooftop, with good views of the area. The wide alley that leads to the Ramoche Temple is lined with curious shops—some merchants selling gold teeth, others gilded temple-top ornaments.

Waiting for you to discover are a host of small temples and shrines tucked into the back alleys. Easy to find are two temples at the back of the Jokhang on the Barkor circuit, on the northeast side. On the edge of the Barkor area, on the southeast side, is **Ani Sangkhung**—one of the three nunneries in Lhasa. Upward of 80 nuns live at Ani Sangkhung: a number of nuns from this place are serving time in Drapchi Prison for demonstrating. The nunnery is difficult to find—keep asking for Ani Gompa. Also in this vicinity are several small mosques, combining Muslim and Tibetan architectural features.

INSTITUTE OF TIBETAN MEDICINE

Tibetan medicine is an amalgam of herbal cures, astrology and Tibetan Buddhism. No surgery is used—for this, the patient would have to go to other practitioners. Diagnosis in Tibetan medicine is done mainly by reading the pulse (urine samples are also checked). By reading the pulse, a traditional physician determines which humour-flow (bile, wind or phlegm) has been blocked, or is excessive—and which herbal remedies to prescribe to set the system in harmony. Apart from the three main "humours" there are over 20,000 "channels" operating through the body. Though this may sound like medieval alchemy, in fact there is strong evidence to suggest the herbal cures, developed over a millenium, have considerable effect.

Since the medical college on Chakpori Hill was razed in 1959, the institute is the only traditional medicine facility left in Lhasa. In its present form—a bland concrete building located just west off Barkor Square—the institute opened in 1977. It has in-patient, out-patient and pharmaceutical production sections, as well as an astro/medical teaching institute.

Put together a small group and you can arrange a short tour of the Institute of Tibetan Medicine (Monday to Saturday, 9–12.30 mornings), which will include a visit to a second-floor museum, and the top floor medical tanka room. Here hundreds of rare medical tankas are stored—teaching devices showing which plants should be collected, anatomical charts with energy channels, and so on. You will be shown copies of the originals. In the same section are three statues of famous medical practitioners—in the middle a white-bearded figure (Yutok Yonten Gonpo, 9th-century founder of Tibetan medical science), flanked on left by the regent of the 5th Dalai Lama (Desi Sanggye Gyatso, 17th-century founder of Chakpori medical college) and on the right by the most renowned physician of the 20th century (Khyenrab Norbu, physician to the 13th Dalai Lama).

BEGGAR WITH A MOBILE PHONE

Lhasa has an air of mystery and intrigue still—but not quite the way you'd think. The big mysteries today are what all those Chinese buildings are, with the guards out the front holding AK-47s or with pistols on their belts. The Chinese military have their own living quarters, exclusive markets, teahouses, restaurants, bars, discos and clubs tucked away—but you can walk into some of them. A lot of buildings are off-limits or Chinese-only or sensitive—and photography is frowned upon. Army bases are self-contained units with high walls—they usually have their own shops and facilities within, including their own video-cinema.

To assist the paranoid Chinese in their endeavours to snoop on Tibetans is a nefarious network of informants—human listening posts—and video surveillance cameras. The video cameras are mounted around the Potala and Barkor areas, and at major intersections of the city. The cameras were initially sold by Western countries to China for use in monitoring traffic flow. Since Lhasa doesn't have a traffic flow problem, obviously they are being put to other uses here. The Chinese network of Tibetan informants includes plainclothes police, monks in robes—and beggars. One Tibetan described these people as "Tibetans who do Chinese work." In the Barkor area, a man in rags was seen begging one moment—and the next using a mobile phone to inform police of what was going on.

The Chinese are convinced that demonstrations by the Tibetans could flare up at any moment. And then there is the threat of bombs. There have been sporadic reports on bomb blasts around Lhasa starting in the mid-1990s. The nature of the bombing is mysterious—Chinese authorities have largely remained silent on the subject. The bombs do not appear designed to cause loss of life—rather, to drive home a message of protest.

In June 1995, police defused an explosive device at the Qinghai-Tibet Highway monument, an obelisk to the west side of the city, opposite the bus station. The monument commemorates the completion of roads linking the TAR to the provinces of Qinghai and Sichuan. Authorities were nervous because the explosive device was discovered a few months before the 30th anniversary of the founding of the TAR, scheduled for September 1995. With about 500 government officials and their families from all over China expected for the celebration, security was considerably tightened, and half a dozen checkpoints established on the Gonggar to Lhasa road. Two European tourists who took photographs of the obelisk a week later were detained and questioned for two hours, and had their film confiscated. In another 1995 incident, a tourist sent a fax from the Holiday Inn speculating about a bomb explosion: Chinese police intercepted the fax, arrested the tourist in the middle of the night, detained him for 48 hours, and then deported him.

In May 1996, Chinese authorities admitted to three bomb blasts in Lhasa, blaming them on separatists. In December 1996, a bomb damaged the gatehouse of the Metropolitan District Government Offices. The blast was confirmed on Tibet Radio, which described the incident as "yet another counterrevolutionary bombing staged by the Dalai clique in Lhasa City" and calling it "an appalling act of terrorism." A substantial reward was posted for information leading to the capture of the person or persons responsible. In June 1998, a bomb exploded outside the City PSB building.

There are closed-circuit surveillance cameras mounted inside the Potala to eavesdrop on the caretaker monks there. Even though the Potala is Lhasa's major tourist attraction, and one of its most sacred sites, its last resident—the 14th Dalai Lama—is vilified by the Chinese. His picture is banned, along with that of the young 11th Panchen Lama (the one chosen by the Dalai Lama). So the whole trade in Dalai Lama and Panchen Lama pictures—once freely pursued in the Barkor—has simply gone underground.

POTALA AREA

THE LINGKOR

The Lingkor is the outer pilgrim circuit of Lhasa, taking about 90 minutes to complete on foot (or half that time by bicycle). Tibetans still follow the full Lingkor circuit, though it has lost much of its sacred appeal on the eastern and southern sides, where small bars and karaoke salons have mushroomed. These places are often fronts for prostitution. Nudes or noodles? Probably a bit of both, washed down with beer. Prostitutes are flown in from Sichuan province. Other fronts: barbershops west of the Potala, and certain restaurants with partitioned sections. How big is the trade? Very big. At Jarmalingka Island bridge, the news doesn't get any better. An old wooden bridge here used to lead to an undeveloped area where Tibetan picnickers would congregate. The bridge was torn down and replaced by a

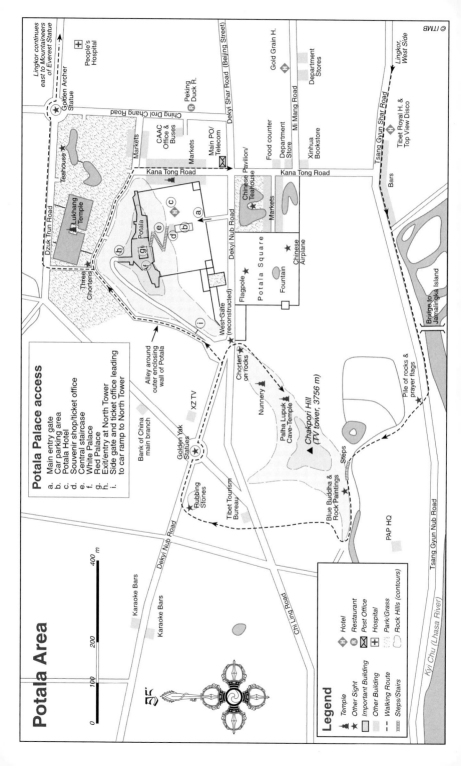

Potala Area

Potala Palace access

a. Main entry gate
b. Car parking area
c. Potala Hotel
d. Souvenir shop/ticket office
e. Central staircase
f. White Palace
g. Red Palace
h. Exit/entry at North Tower
i. Side gate and ticket office leading to car ramp to North Tower

Lingkor continues east to Mountaineers of Everest Statue

Golden Archer Statue
People's Hospital
Peking Duck R.
Ching Drol Chang Road
Dekyi Shar Road (Beijing Street)
Gold Grain H.
Department Stores
Lingkor, West Side

CAAC Office & Buses
Markets
Main PO/Telecom
Markets
Food counter
Department Store
Mi Mang Road
Xinhua Bookstore

Kana Tong Road
Teahouse
Dzuk Trun Road
Lukhang Temple
Kana Tong Road
Chinese Pavilion/Teahouse
Markets
Tsang Gyun Shar Road
Tibet Royal H. & Top View Disco

Three Chortens
Potala
Dekyi Nub Road
Potala Square
Fountain
Chinese Airplane
Bars

Flagpole
West-Gate (reconstructed)

Alley around outer enclosing wall of Potala

Bridge to Jamalingka Island

XZ TV
Chorten on rocks
Nunnery
Palha Lupuk Cave-Temple
Chakpori Hill (TV tower, 3756 m)

Golden Yak Statues
Bank of China main branch
Steps
Pile of rocks & prayer flags

Tibet Tourism Bureau
Rubbing Stones
Dekyi Nub Road

Blue Buddha & Rock Paintings
PAP HQ
Tsang Gyun Nub Road

Karaoke Bars
Chi Ling Road

Karaoke Bars

Kyi Chu (Lhasa River)

0   100   200   400 m

Legend

★ Temple
★ Other Sight
☐ Important Building
☐ Other Building
- - - Walking Route
⫴ Steps/Stairs

⬧ Hotel
⬧ Restaurant
☒ Post Office
✚ Hospital
Park/Grass
Rock Hills (contours)

© ITMB

wider concrete one—to develop Jarmalingka as a casino site, with backers from Macau.

The Lingkor as a sacred circuit really gets under way at a cairn of stones with some prayer flags, just west of Jarmalingka Bridge. This marks the turn-off for a walking track that leads to the Blue Buddha. Apart from walking, you can bicycle the route, but there are steps near the Blue Buddha which require you to carry the bike. Otherwise, it's easy riding, with smooth, flat sections.

Blue Buddha

The way up past the south base of Chakpori Hill is a staircase lined with prayer flags. Further on is an entire cliff face depicting religious figures, which have been carved in bas-relief and painted in bright colours. Some carvings date back over a thousand years, with countless additions over the centuries. The largest carving is the Blue Buddha, shown seated in a meditation pose. In this area, pilgrims pay their respects, and off to the side, carvers chip text into mani stones. If you follow the pilgrims, you'll eventually arrive at Dekyi Nub Road. Right where you arrive at this major road, there's a section with some well-worn rocks. These are special rubbing stones that pilgrims apply their knees or backs to. From here, pilgrims continue past the Golden Yak statues to Lhasa's West Gate—although these were not part of the original Lingkor circuit.

Golden Yak Statues

Two golden yak statues were unveiled in May 1991 to celebrate the 40th anniversary of the "peaceful liberation" of Tibet by Chinese troops. Tibetans have christened the incongruous statues "Tenzin and Raidi"—a reference to the two Tibetan deputy secretaries of the Communist Party in Tibet who are trotted out when the Chinese need to present a Tibetan face to the media. In the background at this site sits the modern office building housing Xizang TV (XZ TV), the main radio and TV broadcasting unit in Lhasa. The operation is solar-powered. The Golden Yak statues are something of a navigation landmark, referred to in this section as the Golden Yak roundabout.

West Gate

As part of the 1995 "celebrations" of the 30th anniversary of the founding of the TAR, Lhasa's West Gate and two accompanying chortens were resurrected. Passing through the chorten-like West Gate was once the only way into the sacred city—and reaching it was the dream of many explorers. It was the gate that British troops marched through in 1904; the gate that Heinrich Harrer and Peter Aufschnaiter reached in rags in 1946, after two years of wandering. Now you see it, now you don't: the original West Gate was completely destroyed in the Cultural Revolution, and then completely rebuilt for the 1995 ceremonies. Tibetan pilgrims pose next to the 1995 version of the West Gate for photos, but Tibetans say that the structure was not properly consecrated by monks—and in any case, there are no hidden treasures within the chorten-like structure that required consecration. Nevertheless, there is some fine artwork lining the interior of the West Gate, especially a mandalic mural on the inside ceiling.

Detours

From the West Gate, there are several hiking options. Some pilgrims make a complete loop around the outer enclosing wall of the Potala and come back to the West Gate, and then visit Palhalupuk cave-temple. Others go from the West Gate to Palhalupuk first, then trace the wall of the Potala north to a site with three chortens, where they diverge past Lukhang Park to Dzuk Trun Road, and then continue eastward past the Golden Archer statue on the Lingkor circuit. Another hike to consider is a climb to the top of Chakpori. This hill was once crowned by the fortress-like medical college of Lhasa—the institute, founded in the 15th century, was razed by shelling in the 1959 uprising. The hill is now crowned with a TV tower—you can climb to the top for views of the Potala.

Palhalupuk Cave-temple

Palhalupuk is an extraordinary cave-temple set into the lower section of Chakpori Hill—you can reach it by a path leading from the West Gate. The brown and ochre-coloured Palhalupuk temple, with a dozen monks in residence, offers a superb viewpoint of the Potala, giving it a foreground of rocks and trees. Close by are two small caves—the larger one is lined with several rows of brightly painted bas-relief images, believed to date back as far as the 7th century (which qualifies them as the oldest in Lhasa). The central image here is Sakyamuni, while at the back is a small statue of Palden Lhamo, the protectress of Lhasa. The intimate scale of the temple and cave make Palhalupuk very special—it offers perspectives that you will find nowhere else in Lhasa. There's a second (minor) cave with an image of Avalokitesvara in the vicinity; above Palhalupuk to the right is a small active nunnery.

Lukhang Park

The park at the back of the Potala was a site where Tibetan aristocracy used to picnic or drink tea. It has lost its noble atmosphere—it's down at the proletariat level now, re-named Jiefang (Victory) Park. However, you can still take tea—and contemplate the excellent views of the Potala. There are three entrances to the park—one at the north side, one at the east, and one at the southeast side. On the western side, the way in is blocked by walls and Lukhang Lake. At the entrances, you pay a token fee (extra for a bicycle). Lukhang Park attracts picnickers, strollers and people relaxing—it's great for cycling around. Toward the northeast corner is a teahouse with outdoor tables and umbrellas—it looks over a small artificial lake, with the towers of the Potala looming above. A plant nursery is attached to the teahouse: potted plants and flowers make this a very pleasant place. You can park yourself over a cup of ba bao cha (eight treasures tea)—this is provided in a cup with a lid, and contains a big lump of rock sugar with dried berries and herbs, to which steaming hot water is added.

Lukhang Temple

On an island in the middle of the lake is Lukhang Temple, a tiny three-storey chapel constructed in the form of a mandala. Building of the temple is attributed to the Sixth Dalai Lama—it was used as a quiet retreat by successive Dalai Lamas. There are a few monks currently in residence at Lukhang Temple. You can visit: not all parts of the building are accessible. There are murals on each of the three storeys: the most interesting are those on the third floor, believed to date to the 18th century. You will need a flashlight to see these gems—they are protected by a wire shield, which doesn't make the viewing easier. The murals show subjects that are rare to find in Tibetan temples today. Among them are depictions of Indian ascetics in yogic poses, and others striking blissful tantric poses. One wall shows the stages of human life, with detailed anatomical pictures acting as a kind of Tibetan medicine primer (in which system an imbalance of humours leads to sickness and dysfunction). Attached to this is a set of murals based on The Tibetan Book of the Dead.

POTALA SQUARE

Potala Square was created in time to mark "celebrations" for the 30th anniversary of the TAR. A large area of ramshackle Tibetan housing was razed to create the paving: the inhabitants were moved to concrete housing north of the Potala. The concept of a large square or plaza is alien to Tibetan town planning: this is a Chinese idea. The

THE MYSTERIOUS SIXTH

The Sixth Dalai Lama was Tsangyang Gyatso, whose name means "Ocean of Melodious Songs." He is thought to have lived from 1683 to 1706. The Sixth took over as Dalai Lama under very unusual circumstances. The Fifth Dalai Lama had died during the construction of the Potala but his death was concealed by the Regent for some 15 years to ensure completion of the work (the Fifth was replaced by a double and was said to be engaged in long meditation retreats). The Sixth Dalai Lama took over as an adolescent, not an infant like his predecessors. He did not take any celibacy vows and was never fully ordained as a lama. He showed little interest in either his political or religious duties. His passions lay elsewhere. He was a prolific rake—no woman in Lhasa was said to be safe from his indulgences:

> *I dwell apart in the Potala*
> *A God on earth am I*
> *But in the town the chief of rogues*
> *And boisterous revelry*

Lukhang Temple has been variously described as the Sixth's personal retreat—and as his favourite trysting place. He was said to sneak out a back gate of the Potala to meet his lovers. Apart from his love of wine and women, the Sixth was renowned as a melodious singer of love songs, and writer of romantic lyrics:

> *Drops of rain wash away*
> *The love songs written in*
> *Black and white*
> *But love, though unwritten,*
> *Remains long after, in the heart*

Despite his behaviour, the Sixth was revered by the people, who came to the conclusion that the living Buddha had two bodies—one which stayed in the Potala and meditated, and the other that got rotten drunk and chased Lhasa women. The Sixth disappeared under mysterious circumstances at the age of 23. One account claims that he had a son by a special lover, and that high lamas—fearing the office of the Dalai Lama would become hereditary—drove the Sixth into exile and imprisoned his lover and their son. Another account claims he was murdered at Litang.

Tibetans would have no use for such a square because it allows the bitter winter wind to roar through. Potala Square has a lot in common with Beijing's Tiananmen Square, including the same chandelier-lamp fixtures with propaganda speakers attached. Tiananmen Square was Mao Zedong's creation—designed for military parades and mass solidarity parades, and meanwhile used for weekend amusement like photo-taking or kite flying.

This is exactly what Potala Square is used for: the military use it as one big parking lot; concerts for the military have been staged here; shows of force and parades by the PLA have taken place; trade fairs with vendors promoting Chinese products have been conducted here. The emphasis at Potala Square is on entertainment, too—angled for the Chinese. In the mid-1990s, Lhasa's biggest Chinese disco, called JJ's, was located in a large building on the west side of Potala Square—it closed down within a year. Toward the back of the square are amusement rides for children, a fountain with a Chinese dragon sculpture, and an old aircraft which is used as a photo-prop. Potala Square is the premier Chinese photo opportunity site. There is a slew of photo-shops just to the west of the square, catering to Chinese tourism. A flagpole at the front of the square is a favourite place for Chinese tourists to have their photos taken. All Chinese dignitaries and military honchos arriving in Lhasa stop near the flagpole to have photos or video taken with the Potala in the background.

POTALA PALACE

The Potala was inscribed on the UNESCO World Heritage List in 1994. The citation says "The Potala, winter palace of the Dalai Lama since the 7th century AD, symbolises Tibetan Buddhism and its central role in the traditional administration of Tibet." Chinese authorities conducted a five-year multi-million-dollar restoration of the Potala, completing work in 1995. Why restore a palace that is former abode of Public Enemy Number One? As a tourist attraction, of course. Unlike the Jokhang or the monasteries around Lhasa, the Potala is run by Chinese tourist authorities: the practice of Buddhism is essentially banned in the palace.

Once humming with activity, the Potala is now a lifeless museum, a haunted castle. A lot of the Chinese restoration was directed at the enclosing walls, which were damaged by Chinese shelling during the 1959 uprising. Adding considerably to the bill is the "wiring" of the Potala. Electrical hook-ups have been enhanced and video surveillance cameras have been installed throughout. The cameras are to monitor the 60-odd caretakers at the Potala—mostly monks who are not permitted to wear robes (it appears that a number of them were replaced by ordinary cleaners in 1997). On a more practical note, fire extinguishers and other devices have been installed (following a disastrous fire that broke out in 1984 due to a short circuit).

Below the Potala, within the enclosing walls, used to lie the Tibetan administrative quarter of Shol. Some buildings in this zone have been destroyed. One building has been turned into a hotel; the others are used as art galleries, souvenir shops, or occupied as residences. In pre-1950 days, Shol quartered the offices of the Tibetan government, Tibetan Army officials, guard offices and a prison. Other sections of the Potala were used to house Namgyal Monastery, as well as a community of monks and a school for monk officials.

History & Architecture

The Potala is a 13-storey castle—rising over 117 metres—built of rammed earth, wood and stone. Crowning a mass of solid rock, the maze-like structure contains over a thousand rooms, and is thought to house 10,000 shrines and 200,000 statues. The architecture at first appears to be regular, but is not—storeys are not continuous, and access to halls may be hidden behind pillars or shrines. The walls—varying in thickness between two and five metres—were strengthened against earthquakes by pouring in molten copper. No steel frame was used, and no nails were used in the woodwork. The Potala is layered structure: successive Dalai Lamas worked on the project. Although original construction dates back to the 7th century, the White Palace was not completed until 1653, and the Red Palace completed by 1694: at this time, the wheel had not been introduced to Tibet, so stones were lugged in on donkey-back, or on the backs of humans. Simple equipment was used to fashion this skyscraper—an achievement on a par with the building of the pyramids.

The skyscraper itself created a transport problem. The Potala had no plumbing, electricity or heating, so there was—in previous times—a constant stream of porters with water for tea, yak-butter for the prayer-lamps, and firewood for the fireplaces. The Dalai Lama was portered in and out of the palace in a palanquin; high lamas were piggybacked up to the entrance of the Potala by porters.

Access

Hours of opening for the Potala seem to chop and change, and may vary with the season. You can follow the logic of the hours described here, but there could well be modifications. In theory the Potala is open to tourists six days a week, from 9.30 am to noon (possibly as late as 12.30), Monday to Friday, and probably also Saturday (could be restricted access on Saturday). Winter hours and days open may vary from this schedule. The entry ticket is $6; a half-price ticket is offered to foreign students with proof of status; there are additional charges for use of a camera or video-camera; a further charge is later levied to get on the rooftop, and into two exhibition halls near the teahouse in the Red Palace. The Potala is open to Tibetan pilgrims, who pay a token entry fee, from 8.30 am to noon on Mondays, Wednesdays and Fridays. Technically, the Potala is closed on Sundays, but because this is inconvenient for group tour schedules, they do visit on Sundays (the entry price doubles, however).

Because Tibetan pilgrims are only allowed to visit the Potala three mornings a week, on these days, key shrines may become very crowded, with long line-ups. Here's a paradox: things are much more lively with Tibetan pilgrims around (you can observe what they are doing—muttering mantras, flinging katas, and spooning yak-butter into lamps at shrines) but at the same time, it's more crowded and uncomfortable. Solution: visit the Potala twice—the first time to see the architecture and statuary on a tourist-only day. The second time, go and mingle with the Tibetan pilgrims.

If you consult the Potala Area access section of the Potala Area map, you can discern the main entry/exit routes. There are two ticket kiosks where you pay to enter the Potala—near the central staircase (d), or near the West Gate, at a large wooden door leading to a car ramp (i) that brings you out to a parking area at the North Tower (h). You can enter and exit using a combination of these options. Group tours usually drive up in vans to the North Tower, and make their way through the Potala, exiting down the central staircase (e), where the vans pick them up again. This requires a minimum of physical exertion, which is what the tour operators want. Freelance travellers can walk up the same ramp to enter the Potala, but most opt for the traditional approach—the route the pilgrims take—which is via the central staircase. You walk slowly up the central staircase (e), reach the rooftop, spiral down through the Red Palace (g), and exit at the North Tower (the exit is difficult to locate—it's at the back of statuary, so just follow the pilgrims). You can then walk back down the car ramp to the West Gate area. A word of caution if you are tackling the central staircase—it's like Stairmaster at altitude. Ensure that you are reasonably acclimatised before tackling these steps—they can knock the wind out of you.

The description in this book follows the entry up the central staircase and exit via the North Tower: if approaching from the reverse direction, read backwards. Only a fraction of the Potala's 1000-odd rooms are accessible to the touring public: the contents of many are rumoured to have been destroyed or carted off. The rooms seem to open and close without rhyme or reason, so the following description may hit the mark—or it may not.

Inside the Potala

The Potala is divided into the White Palace and the Red Palace. The White Palace was secular in nature (used for offices, printing house, and so on), while the Red Palace fulfilled a religious function (comprising the tombs of the Dalai Lamas, scores of chapels and shrines, and libraries of sacred texts). Most of the White Palace is inaccessible; you can see a fair number of rooms in the Red Palace.

The 14th Dalai Lama's Quarters

After huffing and puffing up the central staircase, you arrive near the roof of the Potala, reaching an open area: to the west side of this are the former living quarters of the 13th and 14th Dalai Lamas, attached to the White Palace. The only section accessible here takes you into the former Reception Hall, dominated by a large throne. On the wall nearby hangs a portrait painting of 13th Dalai Lama, but a portrait of the 14th that used to hang alongside it has been removed. So ludicrous is the Chinese removal of 14th Dalai Lama images that in a lavishly illustrated Beijing hardcover about the Potala, he is only seen in one picture—shaking hands with Mao Zedong in 1954.

In the same Reception Hall, near the entrance, is a large mural of the legendary land of Shambhala. Beyond the hall lie the private quarters of the 14th Dalai Lama. You may or may not be allowed to see these—depending on the mood of caretakers. Try tagging along behind an official tour. At the 14th Dalai Lama's tearoom and meditation room, pilgrims leave katas and other offerings; beyond is His Holiness' bedroom, vacant since 1959.

Back out in the open courtyard, you can fork over another dollar or so to take rickety ladders that lead right onto the roof of the roof of the world. Here you can see what the Chinese have wrought in Lhasa—the extent of Potala Square. Chinese tourists hire historic costumes here for photo-taking sessions.

The Red Palace

Entering the Red Palace from the rooftop area, you spiral downward through four levels, eventually exiting at the North Tower. The upper levels of the Red Palace enclose an open skylight space, with chapels arrayed in a gallery-like rectangle around that space. Interspersed through the many chapels and shrines of the Red Palace are the eight gold-plated stupas, each containing the salt-dried body of a past Dalai Lama—from the 5th to the 13th, with the exception of the 6th, who disappeared. Four of the reliquary stupas are on the upper level, and four on the ground level.

Upper Level: The upper level contains access to chapels with the stupas of the 7th, 8th, 9th and 13th Dalai Lamas. You may have difficulty getting permission to see the stupa of the 13th Dalai Lama, which is 14 metres high, made of gold, and fronted by a three-dimensional mandala said to contain 200,000 pearls. The tomb ranges over several storeys and is well lit. One wall bears fine murals of the 13th Dalai Lama surrounded by his ministers and tutors, as well as scenes from his life. Another highlight of the upper level is the former throne room of the 7th Dalai Lama, which contains a beautiful silver image of eleven-faced Avalokitesvara, the bodhisattva of compassion—this statue was commissioned by the 13th Dalai Lama.

Revered by Tibetan pilgrims as the most sacred part of the entire Potala is the Avalokitesvara Chapel (Phakpa Lakhang), on the northwest side of the upper level. The tiny chapel gets very crowded on the days that the palace is open to pilgrims. It is reached by a small triple staircase. The centre of pilgrim attention is a tiny gilded standing statue of Avalokitesvara, thought to have come from Nepal. Legend has it that the image was found miraculously embedded in a Nepalese sandalwood tree when its trunk split open. Flanking it are two other images derived from the same source—one of Avalokitesvara again, the other of Tara. To the right of this chapel is the massive funerary chorten of the 7th Dalai Lama, rising to a height of nine metres, and studded with precious stones. Next to that is the tomb of the 9th Dalai Lama.

Mid-levels: Downstairs, there is a Tibetan-style tearoom with a souvenir shop. There are two levels of galleries here, but rooms on the lower level are most likely closed (these contain murals depicting the construction of the Potala and major Tibetan monasteries). The highlight of the mid-levels is the Kalachakra Chapel (Dukhor Lakhang), which contains a stunning three-dimensional mandala of the palace of the Kalachakra deity. Made of copper and gold, it measures over six metres in diameter. To one side of the mandala is a life-sized statue of the multi-headed multi-armed Kalachakra deity in union with his consort. On shelves nearby are the seven religious kings of Tibet and the 25 kings of the mythical realm of Shambhala.

Very popular with Tibetan pilgrims on this level is the oldest chamber in the Potala—the Chapel of the Dharma Kings, thought to have been the meditation chamber of King Songsten Gampo. This cave-within-the-castle is approached by a ramp; the niches lining the cavern are filled with statuary of past kings, royal family members and ministers. The most highly-regarded statue is that of Songsten Gampo himself.

Ground Level: After negotiating several steep, dark flights of stairs, you come into a large assembly hall with columns—the Great Western Assembly Hall. This is the largest room in the Potala Palace, with dozens of pillars wrapped in raw silk. It contains the throne of the 7th Dalai Lama; the walls are coated in murals and applique tankas.

There are four chapels open on this level. The first you come to is Lamrin Lakhang, dedicated to the ancient lineage masters of the Geluk school, particularly Tsongkhapa. The next chapel, Rigdzin Lakhang, is dedicated to the great Nyingma lineage holder, Padmasambhava, showing eight manifestations of the master; in the same line-up of statues here are seven other great Indian masters.

The next chapel, Dzamling Gyenchik, contains the astounding tomb of the 5th Dalai Lama, which reaches a height of over 14 metres, and is said to contain 3700 kg of gold. It is studded with jewels and precious stones. In this line-up of tombs are eight more dedicated to Sakyamuni Buddha, commemorating the eight major events in his life. In the same chapel are the more modest stupas of the 10th and 12th Dalai Lamas, who both perished as minors, failing to attain their majority. The Dalai Lamas from the 6th through 12th all died young and under mysterious circumstances—possibly poisoned.

The last chapel on the ground level is Tungrab Lakhang, featuring a central double throne with two statues—a gold one of Sakyamuni and a silver one of the 5th Dalai Lama. This chapel contains the tomb of the 11th Dalai Lama; three statues of the Buddha (past, present and future); and statues of the eight Medicine Buddhas.

North Tower Exit

You can exit Tungrab Lakhang by a dark corridor at the back of the statues—this leads out the rear of the Potala at the North Tower. Heading down the hill you get a view of north Lhasa that is not revealed from the rooftop of the Potala. You leave the palace grounds by the doorway near the West Gate.

THE NORBULINGKA

In contrast to the lofty, monumental Potala, the Norbulingka is a small-scale down-to-earth summer palace. In former times, an elaborate procession would wind out of the Potala, escorting the Dalai Lama to the Norbulingka—his home for up to six months of the year. In better days, the walled summer palace exuded an idyllic atmosphere, with picnic pavilions and well-tended gardens, peacocks roaming the grounds, and Brahminy ducks flocking to the lakes. Norbulingka in fact means "Jewelled Garden." Visiting in the 1930s, members of a British delegation were surprised to find roses and petunias flourishing at 3650 metres, as well as hollyhocks, marigolds, chrysanthemums, and rows of potted herbs or rare plants. As well, there were apple, peach and apricot trees—though the fruits did not ripen in Lhasa—and stands of poplar trees and bamboo. The Norbulingka was shelled during the 1959 uprising, and a number of buildings were destroyed. The gardens now lie derelict—the fountains and miniature lakes have dried up. The Norbulingka is mainly identified with the 13th and 14th Dalai Lamas, who commissioned most of the structures you see here.

Access

The Norbulingka is open 9.30–12.30 mornings and 3.30–6 pm (summer hours); closed Sundays. To get to the Norbulingka, you can walk, bicycle, take a taxi, or take a number 2 bus from the Barkor Square vicinity. Although there are several gateways at the Norbulingka, the only one open for entry/exit is the East Gate, with a ticket booth and bicycle parking nearby. When Tibetan opera is held here during the Yoghurt (Shoton) Festival, around August/September, the grounds are crowded with picnickers. Flanking the massive east gates of the Norbulingka are two snow lion statues, draped in katas. Tibetans like to get their photo taken next to the mythical snow lion (the one to the left side shelters a lion cub). The snow lion is the symbol of Tibet—it is reputed to be able to jump from one snowcapped peak to another. Only a few buildings inside the Norbulingka are open—others are locked up, or used as storage, or as residences or offices by those involved with the upkeep of the Norbulingka. Some more recent building additions or renovations are souvenir kiosks—selling drinks, souvenir books and some Tibetan artefacts. There's a restaurant to the northeast side called Snowland Tibetan Flavour Restaurant, operated by Snowland Hotel.

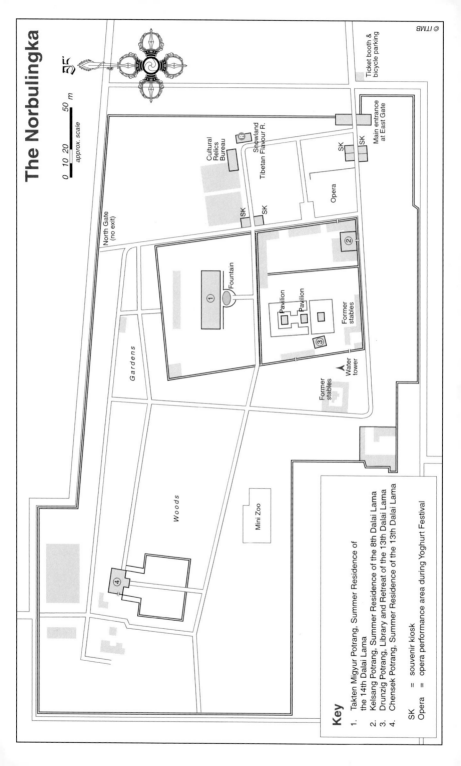

The Norbulingka

0 10 20   50 m
approx. scale

North Gate (no exit)

Gardens

Woods

Mini Zoo

Cultural Relics Bureau

Snowland Tibetan Flavour R.

Opera

Main entrance at East Gate

Ticket booth & bicycle parking

Fountain

Pavilion Pavilion

Former stables

Former stables

Water tower

SK

SK

SK

SK

© ITMB

Key

1. Takten Migyur Potrang, Summer Residence of the 14th Dalai Lama
2. Kelsang Potrang, Summer Residence of the 8th Dalai Lama
3. Drunzig Potrang, Library and Retreat of the 13th Dalai Lama
4. Chensek Potrang, Summer Residence of the 13th Dalai Lama

SK   = souvenir kiosk
Opera = opera performance area during Yoghurt Festival

Residence of the 14th Dalai Lama

The main attraction at the Norbulingka is Takten Migyur Potrang (1), the summer residence of 14th Dalai Lama. It's a pilgrimage site for Tibetans, who leave katas and other offerings in the various rooms here. The building was constructed 1954 to 1956, and was the place where the Dalai Lama meditated before he escaped to India. Access is only to rooms on the upper floor.

In the Assembly Hall, murals portray a detailed history of Tibet, from its mythical beginnings to its early kings to the discovery of the 14th Dalai Lama. Several other rooms can be seen here—the Dalai Lama's study chambers, with a beautiful tanka of Atisha; and his bedroom, with an art-deco bed and a 1956 Phillips radio (a gift from India). A sidedoor leads to a bathroom with state-of-the-art (for Tibet at the time) plumbing. You may be allowed to visit a small library and a meditation room.

In the Reception Hall is a carved golden throne which was used to carry the Dalai Lama when he went outside the Norbulingka for special occasions. One entire wall of the Reception Hall is covered with fine murals, painted in 1956 by artist Amdo Jampa. The murals show—with photo-like realism—the 14th Dalai Lama at the centre, flanked by his mother at the right, ministers and relatives at the left, secretary below him, his four tutors above him, various tribes of Tibet at lower right, and foreign dignitaries at lower left. Under all this is a row of mythical figures. Among the foreign dignitaries you can make out Hugh Richardson (hat and tie) who originally worked for the British and stayed on to represent the new Indian government. Also visible is an Indian dignitary, a Russian wearing medals and a Mongolian ambassador. The opposite wall bears a large portrait of the Great Fifth Dalai Lama, surrounded by smaller portraits of the first through 13th Dalai Lamas. As you exit the doorway, there's a round Shambhala fresco with a Kalachakra mandala. Harder to access are other sections of the building, including the dining room, and various meeting and reception rooms.

Retreats, Vintage Cars & a Zoo

Moving along through the grounds of the Norbulingka, of milder interest is Kelsang Potrang (2), the summer residence of the 8th Dalai Lama, completed in the 18th century. This section may be closed: if it's open, you can view some fine tankas depicting White Tara. On the eastern wall in this area is a viewing pavilion that looks over the opera grounds. The Dalai Lamas would sit here to take in performances, which are still held during the Yoghurt Festival (in August or September). To the west of this, in a separate compound (approached from the west wall) is Drunzig Potrang (3), constructed as the library and retreat of 13th Dalai Lama. It has the atmosphere of a place of worship, with an assembly hall redolent of butter-lamps. It contains a newer wooden statue of Avalokitesvara, and thousands of sacred texts. Nearby is an area with outdoor pavilions—probably used for picnics or drinking tea. The mini-lakes they overlook have dried up.

There are several locations where horses were formerly stabled—though these are hard to pinpoint today. The back of each stable was decorated with bright frescoes of equestrian subjects, ranging from horse anatomy to legends of flying horses. And nearby was the Dalai Lama's garage. In a compound near the water tower (now occupied by a Tibetan family) are the rusted remains of three cars belonging to the 13th Dalai Lama. They were gifts from British political officers, carried in pieces by yaks over the Himalayas from India and reassembled by an Indian chauffeur and mechanic. Two were 1920s Baby Austins (one with the numberplate Tibet 1); the third was a 1931 orange Dodge. They were used for special occasions—the only cars in Tibet at the time, apart from an American jeep. Their range was limited by a lack of roads and lack of gasoline—which had to be carried in from India. By the 1940s, they had fallen into disrepair, but the young 14th Dalai Lama managed to get them running again. He took a Baby Austin out for a spin at the Norbulingka—and promptly crashed into a tree. One of these cars was later adapted to power a generator—for the 14th Dalai Lama's private cinema. Somewhere in the inner gardens of the Norbulingka, there used to be a movie-theatre, constructed in 1949 for the Dalai Lama by Heinrich Harrer (there was another cine-projection room at the British Mission, run by radio operator Reginald Fox).

A fair walk away, in the northwest corner of the grounds, is Chensek Potrang (4), the summer residence of the 13th Dalai Lama. It was built in 1922, and is preserved much as it was in 1933, when the 13th Dalai Lama died. Only the assembly hall here may be accessible. Along the way is a derelict mini-zoo, with some cages lying empty. In residence is a motley collection of bears, spotted deer, rhesus monkeys, foxes, lynxes and Argali bighorn sheep—none of whom look especially thrilled about living on bare concrete.

SKY BURIAL

To the north of Lhasa is a kind of "dead end," with Drapchi Prison, Lhasa Military Hospital, and—to the northeast—a large flat-topped boulder, on top of which sky burials take place. Upon death, the body is thought to return to one of the elements—earth, air, fire, water, or wood. Earth burial is rare in Tibet: the ground is hard to break up, and could be frozen in winter. Cremation (return to fire) is also rare because wood is a scarce commodity. A high lama might be cremated, and the ashes placed in a silver chorten in his monastery. Two other forms reserved for high lamas are wood burial (the body is placed in a hollow tree trunk), and embalming (the body is preserved in a seated pose by an ancient Tibetan embalming technique). Water burial—whereby the body is eaten by fish—is reserved for small children and paupers.

In Tibet, the most common form of dispatching the dead is not under the ground, but the opposite—releasing the body to the air. This is sky burial. The body is taken to a site on a rock on a mountainside and hacked into pieces with machetes. The bones are pounded together with tsampa, and when the work is complete, a signal is given to waiting flocks of vultures—which know the timing well—to feast on the rock. This way, the body is thought to be taken closer to the heavens. Sky burial takes place all over Tibet, but is more common in Lhasa because of the larger resident population.

In the mid-1980s, travellers were allowed to sit near the rock where sky burial takes place. As long as they were respectful of the customs and did not take photos, they were tolerated by the Tibetans. However, a number of ugly incidents involving photo-taking upset the Tibetans. In particular, one Westerner climbed up behind the rock, intending to sneak photos of the site with a long lens. In the process, he scared off the vultures who sit on the ridge above the sky burial site, so they did not come down at the completion of rites—a very bad omen. Since the early 1990s, the site has been off-limits to tourists.

OUTSKIRTS OF LHASA

One of the saving graces of Lhasa is its clean air—far cleaner than in Kathmandu or other Asian cities. In Lhasa, buildings are low-rise, traffic is light, and the place is ringed by mountains. Offering novel perspectives on Lhasa Valley are ridge-top viewpoints—at Bumpa Ri to the southeast side, above Sera to the north side, and at Gephel Ri to the northwest side. The easiest one to tackle is Bumpa Ri. To get to the base of Bumpa Ri, you can bicycle out over Lhasa Bridge—the only bridge to span the Kyi Chu River. The bridge was built in 1965—it is 530 metres long, and is guarded by sentries at both ends. Find a place to keep your bike and climb up toward prayer-flags planted on top of Bumpa Ri. If you want something less strenuous, you can take on smaller hills in this area, also planted with prayer-flags.

At the back of Sera Monastery are fine hiking trails linking shrines. You can take a bus or minivan service to either Sera or Drepung monasteries, bicycle out, share a taxi, hitch a ride, or walk. If you have a mountain-bike, day trips or overnight trips can be mounted—due east and northeast of Lhasa are the best directions to go, as there is less traffic.

Sera

The three great Geluk monastic citadels close to Lhasa—Sera, Drepung and Ganden—developed a considerable rivalry in old Lhasa. They were all established in the early 15th century—Ganden in 1409, Drepung in 1416, and Sera in 1419. Sera's population hovered around 7000 monks, eclipsed by the 9000 at Drepung, while Ganden's quota was probably 5000 monks.

Sera, 4 km to the north of Lhasa, was at one time famous for its fighting monks, who spent years perfecting the martial arts. They were hired out as bodyguards to the wealthy, and even took on the Tibetan Army in 1947 during protests following the imprisonment of Reting Rinpoche. Once a year, the fighting monks of Sera used to race starkers along the Kyi Chu riverbank for several kilometres to toughen up. Sera means "merciful hail"—the origin of the name is thought to derive from the fact that Sera was in constant competition with Drepung ("rice heap monastery") and that the "hail" of Sera destroyed the "rice" of Drepung. Today, only a few hundred monks remain at Sera—a shadow of its former self. You can wander around and view the interiors of the two main colleges—Sera Me and Sera Je—as well as the Main Assembly Hall.

Near the entrance to Sera is a monastery restaurant that serves noodles, vegetables and bread at low prices—there's a pleasant outdoor section at the back, shaded by birch trees, where pilgrims gather.

Hiking Behind Sera: A bigger draw than the temple interiors is the hiking out this way. Behind Sera to the northeast, on a mountainside, is the hermitage of Tsongkhapa—a simple shrine. In the vicinity, are striking rock carvings, painted on boulders. A walking circuit around Sera takes about an hour to complete. If you are well acclimatised, there are more ambitious, longer, steeper hikes behind Sera that offer superb views. Dotted around the hill backing Sera are a number of caves, hermitages and sacred sites—among the oldest in Lhasa. A circuit of sorts leads past Sera to Pabonka, a small temple with two dozen monks; from there you can carry on to Tashi Choling hermitage, and climb a ridge to Chupsang Nunnery, which has 80 nuns in residence. This makes for a fairly strenuous day.

Sera to Drepung

Instead of going back through downtown Lhasa to get from Sera to Drepung, you can take a more interesting shortcut—by traversing a marshy area southwest of Sera. Some of the time there's a dirt road to follow, other times not. It's possible to bicycle most of the route, which leads past a rock quarry. Unless you have a mountain-bike with the gears, it's better not to attempt the steep route up from the base of the hill leading to Drepung. Leave the bike with a shop-owner (with a token payment) and hitch a ride with whatever comes along (most likely a walking-tractor or number 3 bus).

Drepung

If Sera used to be famous for its fighting monks, Drepung was famed for its scholars. Spectacularly sited—enclosed on three sides by boulder-strewn peaks, Drepung is an entire monastic town that once housed a community of some 9000 monks—qualifying it as the largest in the world. There are perhaps 500 monks living here today: their numbers are uncertain following a major re-education campaign in the late 1990s where monks were forced to denounce the Dalai Lama. Drepung has been singled out as a priority for re-education because of its larger contingent of monks and because of its previous involvement in Lhasa demonstrations. Drepung is 8 km west of downtown Lhasa. You can bicycle out this way, or take a number 3 bus—which runs past the Potala and goes all the way up to the gates of Drepung.

Like other large-scale monasteries, Drepung is divided into colleges with attached residences—rather like a campus where different disciplines are pursued. There are four major colleges—Ngakpa, Loseling, Gomang and Deyang. In previous times, all the monks at Drepung would gather on special occasions at the vast Main Assembly Hall. Now the hall is little-used. The hall is three storeys high: you can climb onto the flat rooftop for great views over Lhasa Valley (Drepung lies a few hundred metres above Lhasa). If you like climbing,

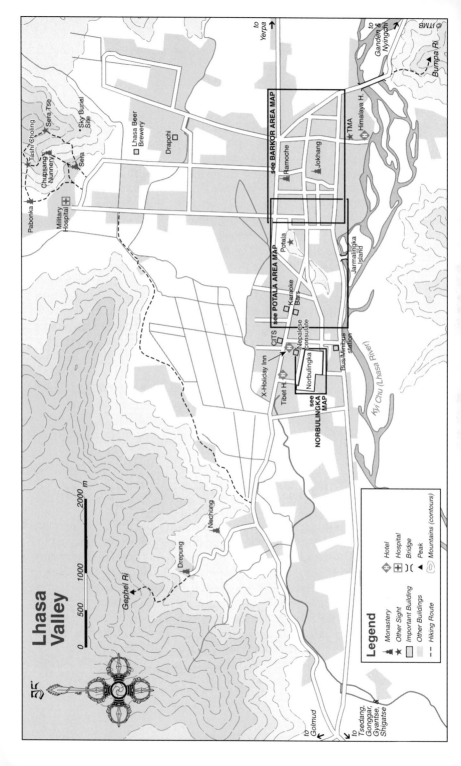

there's a very strenuous hike behind Drepung to the top of Gephel Ri. The climb up and back would take a full day and you need to be very well acclimatised—the top of Gephel Ri is 5200 metres.

Nechung

On the lower slopes of the hill leading up to Drepung is Nechung Monastery, a small temple that fulfilled an important function in old Lhasa. It was the seat of the state oracle, who was consulted by the Lhasa government when making important decisions. The monks who lived at Nechung were trained in the secret rituals that accompanied the trances of the oracle. When in a trance, the oracle was said to be possessed by the spirit Dorje Drakden—the oracle shook, trembled, barked, rolled his eyes and stuck out his tongue. Monk-attendants quickly strapped on the oracle's impossibly heavy head-piece and he would dance around. Questions were asked, cryptic answers were given. The state oracle's last cryptic answers in Tibet concerned whether the Dalai Lama should leave or not—the answer was interpreted as yes. The state oracle himself escaped to India with the exodus of exiles in 1959: he died in 1985, but his successor was found, and the tradition has been kept alive in Dharamsala, India.

In keeping with its unusual function, Nechung Monastery has some strange murals lining the walls—paintings of flayed humans, figures with dangling eyeballs, wrathful deities and other ghoulish artwork. There's a statue of Dorje Drakden in the main assembly hall; adjoining chapels were once used by the various Dalai Lamas when they visited or conducted retreats here. Some 20 monks currently reside at Nechung.

LODGING, FOOD, NIGHTLIFE

Lhasa's handful of hotels and restaurants are nightlife and entertainment venues by default: they are gathering points for information exchange. Source and sauce: other travellers provide the latest information, and you digest it over a steaming bowl of noodles. Tashi I, Tashi II and the Banak Shol's Kailash restaurant function as traveller cafés. This is how people pass their nights—in the "tent" at the Yak Hotel or on the rooftop of the Banak Shol. Chinese nightlife consists of crooning, carousing and chasing Sichuan women around in karaoke bars or places like Top View Disco (some Westerners venture in here too). Tibetan nightlife consists of crowding into tiny video salons where sound distortion and flasks of chang are the big things.

Hotels in Lhasa neatly cleave into low-end backpacker (Barkor area), mid-range group-tour or sports groups (southeast side of Lhasa), and high-end group-tour (west fringe of town). See the Barkor Area and Lhasa Valley maps for precise locations.

Low End

A number of the backpacker hotels have hot showers, laundry facilities, will rent bicycles, and will store baggage while you're off on a trip. The three guesthouses most favoured by backpackers are the Yak, the Banak Shol and the Kirey. Snowland Hotel, tel. 6323687, is close to the Jokhang. This 31-room guesthouse is Tibetan-run, with several storeys arrayed around an inner courtyard. It attracts longer-term foreign residents who may take rooms for a month or more. There are some dorm-rooms available here, as well as regular rooms. There are hot shower stalls available, but otherwise plumbing is lacking. Just north of Snowland is Pentoc Guesthouse, tel/fax 6330700, which is run by Europeans whose connections with the authorities are not exactly clear (given that a foreign-run operation is rare in China, and unheard-of in Tibet). The place is very small—only a handful of rooms—-but the price is right: very clean, plumbing works, good facilities. Here's a refreshing twist: the Pentoc looks Chinese on the outside, but decor is all Tibetan on the inside. The Pentoc has a fax machine and may even have e-mail connections. The management can arrange camping and biking tours in the Lhasa Valley and beyond; the Pentoc also rents camping gear, but prices can be steep.

Moving along, on Dekyi Shar Lam are four Tibetan-run hotels where backpackers stay. The Yak Hotel, tel. 6323496, is a large efficient operation with over 60 rooms, ranging from dormitory (shared facilities) to mid-range/luxury rooms with their own showers. The Yak "tent" is a favourite meeting place for travellers. Further east is the non-descript Gang Gyen Guesthouse, which is lacking in atmosphere but has functional rooms. The nearby four-storey Kirey Guesthouse, tel. 6323462, is popular with backpackers. It has 45 rooms arrayed around a courtyard; baggage storage is free. The Tibetan-run Banak Shol Hotel, tel. 6323829, offers about 100 rooms, ranging from budget upward—the better ones are those on the upper floors, where there's more sunlight. Walls are thin at the Banak Shol—a definite minus. Management is very friendly—a plus. On the roof to one end is a gathering spot—an extension of Kailash Restaurant. This is a pleasant place to sit over a coffee or a beer, or a meal.

Mid-range

Kecho Hotel, tel. 6320234, fax 6330234, on Dekyi Shar Lam, is a small five-storey place with good facilities. It has 21 Tibetan-style rooms, small restaurants and a gift shop. Inside the grounds of the Potala Palace is the Potala Hotel, tel. 6330575, which is in a large converted mansion. Prices for the 22 rooms are reasonable, but windows are a problem—some window rooms open onto an inner courtyard, other rooms have no windows. Management is Chinese.

To the southeast side of Lhasa—a little way out of the action—are two larger establishments, both lacking in atmosphere, but favoured by group tours and adventure tours. The Sunlight Hotel, tel. 6331124, fax 6335675, has 90 rooms (some with attached bath) and a range of services (satellite TV, IDD, bicycle rental). The Himalaya Hotel, tel. 6334082, fax 6334855, operates 116 rooms with attached bath. Sports-related groups are lodged out this way because TIST (Tibet International Sports Travel) and TMA (Tibet Mountaineering Association) have offices in the vicinity.

High End

The most expensive hotels in Lhasa are west of the Potala. Tibet Hotel, 221 Beijing West Road, tel. 6336784, fax 6336787, is a mock-Tibetan abomination of a building that is favoured by Asian group tours. There are 96 guestrooms, ranging from $50-100 and up for a double. The hotel has a few giftshops and bars, plus some travel agents; downstairs is a CAAC office.

Top billeting in Lhasa is at the X-Holiday Inn, 1 Minzu Lu, tel. 6324509, fax 6334117. The X-Holiday Inn, with over 400 rooms, is the only luxury-class hotel in Tibet. Prices range from $70–100 (double/triple) to $120 deluxe; and $180 for a Tibetan-style suite. The X-Holiday Inn boasts three tower wings, with three elevators (the first in Tibet—but not a good place to be in a blackout) and a kidney-shaped swimming pool out the back (another first—nobody seems to use it, maybe because it's poorly maintained). Even if it is a luxury hotel, the X-Holiday Inn has its problems—built in 1985, it is falling apart in places, with water-damaged walls. The hotel has the full gamut of services, including its own telecom and business centre (fax, IDD, and so on), currency exchange counter and several gift shops. Restaurants include the Tibetan-style Himalaya, Chinese-style Kailash restaurant and the Western-style Hard Yak Café. The banquet hall can seat 600. One attraction at the X-Holiday Inn is tiny Chang's Bar, where you can watch CNN and other programs on satellite TV. Chang's Bar used to be called Tintin Bar: the walls bear murals from the comic of the same name. A curious thing: the murals all feature Chang (the Chinese character in the comic) and Tintin appears to have been erased. Politically correct visual revisionism?

THE X-HOLIDAY INN

In late 1997 it was announced that the Holiday Inn management group would not renew its contract for running the branch in Lhasa—the only luxury hotel in Tibet. No reason was given—and the international giant continues to run its numerous other branches around China. Victory was claimed by various campaign groups in the West, particularly the Free Tibet Campaign in England, which launched a boycott of Holiday Inn operations and those of its British parent company, Bass PLC (makers of Bass beer), in 1993. In 1997, Students for a Free Tibet and fifty other Tibet support groups joined the campaign.

Holiday Inn Lhasa, run in partnership with the Chinese government, is the largest foreign currency earner in Lhasa—catering to well-heeled group tours. The original hotel was called Lhasa Hotel, completed by the Chinese in 1986: the Holiday Inn corporation modernised the building and renamed it. A trusted brand name like Holiday Inn brought a certain amount of prestige, a veneer of respectability, and a seal of approval for Chinese operations in Tibet. There were even Miss Tibet contests conducted in 1992 to attract tourism during the slack winter months. You had to wonder how long it would take McDonalds, Pizza Hut and the rest of the multi-national gang to get there in the wake of Holiday Inn.

Although Tibetans work at the hotel, there is no Tibetan presence in the management—profits benefit the Chinese. Top-ranking Chinese military like to stay there, and it appears that the staff are in cahoots with security forces. At the time of writing, it was not clear what the new name of the hotel would be—so it has been designated X-Holiday Inn in this book.

Mystery Hotels

Foreigners may not be permitted to stay in the following hotels. This situation could well change: top secret hotels become declassified and foreign vermin are allowed to trample through. When approached, some of these hotels indicated the rooms were full—even though the reception was dead quiet, and not a guest in sight. What they probably mean is that they're not permitted to accept foreign guests because of the PSB, which would rather keep foreigners isolated in a select number of hotels where they can keep an eye on them.

Refer to the Barkor Area map for precise hotel locations. To the southeast side of the Barkor, the Khada Hotel appears to be for Tibetan truck drivers, as does the Tibetan-style Pata Hotel. Out near the Mountaineers-on-Everest roundabout, the Ying Qiao and Plateau hotels seem to cater exclusively to a Chinese clientele. There are two other hotels where the rules may bend, and foreigners may be permitted to stay. The Gold Grain Hotel, tel. 6330357, is a bland 50-room block on Mi Mang Lam—prices are in the mid-range. The large modern Tibet Royal Hotel, tel. 6333988, fax 6338349, lies on the southern section of the Lingkor. It bears mock-Tibetan trim on the balconies, but is Chinese to the core. Prices are in the high-end range. In the back courtyard of this hotel (which seems to cater to military brass) is Top View Disco, with an advanced light and sound system, and a rabbit-warren of karaoke rooms leading off it. Out on "Karaoke Row" (west of the Golden Yak roundabout) are some glitzy Chinese places with names like Hotel Dream Paris.

RESTAURANTS & FOOD

As an alternative to restaurants, you can throw together your own food in Lhasa. There are places where you can find fresh-baked flat-breads, delicious yak curd (yoghurt), and bananas—start putting these things together and you'll have a great breakfast. It's fun to wander the streets around the Barkor to get your daily yoghurt.

For locations of the following places, see the Barkor Area map: some restaurants are attached to hotels. Simple, inexpensive and nourishing dishes are provided by the Tibetan-run Tashi I and Tashi II (the second place is inside the courtyard of Kirey Hotel). On the menu are yak-burgers, spaghetti, French fries, vegetable dishes and apple momos. Near Tashi I are several Muslim noodlehouses with reasonable fare: these bear green banners with the Muslim crescent moon on them. The Kailash Restaurant (inside the Banak Shol hotel) is Nepali-run and has a larger menu with pizza, spaghetti and Western dishes: there's a rooftop deck where you can lounge in the sun. Kecho Guesthouse may also have a rooftop café—you could try their ground-floor dining hall for breakfast or dinner (could be pricey). At the opposite end of the spectrum—dark and indoors—is the Pink Curtain (so named because of its dirty pink curtains over the windows), which serves up quite palatable Tibetan dishes. If you want to experience real Tibetan atmosphere, try Darkhay Restaurant out near the Ramoche—no guarantees in the food department. Near the Yak Hotel is a place with no name, designated Chinese Noodlehouse on the map—which is what it is.

A few notches up in decor and price is Snowland Restaurant, which is attached to Snowland Hotel but is a separate operation, with Nepali cooks. This place is very comfortable, with a larger section at the back for group tours. On the menu is a selection of Western, Chinese, Tibetan and Nepali food. The Tibetan dishes are curious: yak tongue salad, yak noodle soup, yak fried chilli. The breakfast menu may sound more familiar, serving muesli with fruit and curd (tangy yoghurt), banana milk porridge, or scrambled eggs and coffee. Snowland Restaurant also sells supplies for those off on excursions—you can buy excellent brown bread, canned goods, Swiss chocolate and other delicacies, mostly imported from Nepal.

The X-Holiday Inn has several high-priced restaurants, including the Hard Yak Café (serving yak-burgers) and an ice-cream café (dishes up good gelato). The Himalaya Restaurant at the X-Holiday Inn dishes up a range of food from Indian to German, plus Tibetan dishes like Yak Tartare, or Minced Yak with Tibetan Spices. Traditional Tibetan music groups sometimes perform at the restaurant. Over by the CAAC office is a place called Peking Duck Restaurant—which is what it serves. Best if you assemble a group for this one—you negotiate whole or half ducks. You need to be acclimatised. Huh? Food too?! Yes, that's right—Beijing Duck is rich, fatty food and it's hard on your system. In Beijing there's a phenomenon known as Jet-lag Duck Attack, whereby an unsuspecting tourist arriving with a jetlag hangover is taken straight to a Beijing duck dinery—and promptly keels over after eating the rich food. I guess the Lhasa equivalent would be to step off the plane, go and eat at the Peking Duck Restaurant, and then climb the central staircase of the Potala. Anyway, Beijing duck is delicious—it comes with duck soup, duck crepes and other duck dishes.

If you are feeling really acclimatised, you can wash all this down with some wine. Avoid the cheap Chinese "champagne" on the shelves—this is only good for bathing in. The bottle to purchase is Dynasty White Wine, which is bottled in Tianjin as part of a French joint-venture enterprise. Another good brand is Great Wall Red.

Cafés & Teahouses

There are pleasant teahouses in Lhasa where can soak up the views as well as the drinks. One of these is Lukhang teahouse, in the northeast corner of Lukhang Park—it offers a great view of the back of the Potala and is a peaceful place. The teahouse serves "eight treasures tea"—there are often fresh flowers on the tables from the adjacent nursery. Another viewpoint on the Potala is from the front, at a Chinese pavilion with restaurant and teahouse, overlooking a lake to the Potala's south side. There's a Tibetan-style teahouse inside the Red Palace of the Potala itself. On the rooftop of the Jokhang is a tent teahouse, run by the monks—only in the summer months, and only for tourists. Offering a view across Barkor Square is the upper deck of Barkor Café. Several guesthouses operate rooftop cafés, such as the Banak Shol. Next door to the Yak Hotel is the Crazy Yak Saloon, which has zero views, but does offer profound insights into Tibetan drinking habits and may feature the odd Tibetan musician.

SHOPPING

Whether outfitting for a trip or shopping for Tibetan artefacts, Lhasa has the biggest selection—though it has nothing on Kathmandu.

Trip Gear: For camping gear, try making purchases from other travellers via message-boards. Pentoc Guesthouse rents some camping gear. You can buy (or rent) some gear from Mount Green Trekking Shop, near Kecho Hotel. Department stores sell formless but functional clothing, and there's PLA surplus gear for sale on the streets.

Fresh & Packaged Food: If going on a long trip—as in Kailash—stock up on as much food as you can in Lhasa (the only other place to get supplies is Shigatse). For fresh food, the Tibetan market to the north of the Jokhang has the biggest selection (for items like potatoes, dried fruit and so on). Department stores downtown are a source of packaged goods, such as teabags, chocolate, and biscuits. For muesli, peanut butter and other items imported from Nepal try Snowland Restaurant or Kailash Restaurant (Banak Shol Hotel).

Tibetan Artefacts: The main array of souvenir shops lines Barkor Bazaar—watch out for Chinese clones. Some souvenirs are obviously not Tibetan at all—a few brass Buddha statues are from Thailand; others come from Kathmandu. Much the same stock is sold at giftshops in major hotels are more inflated prices, and at souvenir kiosks at the Potala entrance and at the Norbulingka. Watch out for fake turquoise and other stones if buying jewellery.

You might want to get to the source of items crafted in Lhasa—the factories are a sight themselves. There are several Tibetan tent-making workshops in the city—the easiest to find is in an alley near the Yak Hotel. Among other items, this place sells fine cotton door-hangings with Tibetan lucky symbols hand-embroidered on them. There are several carpet factories in town—one out near Drepung, another to the southeast side of Lhasa. Lhasa Carpet Factory welcomes visitors—there is an exhibition and retail room on the premises. Check out the various designs: a Tibetan dragon has four claws, the Chinese imperial dragon has five claws. A German joint-venture outfit displays yak-leather products at a showroom under the Pentoc Guesthouse—items include wallets and and yak-wool sweaters (and some pretty heavy socks).

INFORMATION & SERVICES

If you can't find it in Lhasa, you're out of luck—you probably won't find it anywhere else in Tibet except in Shigatse.

Traveller Network: Your best information source is other travellers, encountered at cafés like Tashi I. Make other contacts through the message boards at Snowland, Yak, Banak Shol or Pentoc hotels—you can buy or sell medicines, sleeping bags, tents and freeze-dried foods. Assembling small groups for Landcruiser trips is often achieved through the boards.

Books & Maps: You might dredge up the odd map, poster or Tibetan music cassette from the Xinhua Bookstore at the west end of Mi Mang Lam; otherwise, pickings are slim. Prices for maps and books can be absurdly low if produced by the Chinese government. There's a Xinhua bookstore branch out near the X-Holiday Inn. The souvenir shops at the X-Holiday Inn and Tibet Hotel are good for books, though more expensive. Also selling books and postcards are souvenir kiosks near the Potala ticket entrance and inside the Norbulingka. Rule of thumb: when you see something you really want, bargain and buy it—you might not see it again. Other Chinese bookstores are scattered around; there's one at the east side of Barkor Bazaar.

Photoshops: Kodak comes to Lhasa: you can get print film developed at shops south of the main post office or near Potala Square. Prints of Tibetans will make fine gifts. Quality of film purchased in Lhasa varies—some rotten rolls, some good. The price of film in Lhasa is around double that of the same film in Chengdu. Slides cannot be developed.

Staying in Touch: The Potala post office awaits you: the main branch for telecommunications lies near the Potala, on Beijing Road. Sending of regular mail and parcels takes place here; you might want to bring along your own packing materials as none are supplied (for larger items, you might have to open your package for customs inspection). There's a long-distance calling office next door (calls are most likely routed through Beijing); the same office will allow you to send faxes. A second telecom office is located at the Mountaineers-on-Everest roundabout. Faxes can also be sent at the X-Holiday Inn's business centre, but they're more expensive. Pentoc Guesthouse may allow you to use their fax machine, and may even have e-mail. Some hotels handle mail, too—they deliver to the post office. International phone calls can be placed through hotels—even at the budget hotels. The country code (China) is 86; Lhasa area code is 891. E-mail has hit the Holy City: several places now provide the service. Check the Barkor Café and also try Pentoc Guesthouse.

Satellite TV: High-end hotels have satellite TV reception, picking up VTV (India), StarTV (Hong Kong) and CNN. There may be a bar within the hotel where non-guests can watch the tube. The larger the dish, the greater the reception. Satellite receivers require special permission to operate within China, and the foreign programs are not intended for local eyes. Xizang TV is the local station; CCTV from Beijing broadcasts a nightly news service in English, and on Sunday in French.

Banking: The main branch of the Bank of China is located just northeast of the Golden Yak roundabout. It provides full services, including credit card advances (commissions can be high). The BOC is open 10.30 am to 1.30 pm, and 3.30 pm to 6 pm Monday to Friday; from 11 am to 3 pm Saturdays; it may be open on Sundays. There are sub-branches in a few other locations—notably one near the Banak Shol hotel. Major hotels like the X-Holiday Inn have their own exchange counter, but the rate is not as good.

Medical: You're best off moving to a comfortable hotel in the event of a medical problem. High-end hotels usually supply oxygen pillows and may have a doctor on call. Hospitals in Lhasa cost a fortune for foreigners to stay in, and the medical attention is dubious anyway. Lhasa's finest is the Military Hospital at the north end—but that's not for foreigners. The People's Hospital is basic—one unit is supported by an Italian NGO project for equipment and training; there's an X-ray unit here.

ON THE MOVE

RED TAPE

Getting travel permits or visa extensions is tricky in Lhasa—both depend on joining a group with a firm itinerary. You might be better off having an agency approach the relevant offices. Tibet PSB to the east side of town, handles ATPs and travel permits. These are normally obtained through the guide on a trip, and list all passport holders on a single document (usually one sheet of paper). There are several

HAVING A BLAST

Need an blast of oxygen? A high-altitude cocktail? The X-Holiday Inn is reputed to have rooms where oxygen is piped in, though this system no longer seems to function because guests kept going out and leaving the oxygen on. If guests have trouble with the altitude, they are usually given an "oxygen pillow" to make sleeping smoother. There is nothing more scary than sleeping at altitude and waking up in the middle of the night completely out of breath, heart pounding, gulping for air—with a throat like the Sahara. This is where the oxygen pillow comes to the fore—it is a pillow of oxygen with nasal tubes attached. The pillows are also taken along on Landcruiser or minibus trips from the X-Holiday Inn in case a guest is feeling under the weather. Landcruiser drivers may also keep a tank of oxygen in the vehicle—rather like a fire extinguisher unit. Oxygen does not solve the acclimatisation problem—but it provides temporary respite.

Just east of the Golden Yak roundabout, under a sign that reads "Tibet Yak Picture Manufacturing Company" is a shop called KL Oxygen, selling various oxygen devices manufactured in Xiamen. These range from small scuba-like tanks to aerosol spray-cans for those who need a blast of fresh air. You can rent the scuba tanks for a dollar or so a day (with a large deposit)—the capacity is 30 minutes of oxygen.

kinds of permit—ATPs (to visit towns on route), military permits (for restricted areas and getting past military checkposts), and Cultural Bureau permits (for visiting sites of special architectural or cultural interest). While Tibet PSB will not normally issue permits to individuals who apply directly, Shigatse PSB might. The TTB (Tibet Tourism Bureau), near the Golden Yak roundabout, appears to be involved with permit-issuing, but is not approachable directly. It seems that guides need to get TTB permits before they can get ATPs from the PSB for a trip (but in Shigatse, no TTB permits are required from the PSB office). Most Landcruisers in Lhasa carry a TTB sticker on the front window that says "China Tibet Tour."

Lhasa Municipal PSB handles visa extensions, but only if you have a tour booked. If your tour itinerary is for 6 days, then the extension is for 9 days or so (to enable you to complete the tour and leave Tibet). If you have booked a Kailash tour itinerary, you might be able to get a month's extension. The only consulate in Lhasa is the Royal Nepal Consulate-General, tel. 6322881, to the north side of the Norbulingka. You can pick up a Nepalese visa within a day for $30; it's valid for a month (there's a half-price one valid for 15 days). It's not really necessary as you can get the same visa for the same price on arrival in Nepal by air or by road. However, some like the cachet of the exotic visa issued in Lhasa.

GETTING AROUND LHASA

Lhasa is a small town. It's easy to navigate by prominent landmarks like the Potala or the TV tower atop Chakpori Hill. Key roundabouts are conveniently identified by statuary—Golden Yak statues, Golden Archer statue, Mountaineers-on-Everest statue. You could call them the Golden Yak roundabout or the Mountaineers-on-Everest round-about. Although a local minibus system exists, most travellers don't bother with it unless heading out to, say, Drepung. Inquire at your hotel about which bus to take for a longer journey. You can mostly walk or bicycle around town. Foot-powered bicycle-taxis rove the streets—they seat two up front. Regular cabs (imported from east China) cruise the streets—they don't have meters, but you shouldn't have to pay more than a few dollars to traverse the city (bargain).

Bicycling is an excellent way of getting around Lhasa—since the town is mostly flat, you can go a long way on a gearless Chinese roadster. Chinese bicycles can be hired from the Yak, Banak Shol, Snowland or Pentoc hotels (Pentoc has a few mountain-bikes also). Hotels generally prefer bikes to be reserved for use by their own guests, and usually require a deposit. Rental bicycles are often in poor condition—before renting, check that at least one of the brakes works, and that both wheels actually go round. Bike theft can be a problem—make sure you lock yours when you stop, or better yet, leave it in the care of a shopkeeper at your destination. If staying longer in Lhasa, consider buying a Chinese-made mountain-bike from a department store—they cost around $100.

GETTING AROUND TIBET

Buses & Minibus

At the crack of dawn (around 6.30 am) minibuses patrol the streets near the Yak Hotel looking for passengers for Shigatse, Samye or Nagqu. Sometimes they're parked in the alley toward the Ramoche Temple. Also at the crack of dawn are pilgrim bus departures from the west side of Barkor Square, heading for either Ganden or Tsurphu. For Gonggar Airport, there are 6 am departures by CAAC's own bus, leaving from the CAAC office downtown (a second bus may depart in the early afternoon).

Minibuses also congregate in the vicinity just south of the Norbulingka. Around the corner from this is Lhasa's main bus and minibus station, with a large board listing places all over the map—it's unlikely they will sell you tickets to any of those destinations. Destinations they may sell you (after an arm-wrestle) include Tsedang, Shigatse and Damxung. Foreigners have been able to buy tickets to Golmud with some wrangling. Others have got around refusal to sell tickets by ambushing the bus on its way out of town (the fare goes in the driver's pocket?). One foreigner managed to hop on a bus to Chengdu—a trip of about two weeks.

Landcruiser Travel

There are a number of agencies—large and small—that operate Landcruiser trips out of Lhasa, hired by the half-day, by the day, for several days, by the week, by the month. I'm very reluctant to recommend any of them. Travellers have a litany of horror stories to tell: vehicles that break down (or *disintegrate*) in transit, drivers that refuse to follow the itinerary, stroppy guides—the nightmare goes on. Others have had absolutely no problem—just a few loose kidneys at the end of the ride. It would be great to put your money into an agency that employs Tibetan drivers and guides, but in practice a lot of the Landcruiser outfits are Chinese-backed. In addition, agencies that develop a reputation for their honesty may have their licenses revoked overnight, and be shut down by the PSB. The upshot of all this is that you have to cast around and ask a lot of questions. If you find an agency that can supply a Tibetan driver, a Tibetan guide and a vehicle in good condition, then use them again—and recommend them to others. Catch-22: those agencies linked to the military or CITS can arrange permits more easily than others.

Smaller agencies handling Landcruiser rental are found in the vicinity of the Yak Hotel and Pentoc Guesthouse. Some operate out of hotels. These include Potala Folk (Kirey Hotel), TCTS (Tibet Career Travel Service, with an office in the Gang Gyen Hotel) and TNTC (Tibet Nyingchi Tourism Corporation—located under Pentoc Guesthouse). Higher-priced and CITS-linked are the half-dozen agencies operating out of the ground floor of the X-Holiday Inn (CWTS, CYTS, CTQT and CTTT). Across the street is the head office of CITS, with TTC (Tibet Tourist Corporation), Tibet Adventure Travel, and Tibet/China Travel Service all coming under the CITS wing. Operating from the Tibet Hotel is Shigatse CITS; operating from the Sunlight Hotel is Lhasa Travel Service. Handling sports aficionados is TIST (Tibet International Sports Travel), operating from the grounds of the Himalaya Hotel. Close by is the TMA (Tibet Mountaineering Association) which deals with mountaineers. Golden Bridge Travel Service is run by the PLA, and Asian Dragon Travel is run by the dreaded PAP.

The TTB (Tibet Tourism Bureau, aka China Tibet Tour) oversees a lot of the running of the tourist business in Tibet, particularly the registering of guides. Hotels that deal with foreigners invariably carry a TTB seal of approval, as do restaurants catering to big-noses.

Strategy: Four-wheel drive vehicles are the only way to go in Tibet. Toyota Landcruisers are the most common rental vehicles available in Lhasa. A superior version is the Toyota Landcruiser 4500, which has double-capacity gasoline tanks, giving it a range of perhaps 700 km without refuelling. It comes with a range of fog lights and other extras, and is much higher off the ground. Other 4WD vehicles sighted include the Mitsubishi Pajero and the Beijing Jeep Cherokee. In a Toyota Landcruiser you can squeeze in four passengers plus a guide and driver—that makes three in the front, three in the back. However, because of the gearsticks, the front seat won't be comfortable. If you can afford it, go with only three paying passengers. In some situations you may have to go with only three passengers: if you all have a lot of gear the baggage weight alone will limit the vehicle to three passengers. It is possible to go with five passengers (with light luggage)—if you're going to a place like Lake Namtso, you don't need a guide, since Namtso is open without permit, so that frees up the extra seat.

Landcruisers cost about $110–170 a day depending on the route, the distance, the itinerary and so on. If you go into Everest, there's a lot of wear and tear on the vehicle, which operators don't like, so the price might go up for that itinerary. If you go to Lake Namtso and stop for a day there, the vehicle is not using any gasoline that day, so the price might drop slightly if rest stops are included. If you're making a one-way run to the Nepal border, the agency expects a return subsidy to cover cost of gasoline (even though the driver will probably pick up new passengers).

Always arrange to check the condition of vehicle (and crew) before you put any money down. Don't pay everything up front: perhaps put half down, and pay the rest in stages as an incentive for the driver and guide to complete the trip as outlined. Make out a basic contract to confirm conditions you have agreed to verbally: include the itinerary, timing, amounts to be paid and so on. It's extremely important to be flexible with Landcruiser arrangements: you can't push your driver if a bridge is down, and you won't get much out of a driver if you back him into a corner. On a contract, put down a rate for extra days. If a delay is caused by the driver or vehicle breakdown, then the agency covers the cost; if the delay is due to illness of a passenger, the group covers the cost; if the delay is due to bad weather or road conditions, divide the cost between agency and group.

A last thought on Landcruisers: make sure you get along with the others in your group—you'll be seeing a lot of them. If you spend 25 days on the road to Kailash, you'll want congenial company. Compatibility is a very important consideration for long road trips like this.

GETTING OUT OF TIBET

Possibilities by road include the deathly-boring bus to Golmud, and the riveting Landcruiser journey to Zhangmu (and on to Kathmandu). Direct Landcruiser runs to Zhangmu (pure getting there, no sightseeing stops) are cheaper. See the *Lhasa to Kathmandu Route* chapter for road tripping, and see the *On The Road* chapter for more details on the intricacies of long-distance travel to Lhasa by road or by air.

While you can't buy a CSWA ticket yourself when flying into Tibet, you most certainly can buy one in person when flying out. Tickets to Chengdu or Kathmandu, though they can be booked ahead, are generally not handed out until two days before the actual flight (sometimes you can get them a week in advance). Due to computer glitches, some flights get overbooked—be prepared for delays. You can make bookings and pick up tickets at the CAAC office downtown, tel. 6333446. There's a smaller office in the basement of Tibet Hotel (out past the X-Holiday Inn) called TibetAir Travel Service, tel. 6322567. CAAC arranges its own bus to the airport for an extra fee. It leaves the CAAC office around 6 am (there may also be a later bus)—you should buy the ticket the day before. Otherwise club together and arrange a Landcruiser or a taxi to pick you up at your hotel for the one-hour run to Gonggar. Another option is to take a bus out to Gonggar the afternoon before your flight and overnight in Gonggar.

EXPLORING
CENTRAL TIBET
key pilgrimage sites of the region

Lhasa is not Tibet—it is too heavily Chinese-influenced for that. If you want to see more a more genuine Tibet, you have to get out into the countryside, where 80 percent of the Tibetans live. This chapter covers areas within easy reach of Lhasa by Landcruiser. You might also consider combination routes involving Gyantse and Shigatse when on a round-trip out of Lhasa. See the following chapter (*Lhasa to Kathmandu Route*) for details on Gyantse, Shigatse and sites further westward.

While destinations when touring by Landcruiser are commonly monasteries, what's along the way is often more interesting. If you see an opportunity to stop or get off the track, take it. On one trip, we spotted some horse riders in costume. We pulled over and got the driver to ask where they were going. It turned out there was an impromptu horse-racing and archery event not far away. We spent sev-

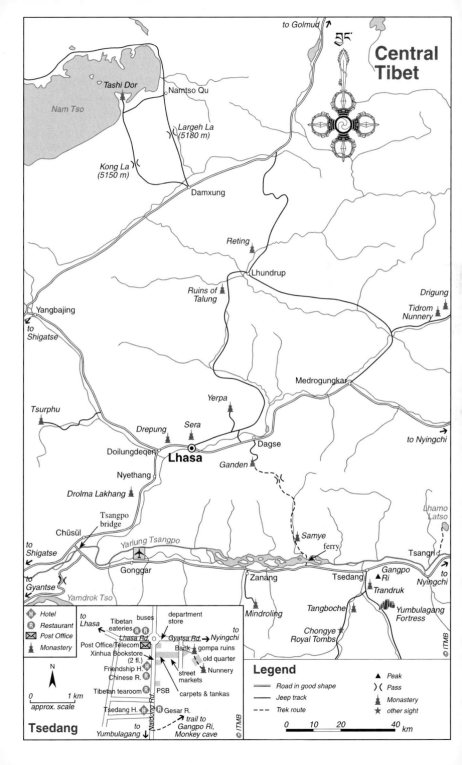

Central Tibet

ༀ་

to Golmud

Nam Tso

Tashi Dor
Namtso Qu

Largeh La
(5180 m)

Kong La
(5150 m)

Damxung

Reting

Lhundrup

Ruins of
Talung

Drigung

Tidrom
Nunnery

Yangbajing

to
Shigatse

Medrogungkar

Tsurphu

Yerpa

Drepung   *Sera*

Dagse

to Nyingchi

Doilungdeqen   **Lhasa**

Ganden

Nyethang

Drolma Lakhang

Lhamo
Latso

Tsangpo
bridge

Chüsül

Yarlung Tsangpo

Samye

ferry

Tsangri

to
Shigatse

Gonggar

Zanang

Tsedang   *Gangpo*
Ri

to
Nyingchi

to
Gyantse

Yamdrok Tso

Trandruk

Mindroling

Tangboche

Yumbulagang
Fortress

Chongye
Royal Tombs

Tsedang

H	Hotel
R	Restaurant
✉	Post Office
⛩	Monastery

N

0   1 km
approx. scale

to
Lhasa

buses

Tibetan
eateries R R

Lhasa Rd.

Post Office/Telecom ✉

Xinhua Bookstore
(2 fl.)

Friendship H. H
Chinese R. R

Tibetan tearoom R

Tsedang H. H   R Gesar R.

to
Yumbulagang

department
store

Gyatsa Rd. →

Bank

Nandong Rd.

PSB

to
Nyingchi

gompa ruins

old quarter

Nunnery

street
markets

carpets & tankas

trail to
Gangpo Ri,
Monkey cave

© ITMB

Legend

	Road in good shape	▲	Peak
	Jeep track	)(	Pass
	Trek route	⛩	Monastery
		★	other sight

0   10   20   40
km

© ITMB

eral hours watching the races and drinking chang. Our Tibetan driver didn't mind—he was enjoying himself too.

If you string together a lot of temples on a Landcruiser trip, you run the risk of becoming "templed out". That is, after visiting the first two or three temples, they all start to look the same. The key to a well-designed trip is variety—visit a temple, a fortress, then take in some countryside, and make impromptu stops along the route. Samye is a good combination of natural sights (crossing of the Yarlung Tsangpo) and temples. A visit to Lake Namtso places more emphasis on natural beauty.

Logistics

Some of the sites mentioned here (Tsurphu, Damxung, Tsedang) can be reached by bus or minibus from Lhasa. Services are intermittent. For greater freedom, hire a Landcruiser with driver and guide for a period of two to seven days, depending on how much ground you want to cover—splitting the tariff between four or five passengers. The permit situation for Central Tibet seems to vary. At the time of writing, few of the places seemed to need a permit. However, Samye probably requires a permit, as does Tsedang. Both of these places have PSB offices that may check on you if staying overnight. If not overnighting, this is less of a problem.

NORTH BY NORTHEAST

Popular destinations north of Lhasa are Tsurphu Monastery and Lake Namtso, and the monasteries of Ganden, Drigung, Tidrom and Yerpa. There are several possibilities for touring this northern sector by Landcruiser. A short itinerary is Lhasa-Tsurphu-Damxung (day one); Damxung over Largeh La to Tashi Dor (day two); back to Lhasa (day three). Apart from hiring a Landcruiser, another option for reaching Tsurphu or Ganden is to take a pilgrim bus, leaving downtown Lhasa early morning from Barkor Square. Some like it rough: you can also indulge in trekking at various points. Resourceful travellers have forged round routes by various non-Landcruiser means. You could, for example, take a pilgrim bus to Ganden, and after seeing the gompa, trek off toward Samye. From Samye, cross the river by ferry, make your way to the highway and pick up a bus coming from Tsedang—all the way back to Lhasa. Or hitchhike back. Another possibility is to take a regular bus from Lhasa to Damxung, then trek out to Lake Namtso and back.

Tsurphu Monastery

The main attraction at Tsurphu is a blessing by the young Karmapa. This takes place at 1 pm sharp—if you're a few minutes late, too bad. Near the entrance to the monastery you can buy katas to offer the Karmapa in blessing. Then join the line-up of pilgrims and wait your turn. Pilgrims are ushered through fairly fast—the bored-looking Karmapa accepts katas, sometimes pausing to drink a Coke. The whole show is over in a matter of minutes.

Tsurphu Monastery is the traditional seat of the Karmapa, head of the Karma Kagyu sect. The monastery was founded in the 12th century by the first Karmapa, Dusum Kyenpa. As the seat of the Karmapa, Tsurphu was headquarters for instruction of monks from far-flung monasteries of the order, some as distant as Kham.

In the 1950s, Tsurphu was home to a thousand monks. In 1959, the 16th Karmapa left for exile in Sikkim, where he founded Rumtek Monastery. Tsurphu Monastery was razed during the Cultural Revolution, but a few parts have been rebuilt, including the impressive assembly hall. About 30 novice monks have again return to the temple precincts. The monastery flies its own flag—a blue and yellow ensign. In May 1997, sacred Cham dances were performed at Tsurphu as part of festivities for Saka Dawa (Buddha's birthday) under the watchful eye of Chinese officials—this dance had been banned for decades. The most curious part of the monastery is a back protector chapel where (dead) animals appear to be the offering: whole stuffed yaks suspended from the rafters, as well as birds—and what appears to be a kangaroo. You have to wonder how a stuffed kangaroo made it to these remote parts.

Getting There: Tsurphu lies 70 km northwest of Lhasa, at the end of a dirt trail off the main road (the turn-off is at kilometre marker-stone 3853). It takes about two hours to get there from Lhasa: there is an inclined rough route to get to Tsurphu, which sits at 4420 metres. Apart from a Landcruiser, the only other transport option is a daily pilgrim bus that departs early morning from the west side of Barkor Square, and returns the same day in the afternoon, after the Karmapa's blessing is bestowed on the pilgrims.

Namtso Circuit

Namtso is Tibet's largest saltwater lake, and at 4700 metres, also one of the highest. You would be unwise to visit Namtso shortly after arriving in Lhasa, as the altitude can be hard on your system. However, if you have been around Lhasa for a while and are contemplating taking trips at higher elevations, Namtso is a good testing ground:

RIFT OVER THE 17th KARMAPA

The lineage of the leaders of the Karma Kagyu sect of Tibetan Buddhism goes back to the 12th century. The 16th Karmapa was born in Tibet in 1924. After fleeing Tibet in 1959, he founded Rumtek Monastery in Sikkim as his principal seat in exile. He died in the US in 1981.

The search for the 17th Karmapa caused a major rift in the Tibetan exile community. Four regents of the Kagyu sect in Sikkim were appointed to conduct the search for the Karmapa: Situ Rinpoche, Gyaltsap Rinpoche, Jamgon Kongtrul Rinpoche and Shamar Rinpoche. In 1990, Situ Rinpoche said he found a letter left by the 16th Karmapa, giving clues about his reincarnate. The letter was not shown to the other regents until 1992: its authenticity was disputed. Nevertheless, in April 1992, with Chinese approval, a search party of lamas left Tsurphu Monastery to find the new incarnation.

A few weeks later, Jamgon Kongtrul Rinpoche was killed in a car accident—he had previously been designated as the person to find and check the incarnate. A boy from a nomad family in eastern Tibet—appearing to match details given in the letter—was brought to Tsurphu in July, 1992. The boy was officially recognised by the Chinese—the first time they have recognised a Living Buddha since 1959. On evidence from the search party, the Dalai Lama then recognised the boy also. In September 1992, eight-year-old Ugyen Tinley was enthroned in an elaborate ceremony at Tsurphu by Situ Rinpoche and Gyaltsap Rinpoche, with Chinese media and government widely represented.

Meanwhile, in Sikkim, violence flared at Rumtek Monastery as rival camps of monks brawled over the Karmapa issue. Indian troops were brought in to hold the peace. The 16th Karmapa's monks were evicted, and Situ Rinpoche's monks forcibly occupied the grounds in late 1993. In 1994, Shamar Rinpoche announced in Delhi that the true Karmapa had been found—a boy from Lhasa by the name of Thaye Dorje. The boy was able to procure travel papers to leave Lhasa by way of Chengdu and Hong Kong to India, which indicates Chinese involvement. The Chinese may actually be fuelling the on-going dispute that has ripped Rumtek apart.

Another great issue remains unresolved: will the enthroned 16th Karmapa be able to fulfill his function as a spiritual teacher within Chinese-occupied Tibet? The 17th Karmapa has failed in

the first test of this. Situ Rinpoche had thought the enthronement at Tsurphu would be a prelude to the 17th Karmapa's
arrival at Rumtek Monastery in Sikkim. Since the enthronement, however, the boy has only been permitted to travel to
Beijing—to proclaim his loyalty to the communist government.

spending a few days here will help you to acclimatise to the 4500-
metre zone.

Along the Lhasa to Namtso route, you pass by **Yangbajing** (elevation 4200m), where a small settlement has developed around geothermal power units supplying Lhasa. Yangbajing hot springs, which are
4 km off the main highway, are nothing to get excited about—the
water is channelled into a large concrete swimming pool with a few
deckchairs lying around. Next stop is **Damxung** (elevation 4400m), a
deadly boring Chinese-built town 170 km from Lhasa. It serves as a
truck-stop on the Golmud road, with several basic guesthouses, so
you can stay overnight here.

A further 40 km from Damxung brings you to **Lake Namtso,**
reached by two rough routes—in a Landcruiser you can enter one
way (motoring over Largeh La, 5180m) and leave by another route
(over Kong La, 5150m). The road runs through a grassland valley,
with the odd nomad encampment visible, and herds of yaks, sheep
and goats roaming around. For the nomads, life is dependent on
yaks: they live in yak-hair tents, and use yak-dung as their main fuel
source. Some travellers hitch a ride in and walk back (about 12 hours),
or trek both ways—a tough hike. You can overnight at Namtso Qu
(tiny village) and Tashi Dor (tiny building attached to nunnery, right
at the shores of Namtso). Bring food, a flashlight, and a good sleeping
bag—there's only floorspace at Tashi Dor. However, beer can be purchased from the nuns.

Namtso is a sacred lake: there are cave-temples, hermitages and a
nunnery for the contemplation at **Tashi Dor.** Hermits from the Kagyu
and Nyingma sects occasionally occupy the caves. Two large rock
towers near the nunnery are considered to be sentinels for the region.
It's worth spending a day or more exploring the area—hiking in the
hills around Tashi Dor, and poking around the cave-temples. The
beautiful turquoise hues of the lake are a source of inspiration, and
the vistas will redefine your sense of space. In the distance, to the
south, the 7088-metre snowcap of Mt. Nyanchen Tanglha looms up,
along with the range of the same name. A walking circuit of Namtso is
a tall order indeed. The lake is roughly 70 km long and 30 km wide,
with a surface area of 1940 square kilometres: it takes nomad pilgrims

up to 20 days to circle it. A short walk to the east of Tashi Dor is a site that operates as a bird sanctuary—between April and November there are good chances of sighting migratory flocks, including, if you're lucky, the black-necked crane.

Northeast of Lhasa

In this direction are a number of ruined or semi-active monasteries, amid spectacular settings. These places are little-visited and take you right off the track into small villages.

Located 40 km east of Lhasa is **Ganden,** a Geluk lamasery founded in the 15th century. Additions in later centuries increasing its capacity to support upward of 5000 monks. Ganden was dynamited to rubble during the Cultural Revolution. Remarkably, a number of its main halls have been rebuilt from scratch. In early 1996, following a ban on Dalai Lama pictures, the 400 monks at Ganden were involved in a riot. PLA troops arrived and fired on the monks—two were believed killed and a number injured. It is thought 100 more monks were arrested; an equal number probably fled into the hills. For a while after this, the monastery was off-limits to travellers: inquire what the current situation is. There's a morning pilgrim bus leaving Barkor Square in Lhasa for Ganden. Ganden is set in a natural hilly amphitheatre. You can hike up in the hills around the monastery for views. For those with stamina and a good food supply, there's an arduous four to five-day trek from Ganden to Samye, over some 5000-metre passes. Some groups arrange a guide and yak-handler to carry gear. Camping out is necessary.

Further to the northeast, about 130 km from Lhasa, are two fine places which are elusive to locate. **Drigung** is a monastery impossibly grafted onto a sheer cliff-face. It was originally the base of the Drigung sub-order of the Kagyu sect, dating from the 12th century. Going up switchbacks in a Landcruiser, you may pass a donkey bearing a body under a blanket: Drigung is reputed to have the best sky burial ceremony of all. It's possible to stay in the village close to Drigung. Not far off is **Tidrom Nunnery,** home to over a hundred nuns. In this area there are numerous hermitages and caves, and a hot springs. There's a guesthouse catering to visitors to the hot springs.

Three other monastic sites worth looking at lie at north of Lhasa: Yerpa, Talung and Reting. **Yerpa,** 45 km northeast of Lhasa (well off the main road), used to be a complex of monasteries, with more than 80 meditation caves tucked away in the hills. The area suffered extensive damage during the Cultural Revolution: restoration is on-going, but in 1998 a major set-back occurred when Chinese officials destroyed several temples and caves.

Further north, the once-great **Talung Gompa** lies in ruins, a victim of the Cultural Revolution. Several temples have been restored and over 100 monks have taken up residence. The monastery overlooks a village.

If you continue along this route past Lhundrup, you'll reach **Reting,** about 150 km from Lhasa. Reting is the former seat of the Reting Rinpoche: this lineage started in the 18th century when the 7th Dalai Lama appointed his tutor as abbot of Reting. Several of the Reting Rinpoches served as regents during the minorities of the Dalai Lamas. The 5th Reting Rinpoche ruled from 1933 to 1947 during the minority of the 14th Dalai Lama, and was actually responsible for his discovery. Involved in political intrigue and sexual scandal, the 5th Reting Rinpoche died in prison in 1947. Very little is left of the splendour of Reting—it was all destroyed in the 1960s. A small assembly hall has been rebuilt, with a few dozen monks in residence. The area is unusual for its grove of juniper trees, which appear to be twisted and gnarled as an arboreal response to the problems of high altitude and high winds. There's nowhere to stay at Reting, but you can find lodging in a basic guesthouse in the village of Lhundrup. Backing Lhundrup is the optical illusion of a perfectly conical mountain.

YARLUNG VALLEY

Southeast of Lhasa lies the cradle of Tibetan culture—the Yarlung Valley. The Adam and Eve of Tibet—a myth involved a monkey and a demoness—were supposed to have dwelt in Tsedang. Most based in historical fact, the Yarlung dynasty kings had their base in the Yarlung Valley—in the 7th and 8th centuries, they unified the Tibetans and strengthened their identity as a nation. The burial mounds of all the Yarlung dynasty kings are at Chongye. However, these are rather dull to look at: the main attractions southeast of Lhasa are Samye Temple Complex and Yumbulagang Fortress. By Landcruiser, you can visit half a dozen sites mentioned here in two or three days. If you're planning to do any hiking, allow more time. You can trek from Samye to Ganden by an arduous route over high passes. You need to be completely self-sufficient for a trip like this. Some group tours tackle the trek with guides, and donkeys or horses to carry gear.

Drolma Lakhang

The exquisite Tara Temple (Drolma Lakhang) is one of the best-preserved in Central Tibet. This temple lies along the main road, 25 km out of Lhasa. It is associated with the Bengali sage Atisha who arrived in Tibet to teach in the 11th century. He died in this area in 1054. The temple is dedicated to the goddess Tara, with whom Atisha had a strong connection. The temple was apparently spared damage in the 1960s because of a request from the government of Bengal, where Atisha is a highly revered figure. The temple is small and active, with 25 monks. The most striking feature is a sutra-chanting chapel where 21 lifesized bronze statues of Tara enclose the space. The main image is a Sakyamuni statue; to the left is a statue of Atisha. On the upper floor is a library, plus some meditation rooms.

Gonggar

The name "Gonggar" is today associated with Tibet's only commercial airport, but in the days before the first planes arrived in the 1960s, it was known to Tibetans as the location of Gongkar Choide. This monastery, about 28 km east of the Tsangpo Bridge, was ransacked during the Cultural Revolution. The main hall was used as a barley silo, and murals were defaced with Mao Zedong slogans. Despite the destruction, the surviving mural work at Gongkar Choide makes it worth the visit.

Gonggar Airport (elevation 3700m), lies further east (95 km from Lhasa), just off the main road to Tsedang. It was constructed in the late 1970s, with elaborate terminal facilities and a second runway added in 1994. Not far from the airport gates is a crossroads with a cluster of small Chinese hotels and restaurants. There's also a ramshackle Tibetan guesthouse here. The airport has a post office. By Landcruiser, it's about 50 minutes from Gonggar to Lhasa.

Mindroling Gompa

Mindroling is the largest Nyingma sect monastery in Central Tibet (a second large Nyingma lamasery is Dorje Drak, on the north bank of the Yarlung Tsangpo). Founded in the 17th century, Mindroling was razed by the Mongols in the 18th century, then rebuilt, and again razed during the Cultural Revolution (and rebuilt). Mindroling's imposing facade is constructed in monastic citadel style; the gompa impresses with its surprising size and austerity, and skilful construction in stone. The most important chapel lies at the back: it houses a huge

Sakyamuni image. To get to Mindroling, turn off the main road near Zanang (aka Zhanang or Dranang): the monastery is a further 8 km away, on a dirt trail.

SAMYE

Samye, an attractive walled temple complex, sits at 3650 metres on the north bank of the Yarlung Tsangpo. A Landcruiser will park on the south banks of the river—the driver waits with the car for a day or two while the guide takes you along on a ferry ride across the Yarlung Tsangpo. On the other side, a truck picks you up for the short run into Samye.

The "ferry" is a barge designed for the transport of goods back and forth from Samye. There have been a number of nasty arguments between foreigners and locals over the cost of the barge and the truck (foreigners are charged at least double the going rate). Bargaining doesn't work well here as this is a monopoly situation and the operators know it. To avoid ill feelings, leave the matter in the hands of the guide, and focus instead on the entrancing Yarlung Tsangpo vistas. Because the barge has to navigate around sand-bars, the trip across the Yarlung Tsangpo can take up to an hour.

Samye Temple Complex

Samye is thought to be Tibet's first monastery and its first university. Samye's layout is based on Buddhist cosmology: it is a mandalic 3-D replica of the Tibetan Buddhist universe. The temple complex has been constructed according to the principles of geomancy, a concept derived from India. Samye has been deconstructed and reconstructed a number of times. The monastery is thought to have been founded in the 8th century by King Trisong Detsen, in consultation with Indian sage Padmasambhava. The temple was destroyed in civil war in the 11th century, by fire in the 11th and 17th centuries, by earthquake in the 18th century, and by Mao Zedong's fanatical hordes in the 20th century.

At the centre of the Tibetan Buddhist universe lies a mythical palace on top of Mount Meru, which at Samye is symbolised by the main temple (Utse). Surrounding this is a great "ocean", with four great island-continents, and eight sub-continents. If the colour-coded chortens (red, black, green and white) look a bit out of place in this scheme of things, it's because they were razed during the Cultural Revolution, and were only reconstructed in the early 1990s—in new brick, with synthetic paints, and without much finesse. Renovation and reconstruction of other parts within the walls is on-going. The ex-

119

Samye Temple Complex

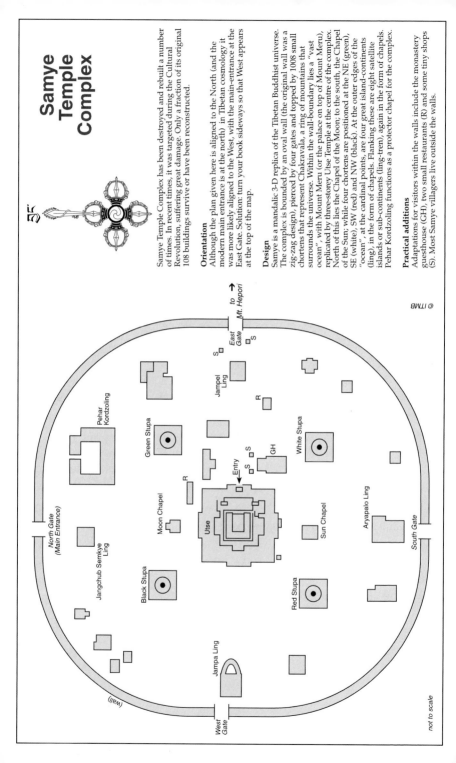

Samye Temple Complex has been destroyed and rebuilt a number of times. In recent times, it was targeted during the Cultural Revolution, suffering great damage. Only a fraction of its original 108 buildings survive or have been reconstructed.

Orientation

Although the plan given here is aligned to the North (and the modern main entrance is at the north) in Tibetan cosmology it was more likely aligned to the West, with the main-entrance at the East Gate. Solution: turn your book sideways so that West appears at the top of the map.

Design

Samye is a mandalic 3-D replica of the Tibetan Buddhist universe. The complex is bounded by an oval wall (the original wall was a zig-zag design), pierced by four gates and topped by 1008 small chortens that represent Chakravala, a ring of mountains that surrounds the universe. Within the wall-boundary lies a "vast ocean", with Mount Meru (or the palace on top of Mount Meru), replicated by three-storey Utse Temple at the centre of the complex. North of this lies the Chapel of the Moon; to the south, the Chapel of the Sun; while four chortens are positioned at the NE (green), SE (white), SW (red) and NW (black). At the outer edges of the "ocean", at the cardinal points, are four great island-continents (ling), in the form of chapels. Flanking these are eight satellite islands or sub-continents (ling-tren), again in the form of chapels. Pehar Kordzoling functions as a protector chapel for the complex.

Practical additions

Adaptations for visitors within the walls include the monastery guesthouse (GH), two small restaurants (R) and some tiny shops (S). Most Samye villagers live outside the walls.

terior wall itself has been hastily restored, using a large amount of concrete—the favourite material of the Chinese.

There are currently about 100 monks attached to the main temple. The monastery was built long before the rise of the different sects in Tibet. In the late 8th century, Trisong Detsen presided over a debate at Samye between Indian Buddhists and Chinese Zen Buddhists over which type of Buddhism should prevail in Tibet. The Indians won. Since that time, the monastery has came under the influence of various sects—the Nyingma, Sakya and Geluk traditions. Even today, influences are eclectic.

Samye Utse: The three-storey temple faces to the east. The upper storeys were removed during the Cultural Revolution, but the gleaming roof was restored in 1989. To the left of the main entrance is a five-metre-high stone obelisk; erected by King Songsten Gampo, it proclaims the Indian school of Buddhism to be the state religion. Inside the main assembly hall of the Utse are statues of the early kings, and images of Padmasambhava and Atisha. The inner sanctum contains a beautiful Sakyamuni image. To the right side of the assembly hall is a Gonkhang or tantric protector chapel with odds and ends like a stuffed snake and an old musket. To the left of the assembly hall is the Avalokitesvara Chapel, with a fine bas-relief portrait of the bodhisattva. Upstairs, you can access several chapels and might even be allowed to view the former quarters of the Dalai Lama. On the second floor is an open gallery with a long string of murals, some depicting the history of Tibet; there is also a mural of the fabled land of Shambhala here.

Ling Chapels: While Meru is connected with the realms of the gods, humanoids are supposed to live on the four island-continents (ling) across a vast ocean, flanked by satellite islands or subcontinents (ling-tren). These are all symbolised by one or two-storey buildings at Samye, some lined with murals, and graced with pleasant courtyards with gardens and potted plants; others lying in a decayed state, awaiting restoration.

Jamphel Ling, at the east side, is dedicated to Manjughosa. It the 1980s it was a commune office. At the southern end, Aryalpo Ling, dedicated to Hayagriva, was where Indian scholars lived during the great debate of the 8th century. It has undergone some restoration of its murals; on the upper storey are strange murals depicting creatures riding scorpions, dragons and bears. The chapel immediately west of this is worth a visit: it has been renovated with a full set of murals.

Jampa Ling, the chapel near the west gate, is dedicated to Maitreya (Champa or Jampa in Tibetan) and is where the Chinese monks resided during the 8th century. At the entrance hall is a mural showing

Samye at it once was. Jangchub Semkye Ling, at the north, was dedicated to Prajnaparamita. Inside is a 3-D scale model of Samye. This building is undergoing restoration—it was used for wood storage.

Just east of Jangchub Semkye Ling is a north-facing red-walled building—Pehar Kordzoling, a protector chapel. Samye's Sanskrit texts were once stored here in the care of the protector deity Pehar. Pehar's mandate was to watch over the monastery's treasures: among these was a leather mask that was believed to come alive, with rolling of bulging eyes. After several centuries at Samye, Pehar was removed to Nechung Monastery in Lhasa, and became the protective deity of the state oracle. There was also an oracle at Samye: Pehar's job at Samye was taken over by Tsemar, the red protector, who sat in judgement of the souls of men once a year: evil-doers were chopped to shreds. Pehar Kordzoling is adorned with unusual mural work featuring skulls; though under renovation, the chapel appears to be a site where special rituals are carried out.

Bizarre Notes

Following Chinese occupation, villagers were encouraged to treat the walled sanctuary of Samye as just another part of the village, so pigs, cows, braying donkeys and sheep are herded through the muddy wasteland. Along with a large band of dogs that hang out on the flagstones near the Utse, this gives Samye a somewhat earthy and surreal air—you round a corner looking for a sacred temple, and instead stray across a pig wallowing in the mud.

Out of Samye

To the east of Samye is Mount Hepori, which offers a great bird's-eye view of the town. Apparently, it also overlooks a military camp, so travellers are discouraged from visiting and taking pictures. Some travellers have been detained and questioned for being "out of bounds" by PSB. Pilgrims climb to the top of Mt Hepori to make offerings at a shrine festooned with prayer flags.

Basics

The best place to stay is the guesthouse attached to Samye monastery. It lies near the front entrance of the main temple. The guesthouse is most likely a former monastery building—it has lots of character, though it's somewhat spartan (and can be chilly at night). The rooftop offers good views of the area, and takes the prize for squat toilets. There's also a private guesthouse somewhere within the walls of Samye.

Just near the main temple is a charming Tibetan-run teahouse which serves good noodle and vegetable dishes. There may be other eateries operating within the walls; there are a few tiny shops, too. Outside the walls lies the Chinese world of the PSB—there have been problems as PSB maintains that permits for Samye are restricted to the walled section only.

TSEDANG
Tsetang, Zedang, Nedong; elevation 3600m; Map reference: see inset on Central Tibet map

Tsedang is a Chinese town—or to put it more bluntly, a Chinese eyesore. This is the shape of things to come, as more Chinese settlers move in. The town functions as a Chinese hub in Central Tibet. In contrast to traditional Tibetan architecture, which blends into the mountain and desert environment, Chinese structures here look totally jarring—with bland concrete blocks finished in bathroom tiling and blue-tinted glass. Although there was an ancient Tibetan town at Tsedang, it has been marginalised—remnants of an old Tibetan quarter exist to the east of the market area. Due to a military presence, there is a surfeit of karaoke bars and bars stocked with young women.

Tsedang is mostly used as a stepping-stone to destinations like Yumbulagang Fortress. There are a few hikes on the eastern side of Tsedang that are of middling interest. One is to a gompa ruins and a small nunnery. A longer hike (about four hours) takes you up a mountain trail to Gangpo Ri monkey cave. This cave is revered as the mythical site where a monkey (an emanation of Avalokitesvara) consorted with an demoness (an emanation of Tara) to give birth to the six children, later leaders of the Tibetan clans. The monkey then instructed them how to cultivate grains in the fertile valley—so Tibet's first cultivated field is supposed to be in the Tsedang area. This tale of the origin of the Tibetan race, involving descent from a monkey, has an oddly Darwinian touch.

Basics

A strange cat-and-mouse game goes on with hotel, guesthouses and restaurants in Tsedang. Tsedang seems to be a PSB-Mafia-dominated monopoly. Travellers who have tried to stay in non-Chinese-operated guesthouses or restaurants have been visited by Tsedang PSB officers and told to move along. Other restaurant owners, intimidated by the PSB, will inform Westerners they cannot eat in the restaurant. PSB officers have been seen trailing travellers around the town. Travellers should make deliberate efforts to break this stranglehold when it comes to restaurants, but there doesn't seem to be a way round for hotels, as PSB can easily close down Tibetan-run guesthouses.

Tsedang is located around a dusty traffic circle—most activity takes place on the street running south of the circle. Up one end is the Chinese-run Friendship Hotel, tel. 20816, fax 21128, with several floors of mid-range accommodation (backpackers find the prices steep here—you can try bargaining but you're up against stroppy staff who know the cards are stacked in their favour). You pay for the privilege of having a TV in the room and plumbing of dubious quality (when I was there, a swimming pool developed on one floor due to leaky plumbing). There aren't many alternatives. Tsedang Hotel, tel/fax 21668, at the south end of town, is the group tour hotel—it's on the expensive side.

Not a lot of choice in restaurants, either. Near the post office are several Tibetan eateries. Right near the PSB is a Tibetan tearoom—drop in to annoy the Beijing Boys. A Chinese restaurant next door to the Friendship Hotel diverts hotel guests into their parlour. The Tsedang Hotel has its own dining hall. Gesar Restaurant, near the PSB office, is a fancy Chinese restaurant with mock-Tibetan décor: it appears to cater to Chinese army officers.

Shopping & Facilities

For trip supplies, try the department store near the main crossroads, and also the street markets nearby. For artefact shopping, the west end of the street markets offer tankas and Qinghai carpets. The post office/telecom building is at the main crossroads: the Tsedang area code is 893. One street south is the Xinhua Bookstore (on the second floor—don't expect much—you might find some posters or maps).

Mobility

The PSB office here seems bent on restricting your movements. They do spot checks on travellers, asking for permits. Make sure your papers are in order before you leave Lhasa. There are buses running to Tsedang from Lhasa. Since the road is smooth, paved and flat, you can get there in record time—three hours should suffice. Tsedang is 196 km from Lhasa and 97 km from Gonggar Airport.

SOUTH OF TSEDANG

The main attraction south of Tsedang is **Yumbulagang Fortress,** 13 km from town. The fortress crowns a hilltop; it is set in a valley with a village below. Now you see it, now you don't. Yumbulagang is in the RRDCR-CR category (reduced to rubble during Cultural Revolution and completely rebuilt). Pictures taken in the late 1970s show nothing left of the fortress—it was shorn from the rock. Pictures taken in the 1980s show the entire fortress again. The present building, reconstructed in 1982, is a pretty good copy of the original, though not quite as big. The architecture is rare and distinctive: Yumbulagang Fortress is believed to have been built by the Yarlung dynasty kings in the 7th or 8th century. Later it was converted into a monastery. Now it is a museum of sorts, looked after by some Geluk monks. You can clamber up through several storeys right to the very top of the tower, where there are observation windows giving fine views of the patchwork of fields in the village below.

On the way out to Yumbulagang, or on the return trip, you can visit **Trandruk Gompa,** originally built by King Songsten Gampo in the 7th century. The monastery is 7 km from Tsedang. Upstairs on the second floor—locked in a dusty glass case—is the monastery's treasure: a precious tanka depicting Avalokitesvara, whose ghost-like image is reputed to be composed of 30,000 pearls, sewn into a tanka.

A different fork from Tsedang leads 17 km south to **Tangboche Monastery,** which, though in a sorry state, is worth checking out for the murals covering the walls of the assembly hall. These murals were commissioned in 1915 by the 13th Dalai Lama (whose image naturally appears among the murals). A further 13 km southwards brings you to Chongye, where the tombs of all the Yarlung dynasty kings are located. **Chongye Royal Tombs** consist of massive earth mounds, which all look pretty much the same except for their size. This has led to much confusion over who is actually entombed within. The largest tomb is believed to be that of the 7th-century warrior-king, Songsten Gampo. On top of this tomb is a small chapel, reached by a flight of stairs—it features a statue of Songsten Gampo, flanked by two of his wives and two important ministers.

To the east of Tsedang, approached from Tsangri, an arduous hike leads to **Lhamo Latso,** the oracle lake. In former times, high lamas would venture out to Lhamo Latso and contemplate the lake to induce visions used in divinations. In the early 1930s, visions conjured up here helped direct Reting Rinpoche's search for the 14th Dalai Lama. The trek into Lhamo Latso is very tough, going over several high passes. Having a guide would be a good idea; you might want to take camping gear and make a two-day trip out of it—that would leave time to contemplate the lake.

LHASA TO KATHMANDU ROUTE

the greatest road route in High Asia

The Lhasa to Kathmandu route ranks, in my mind, as the finest in High Asia. Not in terms of road surface (*?!*&%), but because of the ethereal views. You are motoring across the roof the world, powering over five passes—festooned with prayer-flags—all above 4500 metres. If you take the Gyantse route, winding up to Khamba La pass, you come to stunning views of the Turquoise Lake (Yamdrok Tso) with snowcaps on the Bhutanese border. Three great monasteries—at Gyantse, Shigatse and Sakya—lie along the road route. If you have arranged it with the driver and guide, you can drive all the way to Everest base camp—a magical spot that will (literally) blow you away. Even without the base-camp trip, on a clear day you can see some 8000-metre peaks right from the roadway, including Cho Oyu, near Tingri. And then there's a fantastic drop right off the Tibetan plateau—from high-altitude desert, switchbacking down to tropical Nepalese jungle. There is nothing in High Asia that can compare to this roadshow. Lhasa to Kathmandu is an excellent adventure. Nobody said the trip would be easy, though.

Logistics

On your own, you can catch a bus running to Shigatse from Lhasa, but no buses run on the southern route to Gyantse (the buses go to Shigatse first, and then from Shigatse back to Gyantse). There is an intermittent service to Sakya also, as well as pilgrim trucks headed in this direction. Some backpackers have managed to negotiate rides all the way to the Nepalese border. Three backpackers paid for a ride on a CITS bus that was heading from Shigatse to Zhangmu to pick up a group at the border—but there was no stopping or sightseeing.

If you want to stop where you like, the best option is to club together with other travellers and rent a Landcruiser with driver and guide (or several Landcruisers). There are a number of options here: take the Landcruiser to Zhangmu and cross the border into Nepal, or go to Zhangmu, turn around, and come back to Lhasa. You might want to arrange a mixture: drop some passengers at Zhangmu, and then return to Lhasa. Landcruiser travel gives you flexibility. A factor you have to consider when planning this trip is where to overnight. Apart from the places mentioned in this text, the driver and guide can ferret out small restaurants or places to stay overnight if you are stuck somewhere at nightfall. There's always a guesthouse or teahouse tucked away somewhere.

In theory, the Lhasa to Kathmandu route (the actual highway) is open without permits. However, if you stop anywhere or overnight, the only place that appears to be quite open is Shigatse. You are supposed to have permits for places like Gyantse, Sakya, Everest, Shegar and so on. The guide with a Landcruiser can arrange these. On your own, you may be able to pick up permits for onward destinations at Shigatse PSB—ask other travellers about the current situation.

Timing

A lot of navigation information is carried in the Lhasa to Kathmandu Route map in this book. You can work out turn-offs and where you are by a system of kilometre marker-stones by the roadside. This is the best way, for example, to find Milarepa's cave (which is not visible from the road). The entire route from Lhasa to Kathmandu is 938 km if you go via Gyantse, but 865 km if you take the direct Lhasa-Shigatse route. If you take sidetrips to Shegar and Sakya (highly recommended), you add 56 km to the kilometrage, since Sakya lies 21 km

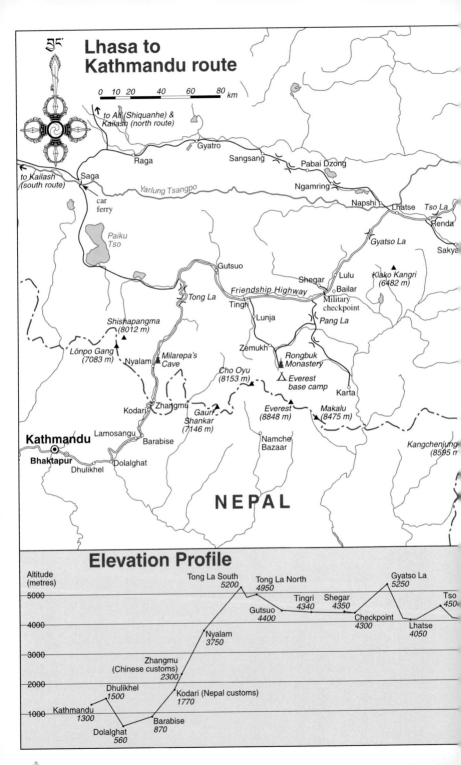

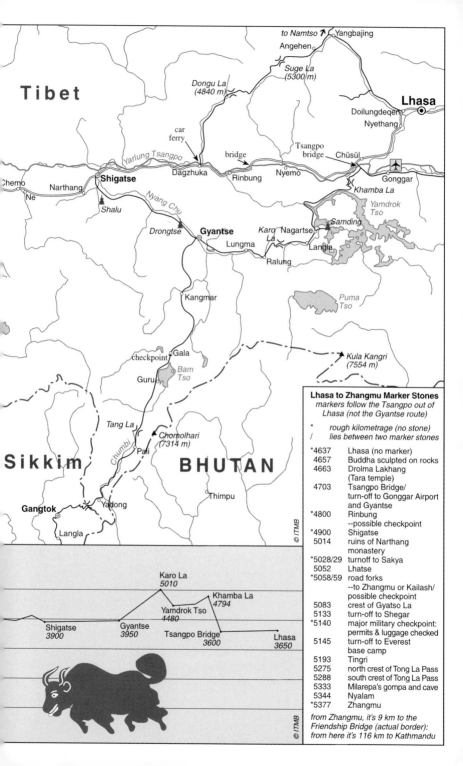

Lhasa to Zhangmu Marker Stones
markers follow the Tsangpo out of Lhasa (not the Gyantse route)

*	rough kilometrage (no stone)
/	lies between two marker stones

*4637	Lhasa (no marker)
4657	Buddha sculpted on rocks
4663	Drolma Lakhang (Tara temple)
4703	Tsangpo Bridge/ turn-off to Gonggar Airport and Gyantse
*4800	Rinbung --possible checkpoint
*4900	Shigatse
5014	ruins of Narthang monastery
*5028/29	turnoff to Sakya
5052	Lhatse
*5058/59	road forks --to Zhangmu or Kailash/ possible checkpoint
5083	crest of Gyatso La
5133	turn-off to Shegar
*5140	major military checkpoint: permits & luggage checked
5145	turn-off to Everest base camp
5193	Tingri
5275	north crest of Tong La Pass
5288	south crest of Tong La Pass
5333	Milarepa's gompa and cave
5344	Nyalam
*5377	Zhangmu

from Zhangmu, it's 9 km to the Friendship Bridge (actual border): from here it's 116 km to Kathmandu off the main route. There's a major detour of 70 km off the main route to reach Everest base camp (see the *Star Treks* chapter).

Without stops or obstacles, fast drivers can make the run from Lhasa to Zhangmu in two days, overnighting at Tingri. With stops, the trip would require a minimum of four days. It's recommended you allow six to seven days, depending on sidetrips. If you include Everest base camp, allow more time. Approximate driving time along the route: Lhasa to Shigatse, 6 to 10 hrs (depending on route taken); Shigatse to Lhatse, 3.30 hrs; Lhatse to Tingri, 4 hrs; Tingri to Nyalam, 4.30 hrs; Nyalam to Zhangmu, 2.30 hrs; Zhangmu to Kodari, 1.5 hrs (includes checkposts); Kodari to Kathmandu, 4 hours.

Reverse Trip

The description here follows Lhasa to Kathmandu for the very good reason that it's more approachable in that direction due to the altitude acclimatisation factor and the visa/permit situation. However, it is possible to do the route in reverse. Some words of caution. Once you enter Tibet at Zhangmu, you do not have an Alien Travel Permit. Technically, the road from Zhangmu to Lhasa is open without permit, but this could be sticky. Really, you are at the mercy of CITS in Zhangmu, who arrange Landcruiser rides to Lhasa for $100-$150 a person. You're in a poor bargaining position—CITS is a transport monopoly. Coming in from Kathmandu, be careful what you bring in your baggage—suspect literature may cause big problems. Going up from 1300 metres in Kathmandu to a 5200-metre pass, you may be in no mood or condition for sightseeing. You may have trouble with altitude sickness. Some Landcruiser drivers carry a small tank of oxygen in the vehicle.

LHASA TO SHIGATSE ROUTES

There are three routes from Lhasa to Shigatse. If on a round-trip from Lhasa, you can combine routes. For example, for a long loop, you could motor via Yamdrok Tso to Gyantse, and then return to Lhasa via Yangbajing, stopping at various monasteries along the routes.

Northern Route: The northern route via Yangbajing is the least-travelled way of getting from Lhasa to Shigatse—but makes sense if you've been off to Lake Namtso. The route is sometimes used if for some reason the main westward route is blocked. Yangbajing supplies geothermal power to Lhasa; there is a hot- spring pool here. Heading southwards from Yangbajing you motor across two high passes—Suge La and Dongu La. On the north banks of the Yarlung Tsangpo you can detour along a rough road to Menri Gompa, a small Bon monastery. You cross the Yarlung Tsangpo by car ferry to Dagzhuka, and join the main western route to Shigatse. Approximate driving time (no stops) on this route is: Lhasa to Yangbajing, 2 hrs; Yangbajing to Suge La, 2.15 hrs; Suge La to Dagzhuka ferry crossing, 2.45 hrs; Dagzhuza to Shigatse, 2 hrs.

Western Route: This road follows a canyon running along the Yarlung Tsangpo—it is used by Chinese military and supply trucks to get from Lhasa to Shigatse in the fastest time. It thus sees the heaviest traffic, with convoys of military trucks heading through. The road runs beneath steep canyon walls: rockfalls may block the road entirely. Slabs of roadway have also been known to disappear into the Yarlung Tsangpo—haven't quite perfected the engineering. The bridge spanning the Yarlung Tsangpo near Rinbung is one-way, meaning that there can be traffic line-ups when the flow is against you. Driving time on this Lhasa to Shigatse route is about 5 to 6 hours if there are no delays or problems.

Southern Route: This route via Gyantse to Shigatse is much more dramatic, taking in the beautiful lake of Yamdrok Tso. This route is longer, more winding and rougher, so it is not used by supply trucks. This means minimal traffic and far superior views. On the southern route, exiting Lhasa, you cross the Tsangpo Bridge and wind up to Khamba La, with stunning views. Down the other side of Khamba La you reach Nagartse, a village with a small restaurant, plus a guesthouse. If you can, arrange a sidetrip to Samding Monastery. From Nagartse, the road climbs over Karo La and heads for Gyantse. Approximate driving time on this route: Lhasa to Khamba La, 1.30 hrs; Khamba La to Karo La, 3 hrs; Karo La to Gyantse, 2.30 hrs; Gyantse to Shigatse, 2 hours.

SOUTHERN ROUTE TO GYANTSE

Drolma Lakhang

Exiting Lhasa on either the western route or the southern route, you can visit this well-preserved temple, about 25 km from Lhasa. See *Exploring Central Tibet* for details.

Yamdrok Tso

From Khamba La, where prayer flags are buffeted by the winds, you get a magnificent view of Yamdrok Tso (the Turquoise Lake), with the large snowcap on the horizon being Kula Kangri on the Bhutanese border. From this vantage point, you can see why the Tibetans consider Yamdrok Tso to be a sacred lake. It is Tibet's largest freshwater body of water.

Winding down from Khamba La toward the shore of Yamdrok Tso, you can see a hydropower plant, with Austrian-built turbines. This plant is part of a hare-brained Chinese scheme that drains the lakewater to produce electricity for Lhasa during peak demand. The plant is designed as a pumped storage plant with 90 MW capacity. The project has been a total disaster since its inception in 1985. In 1986, due to vigorous objections from Tibetans headed by the 10th Panchen Lama, work was halted, but was resumed after the Panchen Lama's death in 1989. Overriding international campaigns, the Chinese went ahead with construction—and reports filtered through of leaking and collapsed tunnels leading from the lake to the turbines. The plant started generating power in mid-1997.

Western environmentalists are concerned that the water level at Yamdrok Tso could drop significantly—or, in a worst-case scenario, that the lake might completely drain away. Authorities in Lhasa insist this is not the case: they say they will pump water back from the Yarlung Tsangpo to replenish the lakewater. But even if this were true, it means snow-fed lakewater would be replaced with muddy river flow, with uncertain ecological results. Pumping water back up into Yamdrok Tso requires a separate power source: a new dam, under construction on the Nyang River, 30 km east of Gyantse, is said to be that source. The building of this dam has spawned an entire town of corrugated roofing, housing Chinese construction workers and engineers.

Samding Monastery

Yamdrok Tso is shaped like the pincers of a crab: in the grip of the pincers lies the monastery of Samding, about 8 km from Nagartse. You can reach it by Landcruiser from Nagartse, or hike in. Nagartse PSB does not seem to like travellers visiting this one, so be discreet when visiting. The monastery is on a hilltop, reached by a set of switchbacks; a few dozen monks are in residence. There are expansive views across the valley from Samding.

Samding Monastery has an odd history. The monastery was probably founded in the 13th century, and was associated with the Bodong sect, initiated by Bodong Chokle Namgyel (1306–1386). The Bodong sect never gained much prominence, although a number of temples within radius of Samding followed its precepts.

At one time, Samding appears to have had both monks and nuns in residence, and was run by an abbess—one of the only female incarnations in Tibet. The lineage goes back to the 18th century. In 1717, legend has it, the abbess (venerated as Dorje Phagmo, or the "Thunderbolt Sow," believed to be a reincarnation of Tara) transformed herself and her cohorts to save themselves from a Dzungar (Mongol) attack.

For centuries, the lineage continued uneventfully, until the year 1937. That year the acting Regent of Tibet announced that the 6th Dorje Phagmo had been recognised in a young girl, even though the 5th was still at large. He argued that the transference of souls actually took place in this case before death. The 5th Dorje Phagmo died the following year, but the Tibetans would not accept the 6th as the true incarnation and three other candidates were put forward. The matter was hotly disputed by the nominated 6th's father, and a costly legal battle drained the funds of Samding and tore its monks and nuns apart with internal strife.

The 6th Dorje Phagmo, it appears, hardly took up residence at Samding, since the legal wrangle carried over into the 1950s. In 1959, she fled to India, but the same year decided to return to Tibet by way of China. She then sided with the Chinese in her loyalties and made it clear she did not wish to be a Living Buddha anymore. She married and had three children, and held a high government position in Lhasa. When last heard of, however, she had resumed her role as head of Samding and was said to be again giving initiations.

If a community of nuns and monks with an abbess at their head sounds like good material for a novel, there is one that draws inspiration from Samding. In his suspense novel *The Rose of Tibet*, author Lionel Davidson combines Yamdrok Tso and Samding to create a place called Yamdring Monastery.

GYANTSE
GYANGTSE, GYANGZE; ELEVATION 3950M

Gyantse was established as the personal fiefdom of King Pelden Sangpo, in the 14th century. His successor, Rabten Kunsang Phapa (1389–1442), extended the fiefdom's range, and constructed Palkor Choide Lamasery and the might Kumbum—both still standing.

In later centuries, Gyantse developed as an important centre of the wool trade in Tibet, and a bustling caravan stop on the trade-route from Lhasa to India. That route—leading to Sikkim and Bhutan—was closed by the Chinese after they took over in 1950. Gyantse has fallen into obscurity, its role usurped by Lhasa under the Chinese. This situation, however, has left Gyantse intact as a Tibetan architectural entity, which is something quite rare amid all the Chinese destruction and reconstruction (in Lhasa itself). Gyantse has a largely Tibetan

Gyantse

Gompa Ruins

Kumbum

Palkor Choide

Main Entrance

Nunnery

Stadium

Horseracing Ground

Carpet factory

Clinic

Tashi R.

Tibetan Truckstop H.

Dzong

Main Entrance

Bakery

Street markets

Minibuses

Karaoke Bar
Department Store

Vegetable Market

Sichuan R.

Yak R.

Gyangze H.

Movie Theatre

Bank

Nyang Chu

to Shigatse & Lhasa by paved North Route

Gyangtse H.

Post Office/ Telecom

Army Camp

to Pala Manor 2 km

TV Station

to Nenying Gompa, Yadong & Bhutan Border

to Lhasa by old South Route

Legend

Fort		Hotel	
Tower		Restaurant	
Important building		Post Office	
Tibetan housing (Old Quarter)		Hospital	
Cultivated area		Bridge	
Walking trail		Entrance	
Old stone-paved road		Ridges with sharp drop-offs (contours)	

0   100 200   400 m

approx. scale

© ITMB

population—perhaps around 15,000. There is a huge fort up one end of town, a walled-in monastery-grounds at the other end, and a ramshackle market-place with older buildings and alley-ways between fort and monastery.

In the late 1940s, Italian photographer Francesco Mele passed through Gyantse. Here's his description of the market:

> Its market is rich, due to the wool trade and the Indian and Chinese imported objects sold there. The shops are near to the main street, and many of them are simply tents. Here women wearing silver and turquoise jewellery sell clothing and household articles.... There are even some Nepalese and Bhutanese salesmen, and a few Muslims who have taken the few weeks' journey from Ladak in order to sell their products in Gyantse. Muslims are often employed as butchers of yak and goat here, since the Buddhist religion forbids Tibetans to kill animals. Fresh and dried beef and mutton hang in every part of the market, giving it an oddly surrealist appearance.

Gyantse market appears to have died: there isn't a whole lot happening around the old quarter anymore. Instead, various smaller street markets are scattered around the town. Nevertheless, Gyantse is a great place to visit, and will give some idea of what an intact Tibetan town must have looked like.

Buildings in Gyantse date back as far as the 14th century. One of these is the massive dzong (fort), occupying a strategic hilltop at the southern end of town. The dzong guarded the road to Lhasa, and the invading British expedition of 1903 found it a formidable obstacle. The British eventually stormed the dzong—the Tibetan defenders capitulated, and there was no further resistance on the road to Lhasa.

Although the last of the British forces withdrew in 1908, several vestiges of British presence remained in Gyantse, in the form of a British Trade Agent, a British wool-agent station, a British post office (with a telegraph line running to India), and later a British-run school for upper-crust Tibetan children. By the 1940s, a great deal of Gyantse's sheep-wool production was slated for export to British India. There was little interest in yak-wool, which was too harsh in quality—although in the pre-synthetic era, the beards worn by Santa Clauses in US department stores were made from yak-tail hair. Gyantse became a funnel for the export of wool due to its location, and wool was brought here from outlying areas of Tibet.

The 1950s saw a period of severe dislocation in Gyantse. In 1954, the town was nearly destroyed by flooding; in 1959 the local industries were virtually dismantled with the exodus of artisans from Tibet, and the removal of others to workcamps. After putting down the 1959 revolt, the Chinese imprisoned 400 monks and laymen at the monastery of Gyantse. During the Cultural Revolution, the monastery itself was ransacked and dismantled—items of value were either destroyed or shipped back to China. Gyantse Kumbum, however, was spared. Since 1980, the Chinese have attempted to stimulate the handicraft production for which Gyantse was so famous. But if there has been any stimulation, there is little evidence of it in Gyantse's present-day market-place.

Orientation

Gyantse cleaves into several distinct zones. To the northern end of town is the old quarter, with Tibetan housing. To the southern end of town, south of the central roundabout, are newer Chinese concrete blocks and Chinese facilities like bank, post office, cinema and so on. At all compass points around the town are cultivated fields. There are stupendous views of Gyantse from the topmost ramparts of the fort.

Horse-racing Festival

The time when Gyantse really comes to life is during the horse racing festival, held in the first week of the eighth lunar month (usually sometime in late July or early August). The horse-racing ground is to the northeast side of town. Festivities last for about five days. The jockeys are young boys: the winners (both boy and horse) are festooned with white ceremonial scarves. Large parades, with dancers and singers, and monks in full regalia, accompany the opening and closing ceremonies.

Old Quarter

Gyantse is a great town to walk around. The Tibetan part of town, toward the gates of Gyantse Gompa, is a fascinating medieval jumble of alleyways, with the odd cow roaming through. Gyantse market used to be located along the stonepaved road close to the main monastery. There's no plumbing in the old quarter—water comes from street taps—and little electrical supply. However, solar cookers have been introduced by the Chinese: these concave-shaped reflectors are found on the flat roofs in the old quarter—they can bring a kettle of water to the boil in a few minutes.

There is a walking trail through from the monastery toward the horse-racing ground—it cuts through a cleft in a high ridge. Along the way is Gyantse Carpet Factory, where all work is done by hand—carding the wool, spinning, dyeing and weaving. This small operation is a shadow of what Gyantse once was. There's also a clothing factory in Gyantse. A worthy destination to the northeast side of town is a nunnery with 30 nuns in residence. A tiny chapel here contains a large wooden prayer-wheel and some lifesize frescoes—including one of the current Dalai Lama (easily identifiable from his glasses). Behind the nunnery is a cliff face with hermit caves; there's a sky burial site in this vicinity.

The Monastery

Pictures taken by Leslie Weir on a visit in 1930 show a complex of 16 monasteries within the high walls at the north end of Gyantse (Weir was a British Trade Agent at Gyantse). The monastic town has been razed with the exception of a few of the larger buildings.

Access: The monastery is only accessible by the south gate, where an entry fee is charged. The Kumbum appears to only be open in the mornings—in any case, this is the best time to visit. Chapels can be dark—bring a flashlight.

The Kumbum: The main sight of Gyantse is the immense chorten or Kumbum in the grounds of the walled monastery at the north end. It was built in the 14th century by Rapten Kunsang Phapa. Kumbum means "having 100,000 images"—and Gyantse Kumbum may well live up to that description. The chorten is a deluxe model and quite innovative in its architecture—there is nothing like it elsewhere in Tibet. It has 70 small interlocking chapels that you visit as you spiral your way to the golden plume at the top. Each chapel contains fine statuary, and murals painted in the 15th century by Newari artists.

In aerial perspective, the chorten is shaped like a mandala, the embodiment of the Lamaist universe. Pilgrims circumambulate this giant wedding-cake structure: the inner spiralling circuit of the chorten is a meditational aid, with the top canopied section representing the highest plane of wisdom. How far you can ascend depends on how adept you are at convincing the caretaker monks to allow you to proceed. The best strategy is to try and follow pilgrims, since entrances to upper regions are hidden behind statues and in dark alcoves (some may be locked). Right near the top you come out below the large all-seeing eyes of Buddha, painted on the upper walls. The chapels here are larger and contain intricate tantric murals and mandalas. Although it may appear you cannot go higher, in fact there are ladders leading above the all-seeing eyes through a trapdoor to an open wooden turret, under the top umbrella-like structure. From here there are panoramic views of Gyantse.

Palkor Choide Lamasery: This monastery is believed to have been constructed 1418–1425 by Rapten Kunsang Phapa. Though in the past it served the Sakya and Geluk orders, it is presently looked after by Gelukpa monks. The monastery has miraculously survived with some original statuary intact. More interesting than the ground floor assembly hall are the chapels on the second floor. On the third or topmost floor is a shrine to Sakyamuni Buddha, with huge tantric wheel murals of Sakya deities.

The Dzong

This brooding 500-year-old colossus crowns a hilltop at the southern end of Gyantse. The fort's foundations are 14th-century vintage, while the thick walls were probably constructed later. Access to the dzong is only from steps at the southeast side—there's a path leading from a roadway bridge here, through village housing, to the outer door. You need to find the gatekeeper to open the dzong's huge doors, on payment of an entry fee. Other buildings in the dzong complex may be locked, too. You can climb right to the top battlements, which offer a superb view of Gyantse town and make a great photo perch. Within the dzong, there's actually little to see. Various buildings and battlements were blown to smithereens by Nepalese invaders, then British invaders, and again by the favourite cohorts of Mao Zedong (the Red Guards)—leaving a lot of rubble lying around. Even so, it is one of the best-preserved forts in Tibet. Two restored sections include a chapel with some dark murals and newish Buddhist statuary, and an anti-British museum.

Bizarre Notes

"Memorial Hall of the Anti-British" is the name of a two-room museum exhibit at Gyantse Dzong. There are pictures; explanations in Tibetan, English and Chinese; a couple of small cannons; and a heroic statue of Tibetans fighting the imperialist British. A guide who was shepherding along some group tourists seemed to think that the Tibetans won the battle at the fort in 1903—which my (British) companion loudly called into question. Later on, we were intercepted by a Chinese official who arrived to question us about the questions we'd asked the guide! At which point, we feigned ignorance. History, it seems, undergoes constant revision within the PRC. Oddly, a

Chinese movie crew making a movie in 1996 about the British invasion of Tibet did not use Gyantse Dzong as a set.

WAX SEALS & POSTAL RUNNERS

After invading in 1903, the British negotiated the right to set up telegraph and post offices in Tibet. This gave the Tibetans access to the international postal system. There were a handful of British post offices—the earliest starting around 1906. The British were not permitted to establish a post office in Lhasa, but three British post offices linked the main trading corridor from Tibet to India: at Gyantse, Phari and Yadong. The mail then went on to Kalimpong, in India.

The postal system for external mail in Tibet was primarily used by Nepalese and Indian traders. Delivery was accomplished by runners; the monasteries, for instance, had their own runners. Ponies were also used, and in the 1930s a Dodge truck operated on part of the route to India. The runners, like most Tibetans, were illiterate and could only identify traders' mail by handmarked symbols on the envelopes. The mail could be delivered in a fairly short time: officials in Lhasa used to subscribe to newspapers in Calcutta, which might arrive a week or so later. Considering the altitude of the passes along the route, the runners did a remarkable job.

In 1910 the 13th Dalai Lama, who had fled to India, asked the British company of Waterlow to design a Tibetan stamp. Waterlow produced some proofs with a Snow Lion on them—the symbol of the Dalai Lama. These were rejected by the Tibetans, but they kept the proofs, and the Waterlow design was copied for the first Tibetan stamp issue of 1912. Tibetan stamps were a very haphazard affair. The 1912 issue, done in five different trangka values, was printed off woodblocks of 12 stamps. Stamp colour largely depended on what inks were available in the market-place. Tibetan cancels never bore dates, and the random print-runs were never announced—the 1914 issue of stamps was not discovered by the West until 1942.

If you were living in Lhasa in the 1930s and you wanted to get a letter to England, life got complicated. There was no British post office in Lhasa, and Tibet was not a member of the International Postal Union. So you needed two sets of stamps on an envelope—Tibetan and Indian. In Lhasa, they'd cancel the Tibetan postage and forward the item to the Tibetan post office in Gyantse. Somehow the letter would make it across town to Gyantse's British post office, and then go on to Yadong and India, where it entered the international postal system.

Incoming mail was virtually impossible to orchestrate unless sent care of a trader in Gyantse or Phari, who would affix the Tibetan postage and forward the letter. In the process, the actual stamps would be dwarfed by a selection of wax seals, handstamps, chops and registration-marks. Red wax seals could only be used by Incarnate Lamas. Few of the Dalai Lama's letters went beyond Sikkim. They were carried by private runners, and enclosed ceremonial silk scarves and perhaps a small bag of gold-dust. They could only leave the Potala on auspicious dates.

By the early 1950s, stamp collectors were rushing to buy Tibetan postage. The majority of fake Tibetan stamps and covers started to appear at this time, though the hobby goes back to 1920. Buyers who are offered earlier Tibetan stamps in Kathmandu will probably be shown forgeries nine times out of ten. Covers are now forged to the point where only a handful of world experts can tell the difference.

—Geoffrey Flack

Near Gyantse

Over a bridge, on the west side of Nyang River, is a junction with several turn-offs. To the southwest you can drive 2 km to Pala Manor, which is an old noble's house in the middle of a small village. The manor belongs to the "feudal" days when an aristocrat ruled the village and surrounding lands. The walled manor, mostly constructed of wood, features the former tearoom and stables. Most likely this manor, being extensively restored, will be a showpiece on how the people of Gyantse were exploited by Tibetan nobles (that's before all the major buildings of Gyantse were blown up by the Chinese).

Another turn-off leads directly south to Nenying Gompa, about 20 km from Gyantse. This is an active monastery set in a small village. The monastery was nearly destroyed by the invading British in 1903, and later rebuilt, only to be destroyed again during the Cultural Revolution (and then rebuilt). The road here leads southward all the way to Yadong, at the border of Sikkim. There's a military checkpoint at Gala, beyond which you are most unlikely to be allowed to proceed (after that, there are views of Mount Chomolhari from the road).

The main turn-off from Gyantse is the one leading to Shigatse. It's a fast, flat run from Gyantse to Shigatse—the ground can be covered in a matter of several hours. There are two monastery stops you can make. The first is at Drongtse Monastery, a small place famed for its slate bas-relief carvings—iconography etched in slate. Drongtse is about 9 km from the junction in Gyantse. A second possibility is Shalu Gompa, which is reached by a turn-off 18 km short of Shigatse. The gompa is 4 km off the main route (you can also visit Shalu on a day-trip from Shigatse—see that entry).

Basics

In the old quarter is a ramshackle Tibetan truck-stop hotel, with basic dorm-type rooms: a tap in the yard provides the plumbing. Closer to the bank is Gyangze Hotel, a Chinese blockhouse with softer beds—but the plumbing, though it may look impressive, fails to perform. The classiest place in town (the plumbing actually does work) is Gyangtse Hotel, to the southwest side—this is the place for group tours, with dining hall and souvenir shop. Amenities at this establishment include StarTV and hot water; oxygen pillows can be requested; there a yak tethered near the entrance—available for photo opportunities for a fee. The hotel rents bikes but they're too expensive.

Scattered around town are small eateries—some with only two or three tables. Near the Tibetan truck-stop hotel is Tashi Restaurant, a Tibetan-style teahouse also serving food. If the server bursts in through the front door with your food that's because the kitchen is across the street. A special bonus: a layer of dust on your food as the chef carries it from the kitchen across the street to your table. The Yak Restaurant is passable—another Tibetan-run establishment. At the Chinese end of town is small Sichuan Restaurant, with palatable fare. In the mornings, try the tiny bakery to the east of the dzong for hot baked goods.

Facilities

Facilities in Gyantse are limited but include a half-hearted attempt at a department store (shelves bare) and a half-hearted attempt at a bank (staffed by Chinese who appear to have perfected the art of camouflaging themselves as non-bank workers). Further down the street is the post office, with long-distance telecom capabilities if you goad the staff. Try and avoid the clinic at the northeast side of town—it's unsanitary. Gyantse is quiet at night apart from the occasional tuneless wailing from karaoke bars; there's also a movie theatre with an antiquated sound system.

If arriving by Landcruiser and overnighting, park the vehicle within your hotel grounds. Minibuses congregate at the central roundabout of the town early morning for departures to Shigatse. You can also try your luck hitching—walk partway in the direction you want to travel.

SHIGATSE
Xigaze, Zhigatse; elevation 3900m

Shigatse, the second largest town in Tibet, has a population of around 60,000. The massive monastery of Tashilhunpo dates from the mid-15th century. Shigatse was the power-base of the King of Tsang in the 16th century: he was defeated in battle in 1642 by the Mongol leader, Gushri Khan. In 1652, the 5th Dalai Lama bestowed the title of Panchen Lama on the abbot of Tashilhunpo Monastery. From that time on, the authority of the Panchen Lama outweighed that of the Lhasa-appointed district governor, who occupied the defeated king's castle (the present-day ruined dzong) in town.

Apart from Tashilhunpo Monastery and a small Tibetan quarter, Shigatse is heavily Chinese in character, which means an ugly concrete sprawl. There's a weird wind blowing through Shigatse. It's the wind from Beijing—the dusty wind of the Gobi. Look at a Chinese map of Shigatse and you can get some idea of what has transpired. A Chinese map I picked up barely mentions any Tibetan features—except for an entry that says "Trashilhunpo Temple" (can't even get that one right). Apart from the usual "No. 1 Bus Team", "No. 2 Guesthouse," is this curious entry: "Building for Overseas Tibetans." Could this be the fabled shop where Tibetans from Nepal come to buy their souvenirs?

Some glaring omissions on the map are the large army bases that ring the town. Shigatse is something of a glorified army base, with huge barracks punctuating the landscape. The arrival of the PLA en masse was not auspicious. In 1960, the PLA surrounded Tashilhunpo Monastery (which had hitherto escaped reforms) and seized all 4000 monks within. Some were later executed, some committed suicide, and large numbers were taken to labour camps. Only 200 monks remained at the Tashilhunpo.

Because of the status of the Panchen Lama and Chinese attempts to manipulate the high lama, Tashilhunpo Monastery was largely spared Red Guard destruction. By the 1980s, the number of monks in residence crept back up to around 800. In 1995, another major showdown took place at Tashilhunpo Monastery between the monks and Chinese authorities. The dispute erupted over the unfortunate Chinese choice of 11th Panchen Lama, resulting in tremendous upheaval. Many monks were imprisoned or ousted, to be replaced by pro-Chinese monks or those more timid. The head abbot was later sentenced to six years in jail for his part in the proceedings.

Old Quarter, Freemarket & Dzong

The Tibetan quarter, near the dzong ruins, is quite lively, with a skein of alleys to wander around. There's an extensive freemarket selling all kinds of souvenirs, Tibetan boots, stirrups, hats, bolts of cloth, and dried legs of lamb. The target audience is Tibetans (leg of lamb) and tourists (souvenirs). Nearby are several Tibetan teahouses and chang-drinking hangouts.

Photos from the 1930s show Shigatse Dzong looking like a mini-Potala, with the same classic lines. The fort continued to function as the offices of the dzongpon (district governor) until 1950; it was dynamited to rubble during the Cultural Revolution and has not been rebuilt. You can climb up and clamber around the ruins for good views overlooking the old quarter rooftops.

Pilgrim Circuit

Just as interesting as Tashilhunpo Monastery is the cross-section of pilgrims who come from far and wide to pay homage. Pilgrims follow a circuit that starts at the monastery gates and circles clockwise around Tashilhunpo Monastery. Off to the northwest side of the circuit is a sky burial site. Instead of completely looping around Tashilhunpo, most pilgrims continue on a path eastward that finishes at the market in Shigatse's old quarter. There are lots of prayer flags and mani stones that mark the route—just follow the pilgrims, and keep an eye out for dogs. The entire circuit takes about an hour and a half.

Carpet Factory

A short walk from the front gate of Tashilhunpo Monastery is Ganggyen Carpet Factory, which first started operations in 1987 as a project initiated by the 10th Panchen Lama. To get the project off the ground, the 10th Panchen Lama invited the same Tibetan businessman who started up the highly successful Tibetan carpet weaving venture in Kathmandu. Ganggyen Carpet Factory employs several hundred Tibetans—most of them women. If work is in progress, you can drop in and walk around, and see hand-looming at work. Women weavers

THE RENEGADE LAMA

The Panchen Lama, Tibet's second highest incarnate, traditionally has a seat at Tashilhunpo Monastery in Shigatse. The Panchen Lama ("Precious Scholar") was also known as the Tashi Lama. There is considerable confusion over the number of Panchen Lamas in the lineage. This is because, in the 16th century, the 5th Dalai Lama declared Losang Chokyi Gyeltsen (then the abbot of Tashilhunpo Monastery) to be the 4th reincarnate in a line that retroactively dated to the 14th century. He also declared him to be a manifestation of the Buddha Amitabha. From this time on, the elder of either the Panchen Lama or the Dalai Lama served as tutor for the other.

The Tibetan people have never recognised the Panchen Lama's authority to rule over the country of Tibet: his jurisdiction was always restricted to the Shigatse area. However, the Chinese are seen fit to promote rivalry between the Panchen Lamas and the Dalai Lamas.

The 10th Panchen Lama was born in 1938 in the Koko Nor region (Amdo). He fell into communist hands and was certified in Xining in 1949; his qualifications as an incarnate were accepted under duress by Lhasa. The 10th Panchen Lama was brought to Shigatse in 1952 by the PLA as the Chinese were determined to belittle the Dalai Lama's authority. After the Dalai Lama fled Tibet in 1959, the 10th Panchen Lama developed, by early accounts, as a mouthpiece for the Chinese. However, after the PLA raided Tashilhunpo Monastery in 1960 and disbanded the monks, the Panchen Lama changed tack and started to openly support the Dalai Lama. In 1961, when asked to move to the Potala to replace the Dalai Lama, the Panchen Lama flatly refused to do so, and dropped out of public view. In May 1962, he delivered a blistering 70,000-character report on conditions in Tibet to Mao Zedong, and demanded that mass arrests be halted and religious freedom restored. This document was kept secret for three decades until an anonymous source turned it over to Tibet Information Network in London. TIN had it translated and issued in book form in London in 1998 under the title "A Poisoned Arrow", which is what Mao Zedong called the petition.

In 1964, the Panchen Lama was asked to denounce the Dalai Lama at the height of the Monlam prayer-festival in Lhasa. A crowd of 40,000 gathered outside the Jokhang—and the Panchen Lama delivered a stunning speech of solidarity with the

Dalai Lama, and in favour of Tibetan independence. He was promptly placed under house-arrest, denounced as a reactionary and brought to trial. After being beaten to induce confessions, the Panchen Lama disappeared, along with his parents and entourage.

The Panchen Lama was taken to Beijing and sentenced to ten years in prison in 1967, much of it spent in solitary confinement. From time to time he was taken out for "struggle sessions" in a Beijing sports stadium, where he was humiliated in front of thousands of people. In 1978 he was set free again, supposedly a fully reformed man. He lived in Beijing, where he held an important government post. He was married to a Chinese woman and had a daughter: while he was alive, his wife pretended to be his personal secretary to preserve the Panchen Lama's spiritual standing among Tibetans, since none of Panchen Lama lineage holders had married.

Eventually the 10th Panchen Lama managed to return to Lhasa and Shigatse for extended visits, during which he again became increasingly critical of Chinese policy in Tibet. In 1989 he was found dead of a heart attack in Shigatse, at the age of 50. Although seriously overweight and a prime candidate for a heart attack, many Tibetans believe he was poisoned. When he died, the Chinese infuriated his wife by trying to bar her from memorial ceremonies at Tashilhunpo Monastery. She obstinately continued to live in Panchen Lama's Palace in Beihai Park, Beijing—in a building that is destined for the Chinese-sanctioned incarnate, the 11th Panchen. The 11th Panchen Lama is one the most hotly disputed reincarnates in the history of Tibet. For the full story, see the *Context, Subtext* chapter at the back of this book.

often sing as they work—most of the weaving is done from memory, which is quite a feat considering the intricate designs. In addition to carpets, the factory sells wool jackets, sweaters, belts, scarves, bags and blankets. Tibetan horsemen use carpeting as a saddle base: these horse carpets are made here.

New Panchen Palace

South of Tashilhunpo Monastery is a compound with a high wall where the Panchen Lama supposedly stays when in Shigatse. The compound hosts Tibetan-style palatial buildings with fine decoration: none of this is accessible to the touring public.

Tashilhunpo Monastery

The Tashilhunpo is the seat of the Panchen Lama—a topic that raises blood pressures on all sides. The monastery is highly sensitive because of the controversy surrounding the 11th Panchen Lama. Pictures of the Chinese-appointed 11th Panchen Lama abound as icons at the monastery. There are monk-stooges hanging about: take care what you do or say here. Tashilhunpo is immense—a monastic city with temples, assembly halls, living quarters and administrative offices. At its height, it housed up to 5000 monks. Today, the figure is probably closer to 700.

Access: The grounds are only fully accessible in the morning. In the afternoon you may be able to see some of the chapels. Although there are a number of gates (including one at the northeast wall), only one is sanctioned for entry and exit—you pay a foreigner's entry fee. Pilgrims follow an internal temple circuit which is described here, and also an external circuit around the monastery walls.

Main Structures: As you look northward from the front gates of Tashilhunpo Monastery, you will see several buildings that stand out—taller than the rest. You can roughly identify these off the plan in this book. At the back right wall is an enormous tanka-unfurling wall—the height of a nine-storey building. This is where massive tankas of Buddha are unfurled during summer festivities. To the left of the grounds, the largest building is the Maitreya Chapel: it is here that pilgrims begin their tour of the monastery.

The Maitreya Chapel (A) houses a 26-metre-high statue of Maitreya, the Buddha of the Future (Champa in Tibetan), seated on a lotus throne with right hand in a symbolic teaching pose (which looks like the "okay" gesture). The statue is gold-plated: the structure is made of tons of copper and brass, moulded on a wooden frame. Tibetans believe that Champa will return to preside over the world when all human being have earned deliverance from suffering. Pilgrims crowd in to make offerings and murmur mantras as they make an inner circuit around the statue itself. The fortress-style building that houses the Maitreya was built 1914–18 by the 9th Panchen Lama.

The newest building at the Tashilhunpo is the Tomb of the 10th Panchen Lama (B). It was completed in 1993—the Chinese government is reported to have donated 500 kg of gold for use in the tomb's construction, which may explain the Chinese-style roof. A gilded jewel-encrusted stupa encloses the embalmed body of the 10th Panchen Lama, who died in 1989. A life-sized statue of the Panchen Lama is shown at the front of the tomb. Surrounding the stupa are intricate murals. If you go up a few flights of stairs, you reach a room

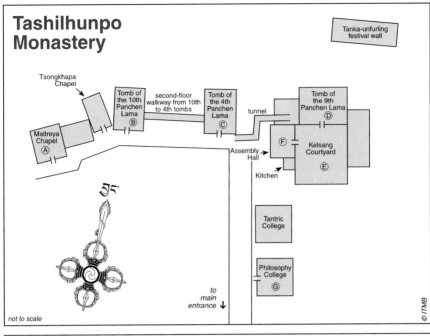

Tashilhunpo Monastery

Tsongkhapa Chapel

Maitreya Chapel (A)

Tomb of the 10th Panchen Lama (B)

second-floor walkway from 10th to 4th tombs

Tomb of the 4th Panchen Lama (C)

tunnel

Tomb of the 9th Panchen Lama (D)

Tanka-unfurling festival wall

Assembly Hall

Kitchen

(F)

Kelsang Courtyard (E)

Tantric College

Philosophy College (G)

to main entrance ↓

not to scale

© ITMB

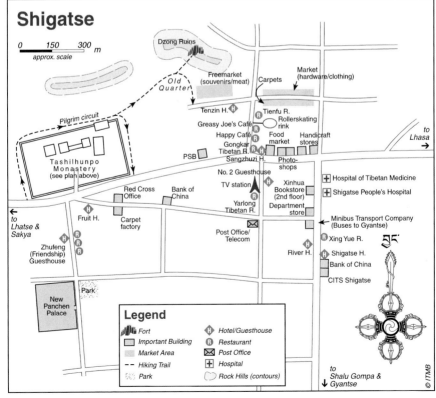

Shigatse

0   150   300 m
approx. scale

Dzong Ruins

Old Quarter

Freemarket (souvenirs/meat)

Carpets

Market (hardware/clothing)

Pilgrim circuit

Tenzin H.

Tienfu R.

Greasy Joe's Café

Rollerskating rink

Happy Café

Food market

Handicraft stores

Gongkar Tibetan R.

PSB

Sangzhuzi H.

Photo-shops

Tashilhunpo Monastery (see plan above)

No. 2 Guesthouse

TV station

Xinhua Bookstore (2nd floor)

Department store

to Lhasa →

+ Hospital of Tibetan Medicine

+ Shigatse People's Hospital

Red Cross Office

Bank of China

Yarlong Tibetan R.

Minibus Transport Company (Buses to Gyantse)

to Lhatse & Sakya ←

Fruit H.

Carpet factory

Post Office/ Telecom

Xing Yue R.

Shigatse H.

Zhufeng (Friendship) Guesthouse

River H.

Bank of China

CITS Shigatse

New Panchen Palace

Park

to Shalu Gompa & Gyantse ↓

Legend

- 🏯 Fort
- ⬜ Important Building
- ▨ Market Area
- - - Hiking Trail
- ⛰ Park
- 🏨 Hotel/Guesthouse
- Ⓡ Restaurant
- ✉ Post Office
- ✚ Hospital
- ⬭ Rock Hills (contours)

© ITMB

with a gigantic 3-D mandalic sculpture and impressive mandala murals on the walls.

If you carefully follow the pilgrims on an upper floor here you'll come into a corridor-walkway lined with small dark chapels heading east. This corridor is lined with Buddhas large and small, Tibetan scriptures, tankas, and with sidechapels displaying statues of Tsongkhapa and the Kalachakra deity. The corridor leads from the Tomb of the 10th to the Tomb of the 4th Panchen Lama (C). This tall, russet gold-roofed building houses a large silver stupa, enclosing the embalmed body of Losang Chokyi Gyeltsen, the 4th Panchen Lama.

Moving along, through a tunnel, you come to the gold-roofed Tomb of the 9th Panchen Lama (D). It was completed in 1988 and was consecrated by the 10th Panchen Lama only a week before his own death. During the Cultural Revolution, the bodies of the 5th through 9th Panchen Lamas were hidden and their identities were confused, so eventually all the remains were placed in a single tomb.

This tomb is attached to an elaborate complex that is the oldest part of Tashilhunpo Monastery, Kelsang Courtyard. The courtyard is enclosed by multi-storey galleries. Strolling around the different galleries gives you an idea of what the place looked like in centuries past. On the east side of the complex is a printing studio where scriptures are made from woodblocks. To the west side at the mid-levels is a large Assembly Hall (F) where monks congregate for sutra chanting. Leading off this is a medieval kitchen with mammoth copper cauldrons, giant implements, and fires burning away on a scale that would've had Macbeth's witches cackling. This is where food for all the monks is prepared. Debating between monks may take place in Kelsang Courtyard.

Heading back southward, you come to the Tantric College, where, if your timing is right, prayer ceremonies may be in progress in the assembly hall. In the courtyard of the Philosophy College (G), monks gather in the mornings to debate the finer points of Buddhist philosophy—vigorously emphasising points with their unique overarm slapping technique.

Bizarre Notes

At the rollerskating rink near Greasy Joe's Café, couples whirl around—hand in hand—to music blaring on loudspeakers. "Couples" means you might see two PLA soldiers hand-in-hand: in China, holding hands with the same sex is okay, but holding hands with the opposite sex is frowned upon. It's just difficult to get used to the idea of soldiers holding hands—and rollerskating on ancient skates.

148

Near Shigatse

To the south of Shigatse (18 km away, then an extra 4 km off the road) is Shalu Gompa. Shalu is most associated with 14th-century scholar Buton, a prolific translator and writer of sacred texts. During the Cultural Revolution, these precious texts were destroyed. The upper part of the monastery was destroyed—donations from Chinese patrons account for the present-day green-glazed tiling on the Mongolian-style roof. Parts of the monastery lie derelict, with faded murals, due to lack of funds to renovate. There are about 60 monks living here.

Basics

The best choice for a lower-priced hotel is the Tibetan-run Tenzin Hotel, overlooking the market. This 20-room place has lots of character. It's several stories high, with rooftop views and friendly staff—even has a hot shower powered by rooftop solar panels (so you had better attempt a shower in the afternoon, not the morning). Rooms range from dormitory-style to two-, three- or four-person rooms. There's also a Dalai Lama suite, which is pricey and may be occupied by monks. One disadvantage of the Tenzin is that it is near the markets: at night the hounds of Shigatse rule the streets and the "dog orchestra" rules the night. Near Tashilhunpo Monastery is a large Chinese-run concrete block known as the Fruit Hotel (you have to resist the temptation to call it "the Fruit Palace"), which is functional but terribly boring. The name comes from Ganggyen Fruit Orchard, which is behind the hotel. The phone number is 22282.

Apart from these two choices, you might try the Sangzhuzi Hotel, another featureless blockhouse hotel which seems to have Tibetan guests. Rates for the Tenzin, Fruit and Sangzhuzi hotels are roughly the same, with Tenzin a little higher. The group tour or expedition hotel is Shigatse Hotel, tel. 22556, fax 21900, at the southeast side of town: the 120 rooms are in the $50 range, and higher for suites. This hotel has a dining hall, bank exchange counter, gift shop and bar. Dark horses (possibly for Chinese only) include Number 2 Guesthouse, Zhufeng Guesthouse, and River Hotel.

One positive thing the Chinese brought to Shigatse is stirfied food. The best place to get fresh food is at a strip of small restaurants around the corner from Tenzin Hotel. Several places have English menus. Or you can simply point out the vegetables you want, and the chef will stir-fry them. Another tactic is to shop for fresh vegetables at the small market near Sangzhuzi Hotel and take these to the restaurant, where, for a fee, they will cook it all up. Greasy Joe's Café is good, as are Tienfu Restaurant and Happy Café. For breakfast, these places offer excellent fresh yoghurt, which you can combine with fruit. More dubious cuisine comes from Gongkar Tibetan Restaurant down the road on the corner. This place sells fish from the Yarlung Tsangpo—but most Tibetans avoid eating fish due to their religious beliefs. Near the TV station is another Tibetan place, Yarlong Tibetan Restaurant. Across town near Shigatse Hotel is Ying Yue Restaurant, which is an expensive Chinese restaurant with classier décor.

Shopping

Shigatse is one of the best places in Tibet to replenish your stocks or add to them, whatever. It is second only to Lhasa. For trip supplies, check out the department stores—these carry canned and packaged goods. Shopping for Tibetan artefacts is best in the Tenzin Hotel area—at the freemarket, and further east for carpets and handcrafted items. There are also several handicraft shops in town, and a gift shop at Shigatse Hotel.

Information & Services

Shigatse Hotel gift shop has the best stock of maps and books in town, and may even have film. The Xinhua Bookstore up the street is fairly useless, though you might stray across a map or poster here. There are some photoshops downtown that can develop black and white film. The post office and telecom building can handle long-distance calls: the Shigatse area code is 892. The Bank of China is near Shigatse Hotel. There are two hospitals in town—neither is of much use to travellers.

Mobility

If you need onward permits, the PSB office to the east of Tashilhunpo Monastery may oblige with ATPs. Some travellers have scored permits for Samye and even Everest here. Sometimes a permit is required for Gyantse—you can get that here. You may be able to get visa extensions too. To get around Shigatse, you can walk to most places. Nobody seems to rent bicycles but there are bicycle trishaws that carry two people—negotiate before setting out. You can also flag down a walking tractor for a ride across town—just jump on the back and pay when you arrive. The minibus transport company to the southeast side runs buses to Gyantse and to Lhasa. CITS Shigatse has a few Landcruisers and minibuses in its stable—these could be expensive to hire.

SHIGATSE TO TINGRI

About 15 km west of Shigatse you pass the ruins of Narthang Monastery, formerly one of Tibet's three great woodblock printing lamaseries. The other two were at Kumbum (Amdo) and Derge (Kham)—only Derge Monastery survives as a large-scale printing works for sacred texts. The high crumbling walls of Narthang are visible behind a roadside village: a few monks have returned to the lamasery and several minor buildings have been restored. Further westward, you cross Tso La; shortly after this, at a place between marker-stones 5028 and 5029, is a turn-off to Sakya—a highly recommended detour of 21 km. Then you can motor on to Lhatse (aka Lhaze or Lhartse), elevation 4050m. Lhatse could be renamed "Karaoke-ville." Everything in Lhatse is strung out along the highway—karaoke bars, eateries, a few truck-stop hotels, a theatre and a gas station. The road forks just west of Lhatse—with a branch heading northwest to Kailash, and southwest to Kathmandu. There may be a checkpoint near the junction. After crossing Gyatso La (at 5250m the highest pass on this route), you reach the Shegar area.

SAKYA
SAGYA, SAG'YA; ELEVATION 4000M

Sakya ("Grey Earth"), 21 km off the main Shigatse to Tingri route, was once the base of the Sakyapa sect which rose to power in the 13th century. The founder of the Sakyapa was Drokmi, who set up a monastery in Sakya in the 11th century. The Sakyapa were strong on magic and sorcery, and permitted their abbots to marry and to drink liquor. This led to hereditary rank (the post alternates between two families), and to a rather unsavoury reputation for worldliness among the monks. Although rank is hereditary, it is believed that seven incarnations of the Buddha of Wisdom (Manjushri) have appeared in the lineage of the Sakyapa.

The rise of the Sakyapa was largely due to "the Mongol connection". In the mid-13th century, Mongol warlord Godan Khan invited the leader of the Sakya sect, Sakya Pandita, to educate his people spiritually. Sakya Pandita accepted the task and under Mongol overlordship, the Sakya school gained great political influence. The Mongol link continued with the succession of Phagpa (nephew of Sakya Pandita) and Kublai Khan. The power of the Sakyapa declined in the late 14th century as the fortunes of the Geluk tradition rose, but Sakya retained its links with Mongolia over the centuries.

In 1959, at the age of 14, Sakya Dagtri Rinpoche was enthroned at Sakya Gompa, becoming the 41st Patriarch (his title is also the Sakya Trizin, or throne-holder). Almost immediately after the event, he and his entourage of teachers and personal staff fled to India. It took Chinese soldiers several months to get to Sakya after the 1959 uprising in Lhasa. The Chinese told the 500 monks at Sakya Gompa that they had supported the Khampa rebels, so the monastery was seized, grain-stocks confiscated, and monks and nuns were submitted to *thamzing* (struggle-session). After getting used to such strange phenomena as trains, cars, buses and airplanes, the Sakya Trizin set up a base in exile at Dehra Dun, in Uttar Pradesh, with a Sakya centre and college established in the 1960s. Today there are Sakya centres all over the world, and the throne-holder has toured extensively—teaching in Europe, America and Asia.

Sakya Gompa

The immense Mongolian-style outer walls of Sakya Gompa dwarf any other structure in the town. At the corners of the gompa walls are corner-turrets and watchtowers. The monastery is thought to date to the 13th century, at which time the Sakyapa were powerful enough to employ not only large numbers of Tibetan works and artisans, but also artisans from India, Nepal and central China to decorate the monastery.

Access is only by the east gate, where an entry fee is charged. You cross a courtyard to gain entry to the inner temple, which surrounds another open courtyard. You can tour the main structures here in a clockwise circuit, keyed to the map with this text.

At Phuntsok Potrang (1), only an upstairs chapel may be accessible, containing fine murals and statues. Phuntsok Potrang (Palace) is the former residence of one of the principal lamas of Sakya. The post of leadership in the Sakya sect alternates between two families—one formerly occupying Phuntsok Potrang, the other occupying Drolma Potrang opposite. The next in line for Phuntsok Palace lives in exile in Seattle, USA. Manjushri Chapel (2) is a large chamber once used for important rituals. It contains a number of bookcases, and glass cases enshrining several thousand bronze statues. The statues of Manjushri and Sakyamuni Buddha here were rescued from the rubble of Sakya's northern monasteries.

The Great Sutra Chanting Hall (3) is lofty and spacious—the roof is supported by four rows of pillars, with 10 pillars in each row. At the base of the massive tree-trunk pillars are lotus-patterned stone pedestals; between the pillars are low carpeted benches with

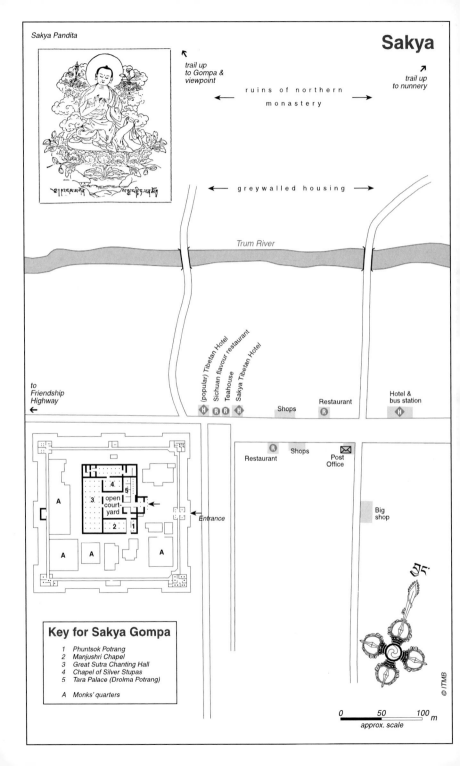

Sakya Pandita

Sakya

trail up to Gompa & viewpoint

trail up to nunnery

r u i n s   o f   n o r t h e r n
m o n a s t e r y

g r e y w a l l e d   h o u s i n g

Trum River

to Friendship Highway

(popular) Tibetan Hotel
Sichuan flavour restaurant
Teahouse
Sakya Tibetan Hotel

Shops

Restaurant

Hotel & bus station

Restaurant

Shops

Post Office

Big shop

Entrance

open court-yard

4
5
3
2
1

A   A   A   A

Key for Sakya Gompa

1   Phuntsok Potrang
2   Manjushri Chapel
3   Great Sutra Chanting Hall
4   Chapel of Silver Stupas
5   Tara Palace (Drolma Potrang)

A   Monks' quarters

© ITMB

0   50   100 m
approx. scale

seating for some 400 monks. If you're lucky, Sakya monks may be conducting a sutra-chanting session, in which case you'll experience the acoustics of the hall. The main visual focus of the hall is the row of massive gilded Buddha statuary at the west wall. These statues are surrounded by thousands of artefacts, seals, ceremonial props, ritual vessels and books amassed from all over Tibet. A small doorway leads to a large hidden library behind the statues.

Continuing the clockwise circuit, you come to the Chapel of the Silver Stupas (4) which contains 11 silver stupas enclosing the remains of the past throneholders of the Sakya lineage. Six more stupas (enclosing the remains of important past abbots of Sakya) are found in a small chapel just north. In the Tara Palace (5) are five stupas of important throne-holders from this family branch. The Tara Palace or Drolma Potrang is the former residence of the current Sakya throne-holder, now living in Dehra Dun, India. Only the upstairs chapel is open, displaying superb murals; the altar has images depicting the longevity triad of Amitayus, Vijaya and White Tara.

Bizarre Notes

At the back of the Great Sutra Chanting Hall is a library that runs the entire length of the north-south wall, with shelves of sacred texts reaching from floor to ceiling. The library is hidden from view: to get in, you might have to convince a monk to unlock a small wooden door that allows you to go around the back of all the statues on display. It's pretty dark so a flashlight is needed. The musty atmosphere is positively medieval—evoking the fabled lost library of Alexandria. The library shelving here is about 60 metres long, 10 metres high and one metre deep—and filled with thousands of dusty Buddhist scriptures, many handcopied by Tibetan calligraphers and illuminated in gold or silver ink. Near the northwest corner is a huge manuscript illuminated in gold called the Prajnamparamita Sutra. The book is so large it requires its own special rack: the pages are 1.75 metres wide. Apparently Sakya's library survived the ravages of the Cultural Revolution because the books were hidden underground. Above the portico leading to the monastery's central courtyard is another room housing rare Sanskrit palm-leaf manuscripts: this section is out of bounds.

Hiking at Sakya North

On the north side of the river there used to be a monastic complex of 108 chapels. Most were destroyed during the 1960s; others were converted into Tibetan housing. Today, the north side is mostly composed of grim grey-walled Tibetan housing, with brushwood and yak-dung lining the ramparts of dwellings, and livestock living in the courtyards. You can hike on the northwest slope up to a small restored gompa and viewpoint (you need to find someone to open the doors here). Another hike takes you up a pathway on the northeast ridge to Rinchen Gang Labrang, an active nunnery rebuilt in 1988. Sakya is right off the main road, so it lies in a completely rural area—there are other directions you can walk into the countryside. Or the countryside may come to you—herders and traders propel yaks, donkeys or sheep right through Sakya town.

Sakya Basics

Not a lot of choice for lodging. There are two Tibetan hotels with—I almost choke on the word—"beds". The more popular is the one closest to Sakya Gompa. At the bus station is a small guesthouse, providing another run-down possibility. There are hole-in-the-wall eating houses around Sakya: a Tibetan teahouse, a place called Sichuan Flavour Restaurant, and several others with no signs (marked "restaurant" on the Sakya map). Some tiny shops can also be unearthed. Sakya has a post office, and a small bus station. Minibuses and vans make the trip to Lhasa. You might also find a pilgrim truck running on this route. Sakya is reached by a dirt road—it is 21 km from the main highway.

SHEGAR
Shekar, Shelkar, Xegar, Xin Tingri, New Tingri; elevation 4350m; see inset/Trekking in the Everest Region map

Shegar, set back 7 km off the main route, is a small Tibetan settlement with an active monastery at the northern end, at the base of a peak. Right up the rock peak are the imposing ruins of Shining Crystal Dzong. The castle was formerly the residence of the governor of Shegar. In 1924, a member of the British Everest expedition marvelled at the fantastic castle, perched on the 5000-metre mountaintop, appearing to be fused to the rock. Today barely a single piece stands upright—it was destroyed during the Cultural Revolution.

At around the same time, the extensive monastery of Shegar was also destroyed. It once housed 300 Geluk monks: today there are only a few reconstructed buildings, with a handful of monks in residence. It's worth visiting the monastery building at the base of the mountain, and then hiking up through the ruins toward the peak, where, on a clear day, you are rewarded with views of Everest (watch out for the nettles). The old quarter of Shegar is the village clustered closer to the gompa. The Chinese section is further southwest, in the vicinity of the post office.

Basics

Shelkar Hotel is a Chinese concrete compound with lack of plumbing, overpriced rooms and surly staff. The alternatives to this dismal place are two low-priced truck-stop hotels near the main highway and the higher-priced Qomolungma Hotel (see following entries). For food in Shegar, there's a Chinese restaurant opposite Shelkar Hotel, and there are several shops with a spotty and narrow selection of consumer goods. The post office in Shegar is said to be the highest in Tibet.

SHEGAR TO TINGRI

Just west of Shegar lies an important military checkpoint, and the main turn-off for Everest base camp. A major hotel lies about 600 metres from the Shegar turn-off. It's called the Qomolungma Hotel—a large Chinese-run operation with a glitzy restaurant and gift shop. Group tours stay here before heading off to Everest base camp. The 50-odd rooms here are expensive, but there are some cheaper dormitory-type rooms—so inquire. Right at the Shegar turn-off are two low-budget truckstop inns with a couple of rooms—a Chinese one (8 beds, offers food) and a Tibetan one (10 beds, has a rudimentary teahouse).

Seven km west of the Tibetan truckstop hotel is a military checkpoint (at roughly marker stone 5140). This is the most important checkpoint on the Lhasa to Kathmandu Route—your documents will be checked, and your luggage may be searched. Have passport and papers ready. From here, it's 5 km west to the Everest turn-off at marker stone 5145. See the *Star Treks* chapter for more details on this major sidetrip.

TINGRI

Dingri, Old Tingri, Lao Tingri, Tinggri West; elevation 4340m; see inset/Trekking in the Everest Region map

Tingri is a Tibetan village arrayed over a hillside. It was once a Tibetan-Nepali trading centre for grain, goods, wool and livestock. This trade largely died out after 1959 but you can still see the odd Nepali trader in Tingri—they occasionally come in with a few yaks over Nangpa La pass.

Tingri is essentially one big army base disguised as a village. Tibetan housing hugs the hillside, but at the north end are walled army compounds and an army telecommunications centre; at the south end are more army compounds. The compounds at the south end are curious—at first sight they appear to be Tibetan buildings. Closer inspection reveals they are Chinese—a new form of camouflage?

Tingri lies at the edge of a vast plain. There are great views of the Himalayan giants to the south, assuming there's no cloud cover. Everest, or the topmost part of it, is visible to the far left, but from this distance doesn't look like a mammoth. However, Cho Oyu, straight ahead, looks stunning. It's worth taking a short hike to the south of Tingri for better views; another viewpoint is from the top of the hill above the village, where there are some old fort ruins. Something to think about as you gaze across the plains: the area was once full of gazelles, blue sheep, antelopes, and wild asses—which were remarked upon by Everest expedition members in the 1920s and 1930s. This fabulous wildlife sanctuary has completely disappeared—now all you can see are the odd herds of domesticated sheep, goats or yaks.

Basics

Facilities in Tingri are strung out along the highway. Basic rooms are found at two small Tibetan inns—the Himalaya Hotel and the Everest View—with about a dozen rooms each. The Everest View has a teahouse with a great atmosphere—carpeted seating low on the floor. You can order momos and potatoes here. Opposite the Everest View is the Himalaya Restaurant, with a more varied menu of Chinese food, at higher prices. A few small shops complete the "strip" here. Further into Tingri village, there's very little—you might stray across a Tibetan teahouse or a tiny shop.

TINGRI TO KATHMANDU

From Tingri westward, in clear weather, you get spectacular views of Himalayan peaks, especially from passes. Tong La is a double pass—north crest at 4950 metres, and south crest 5200 metres. You may be able to glimpse the 8000-metre hulk of Shishapangma from this vicinity. After this, it's downhill all the way down to Nyalam, and on to Nepal.

Milarepa's Cave: Nearing Nyalam, close to kilometre markerstone 5333, is Milarepa's gompa and cave. The gompa is hidden from view at the roadside—but your guide should know where it is. If not, find some local kids to show you the way. You need to find a caretaker with keys to the cave and gompa—might require some funds.

Milarepa, the 11th-century sage who enlightened his students through music and poetry, never founded any monasteries. He lived a mostly itinerant existence in remote areas—living in caves and dining on nettle soup. The mystic is easily recognised in pictures and statuary due to his greenish skin and right hand cocked to his ear. Milarepa's cave is set inside a tiny gompa, which was destroyed during the Cultural Revolution but rebuilt in the early 1980s with the help of the Nepalese. In the cave you can see handprints made by Milarepa when he employed his mystical powers to prevent a huge overhanging rock from falling while a disciple moved a smaller rock in place as a support pillar. Although the cave first belonged to the Kagyu sect, it was taken over by the Geluk order centuries ago.

NYALAM
ELEVATION 3750M

Nyalam is a truck-stop on the Lhasa to Kathmandu route, with a fair range of hotels and small restaurants. The centre of town is a large parking lot for trucks and other vehicles. Because the town is easily supplied from Zhangmu, there is a much greater range of food and goods available here. Along the main road, commerce is mostly operated by Chinese or Nepali merchants, although some shops are run by Tibetans. Take a sidestreet to the west to find the old Tibetan quarter, with traditional-style buildings.

Further afield, Nyalam is the base for trekking to Shishapangma base camp (see *Star Treks* chapter). Even if you have no intention of trekking to the base camp, the initial part of this route—accessed from the northwest end of Nyalam—is well worth a day-hike, or an overnight hike if you take a tent and sleeping bag.

If you're coming from Lhasa, a highly unusual treat in Nyalam is...trees. Stacks of wood are piled up, used as a fuel source. Nyalam is low enough for poplar trees to grow; other wood is brought in from forested slopes lower down.

Basics

Nyalam is well supplied with hotels, small restaurants and shops. The Tibetan-style Snowland Hotel is one of the best choices here—it has a rooftop deck. Among the other hotels and guesthouses are Nongjyale, Nagaden, Power Station Trade Union, Nyalam Garment, and Road Worker hotels. A string of restaurants lines the main road near the truck parking area. A lot of these are Chinese, with names like Rong Rong and Chong Zhou. The Nepali Restaurant is good—serving large silver platters with dhal and lots of sidedishes.

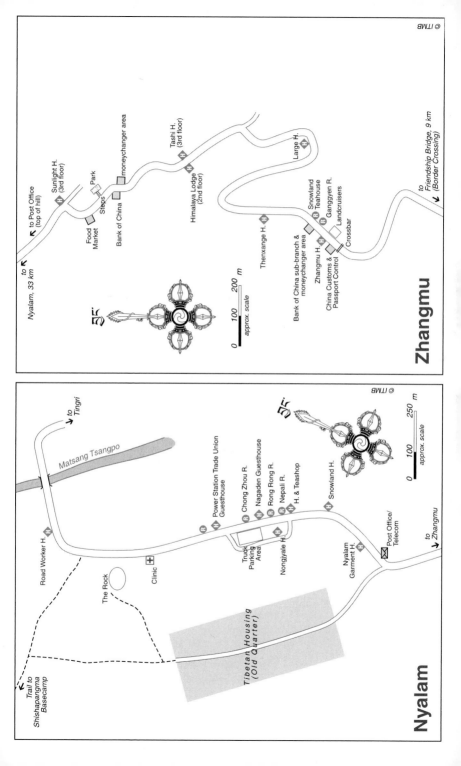

© ITMB

Zhangmu

to Nyalam, 33 km

to Post Office (top of hill)

Sunlight H. (3rd floor)

Park

Steps

moneychanger area

Food Market

Bank of China

Tashi H. (3rd floor)

Himalaya Lodge (2nd floor)

Large H.

Thenxange H.

Snowland Teahouse

Zhangmu H.

Ganggyen R.

Bank of China sub-branch & moneychanger area

China Customs & Passport Control

Landcruisers

Crossbar

to Friendship Bridge, 9 km (Border Crossing)

0   100   200 m
approx. scale

Nyalam

to Tingri

Matsang Tsangpo

Road Worker H.

The Rock

Clinic

Trail to Shishapangma Basecamp

Tibetan Housing (Old Quarter)

Power Station Trade Union Guesthouse

Chong Zhou R.

Nagaden Guesthouse

Rong Rong R.

Nepali R.

H. & Teashop

Snowland H.

Truck Parking Area

Nongjiyale H.

Nyalam Garment H.

Post Office/ Telecom

to Zhangmu

© ITMB

0   100   250 m
approx. scale

From Nyalam, there's an amazing drop off the plateau, down through lush jungle terrain with gushing waterfalls and singing birds—all the way down to Zhangmu. This is one altitude shift you'll remember for some time to come. Because of cascading water (sometimes springing straight over the cliffsides near the road) the route here is prone to rockfalls and landslides, especially in the monsoon season. Because it is at a much lower elevation, Zhangmu is prone to much heavier monsoon rains than, say, Nyalam.

The Chinese name for the entire route between Lhasa and Kathmandu is the "Friendship Highway". The Chinese name a lot of border features into neighbouring countries like this: Friendship Gate (Youyi Guan, border crossing into Vietnam) and Friendship Bridge (Youyi Qiao, border crossing into Nepal). It's not clear whether the Chinese constructed the Friendship Highway as a military route into Nepal: the Chinese designed and built the road on the Nepalese side all the way into Kathmandu. The two countries remain on very good terms—for the moment.

ZHANGMU
DRAM, KHASA; ELEVATION 2300M

There's little to see in the border town of Zhangmu (pronounced Jang-moo) unless you like watching Nepalis, Tibetans and Chinese unload and reload goods and haggle over currency exchange rates. Zhangmu is no longer Tibet—it's more like a Nepali trading town, with Nepali products everywhere, Nepali moneychangers, Nepali merchants and scores of Nepali porters. The town is arrayed along some steep switchbacks that snake down to the Chinese customs and immigration post.

Out of Synch

Nepal is two and a quarter hours behind Tibet, which operates on Beijing time. Thus when it's 12 noon in Zhangmu (Chinese immigration post), it's 9.45 am in Kodari (Nepalese immigration). Bear this in mind when considering banking hours and immigration post hours of opening. Sunday can be a non-working day in Zhangmu.

Customs, Immigration, Money

If exiting Tibet, you can change residual Chinese yuan back into US dollars (with original bank receipts). A much better deal is to change Chinese yuan into Nepalese rupees. Change either at the Bank of

China (two branches) or with moneychangers close by (it's preferable to do these transactions inside a shop rather than on the street: always carefully count the money offered before presenting your part of the deal). In Zhangmu you can pay for goods in either Chinese yuan or Nepalese rupees, but once out of Zhangmu, Chinese yuan are useless anywhere in Nepal (you can, however, trade them with travellers at guesthouses in Kathmandu). On exit, Chinese customs may search baggage looking for "antiques" which means anything older than 1959. Immigration checks are simple—you are stamped out.

If entering Tibet at Zhangmu, there are several hurdles. The first is clearing immigration and being stamped in. The second is baggage check: customs may be thorough—they will be looking for pro-Tibetan material that is available in Kathmandu. After changing money, you will most likely be waylaid by a man from CITS (with an office in nearby Zhangmu Hotel) who will tell you that you have to form a group (four travellers) to take a CITS Landcruiser to Lhasa.

Basics

The rickety Himalaya Lodge is the backpacker special. It does have electricity, which is a plus, and paper-thin walls, which are a minus—and some views to the west, which are a plus. Right across the street is the Tashi Hotel, with reasonable accommodation on the third floor. Right up the hill is the Sunlight Hotel which may or may not let you stay, depending on how persistent you are. At a bend in the lower intestines of Zhangmu is a large Chinese hotel with no shingle hanging out—rooms are basic and staff are rude. Further down toward the customs post is the Chinese-run Thenxange Hotel. The group tour hotel in town is the cavernous Zhangmu Hotel which is in cahoots with CITS. Landcruiser drivers, linked to CITS, lie in wait near the customs post, ready to prey on travellers coming through from Kathmandu. Although the rooms at Zhangmu Hotel are expensive, you can talk your way into far cheaper dorm rooms downstairs.

In the food line, you can riffle through the shops in lower Zhangmu, bearing good stocks of Nepalese and Indian goods. There's a small food market at the northern end of Zhangmu. Near the customs checkpost is Ganggyen Restaurant and Snowland Tea-house. Group tours eat in the dining hall at Zhangmu Hotel.

ZHANGMU TO KODARI

Once you leave Chinese customs, you head 9 km down to the Friendship Bridge. If you have a Landcruiser driver, he will be charged for permission to drive past the Chinese customs post. The bridge is the real border crossing. It has been washed away several times in the past. Halfway across the bridge is a dividing line—one half of the bridge belongs to Nepal, the other half to China. At exactly this point, it seems, you should switch sides of the road—from right-hand drive (China) to left-hand drive (Nepal). Nepal immigration is in Kodari, 2 km from the Friendship Bridge. Your passport is checked here—if you have no visa, you will be stamped in. You just provide $15 in US cash for a 15-day visa, or $30 for a 30-day visa, plus a passport photo. Nepal customs is a bit further down the line near Tatopani.

KATHMANDU

A ride of 114 km along a paved road from Kodari brings you into the bazaars of Asan Tole, in old Kathmandu—in former times, the trading crossroads of the empires of India, China and Tibet. You'll find more Mars bars, apple pie, fresh croissants, shampoo and English newspapers in a 200-metre stretch of a street in Thamel than you will in all of Tibet. The trick is not to go berserk when faced with such myriad choices. The sudden change of diet can wreak havoc on your system: switching to steaks, apple pie and ice cream after months of living off biscuits in Tibet can be traumatic. Still, hot showers, clean white sheets, Swedish massage and other luxuries won't hurt. They may even be therapeutic.

Kathmandu has great resources for things Tibetan: there are Tibetan monasteries scattered around the valley; there are Tibetan-run hotels, shops and travel agents in Kathmandu's Thamel district. If you are incoming from Tibet, Kathmandu has all the forbidden and seditious material on Tibet that Chinese officials so diligently search baggage for. Kathmandu has one of the highest concentrations of English bookstores of any place in the Indian sub-continent. Lots of second-hand books are available as well. You can find Free Tibet T-shirts, flags, and many handcrafted Tibetan items that are superior in quality to those in Tibet—carpets, for instance.

STAR TREKS
high-altitude forays to Everest, Kailash & beyond

This section describes some treks in western Tibet that individuals have successfully tackled—but which are highly challenging, both in terms of physical effort and dodging demands for permits. The rewards? We're talking about a backdrop of the highest peaks on earth here—moonscapes, star treks, stellar vistas! Trekking in Tibet is expeditionary in nature. If you go with an organised group, then yaks and porters will ferry in supplies. If you plan to go on your own, you need good equipment and supplies—trekking here is fraught with all kinds of logistical problems. You have to be self-sufficient, and that includes food.

There are two excellent guidebooks that cover trekking routes in Tibet in detail: Gary McCue's *Trekking in Tibet* and Victor Chan's *Tibet Handbook* (with 60 detailed pilgrimage and trekking itineraries). A handful of classic Tibet treks—enough to keep you busy for quite some time—are described in the following section. The approaches and trailheads are all reachable by Landcruiser.

TREKKING IN THE
EVEREST REGION

There are three main targets in the Everest area: Rongbuk (Everest north base camp), Karta (Everest east base camp), and Cho Oyu base camp. You can reach Rongbuk by Landcruiser. Two staging-points to bear in mind: Shegar in the east, and Tingri to the west.

Everest is not in the same class as Kailash when it comes to a sacred peak. For one thing, the monastery at Everest was only established early in the 20th century (the shrines at Kailash go back to the 13th century). More importantly, Kailash has always been off-limits for climbers, and there are no throngs of Tibetan pilgrims headed for Everest because you can't circumambulate the mountain. Nevertheless, Everest is known to the Tibetans as Chomolangma, which transliterates as Queen (Jhomo) on an Ox (glangma), otherwise more prosaically rendered "Mother Goddess of the World". Tibetans believe that the goddess Miyo Langsangma (one of the five Tsering sisters) resides at Mount Everest: her mount is an ox, although other images show her astride a tiger.

The goddess is not one to tangle with lightly. Witness what happened to the first expeditions. In 1921, Tibet opened expedition attempts on Everest to British climbers. The monks at Rongbuk were none too keen on the idea of climbers wending their way up a sacred peak: they predicted dire things would come to pass—which, in the case of Mallory and Irvine did come to pass. The monastery practice of blessing climbers rather than cursing them appears to have started in the late 1920s or 1930s when Nepali Sherpas were employed by the British as porters and cooks. Because Sherpas are Tibetan Buddhist, monasteries started dispensing blessings for safe passage on the mountain. Sherpas climbing from both sides visit monasteries before going to base camp, where they light butter lamps in supplication of various deities. At base camp itself, Sherpas make offerings of tsampa and chang to the goddess Chomolangma in the belief that the wrathful goddess will turn a blind eye and allow them passage. Tsampa is thrown skyward; ice axes and other gear also get a ritual blessing before climbers go higher.

DRIVING TO RONGBUK

Everest base camp is remarkable in that it's a drive-in approach. The rough road to the base camp at the north side of Everest was engineered in 1960 for Chinese mountaineering attempts on the summit. The common approach by road is from the Shegar end, though it's also possible to drive in on a rougher route from Tingri. You can commandeer a Landcruiser in Lhasa and drive right to Rongbuk Monastery, which is about 12 km short of Everest base camp. You can also try hitching in on this route, picking up a supply truck of some sort. There's primitive lodging at Rongbuk. Landcruisers can cover the distance from Shegar to Rongbuk in about seven or so hours if there are no holdups like flooding.

If arriving from Shegar, there are two major checkpoints on the way to Everest. The first is the military checkpoint close to the Shegar turn-off. There are cursory checks of passports and baggage here. At the village of Chay, each passenger must pay a fee of $7 for entry into what is billed as being "Chomolangma Nature Reserve".

From the Rongbuk area you can also drive further to Everest base camp and have a poke around. There are great day hikes around Rongbuk: you can clamber around and get fantastic views of the north face of Everest. The Big E will blow you away—literally, if a wind comes howling down the valley. Everest does not always co-operate—it might be obscured by low cloud. But if the sun is out and it's clear, Everest will take your breath away. You are looking at the highest face on earth—the north face of Everest.

TREKKING TO RONGBUK

There are two routes into Rongbuk on foot—from the Shegar end, or from the Tingri end. Trekkers tend to favour the walk in from the Tingri end because there's no checkpoint to contend with and it's easier to hire pack animals in Tingri. However, there's zero chance of hitching a ride from the Tingri end—if your equipment is not so good, or your intention is to get a ride in and trek back, then you should stick to the Shegar route, which has more in the way of lodging and teahouse support. You can combine the routes—take one route in, the other route out (and consider a sidetrip to Cho Oyu base camp on the Tingri route). You might want to think about hiring a donkey (or yak) and handler to carry supplies and food. The handler will also act as a guide. Animals are scarce when harvest is in progress; if you're going one-way with a pack animal, the handler may want compensation for the return journey.

From Tingri: The walk into Rongbuk takes about four days. The first day's target is not particularly strenuous: the village of Lungjhang (4500m), with beds available. The next day is strenuous— it's best to work your way toward the base of Lanma La and camp out near a herder's camp. The next day, you can trek over Lanma La

(5150m) and make it to the village of Zhommug, where basic lodging awaits. Zhommug is not far from the jeep road that winds in from Shegar: you should be able to reach Rongbuk by the end of the fourth day of trekking.

From Shegar: You essentially walk along the jeep track to Rongbuk. The trek takes three to four days; there are enough lodges along the way to qualify this as Tibet's first "teahouse trekking" route. Starting out from the Tibetan truck-stop at marker-stone 5133, you can hitch or walk to the Everest turn-off at marker-stone 5145. If you're on foot, you may have to pay an entry-fee at the Chay checkpoint, but you're in a better position to bargain than those in Landcruisers because the fee is supposed to be collected for road maintenance. You can negotiate hire of a donkey at Chay for the trip as far as Peruche, where there is a Tibetan-run lodge—albeit a filthy one—and also a few shops. On the next leg of the journey, between Peruche and Chosang are two villages where you can stay: at Tashizom and Passum. Both have teahouse-lodges with cheap beds. These places are at around 4100 metres in elevation. The last place with beds is Chosang, but trekkers have found the folk here particularly light-fingered and cold-hearted, so you may want to skip this place. From here is a steady climb to Rongbuk.

Trek Alert

Tibetan villagers in the Everest region are notoriously prone to thievery. You have to consider that there are not a lot of shops out this way: taking things from visitors is somehow considered fair game. Even hosts at village inns will brazenly take small items, and when confronted, think it is no big deal. Keep an eye on gear that you can't do without—watch those waterbottles. Always negotiate carefully and establish prices before consuming any food or drink at teahouses in the area—there have been problems. Another alarming problem: innkeepers in the Everest region have been known to beat up their wives. So what do you do—ignore this late at night, or try to step in? It's a tough call. Donkey and yak handlers can be hard to get along with and argumentative—this has little to do with language, more to do with temperament.

RONGBUK
Dza Rongphu, elevation 5030m

Rongbuk Gompa, the highest monastery in the world, was established sometime in the early part of the 20th century, under the

Nyingmapa sect. Its history is sketchy. Rongbuk Valley was known as the "sanctuary of the birds". There was a strict ban on killing any animal in the area. Domestic animals could be eaten as long as they were slaughtered outside the valley. The British Everest reconnaissance party, arriving at Rongbuk in 1921, found the animals of the valley extraordinarily tame: wild blue sheep would come down to the monastery. There were hundreds of lamas and pilgrims engaged in meditation in a cluster of brightly coloured buildings. The British did not meet the Head Lama as he was off doing a year's "time" in a cave. It was common for hermits to go on meditation retreats in caves in the valley, subsisting on water and barley passed to them once a day.

The monastery was razed in the 1960s. At the instigation of Red Guards, Tibetans were encouraged to disassemble the buildings for raw materials, such as precious wood beams. The monastery's stupa was split in two and ransacked of its treasures. The abbot of Rongbuk fled over the Himalayas and established a new monastery at Junbesi in Nepal.

In the late 1980s and early 1990s, rebuilding took place at Rongbuk and its monastery has been resurrected, along with the stupa that figures prominently in tourist photography of the scene. A dozen monks and 30 or so nuns live at Rongbuk Gompa. Surrounding the monastery is a village; further up the valley is a nunnery, and there are cave-retreats scattered around the hilltops. You can stay at a simple stone building attached to Rongbuk Monastery. There's an outhouse, and hot water in thermoses can be obtained for a payment from the monastery, but don't expect luxuries here—nights can be very cold, and there's no electricity.

NORTH FACE BASE CAMP

From Rongbuk, you can drive or walk the final 12 km out to the North Face base camp, at elevation 5150m. Base camp is marked by a single concrete building, and possibly by a lot of expedition tents, depending on the season. The area is a glacial moraine—a bleak and desolate place—but awe-inspiring because it is so close to the Big E. Beyond base camp lies a trek described by Gary McCue (*Trekking in Tibet*) as "the Highest Trek in the World…an incredible journey to Camp III (6340m) and to the base of the North Col via the East Rongphu Glacier." The ascent is possible without climbing gear, though it would be advisable to have items like crampons when traversing the glacier. You need excellent back-up and considerable logistics to undertake such a strenuous—and potentially hazardous—journey.

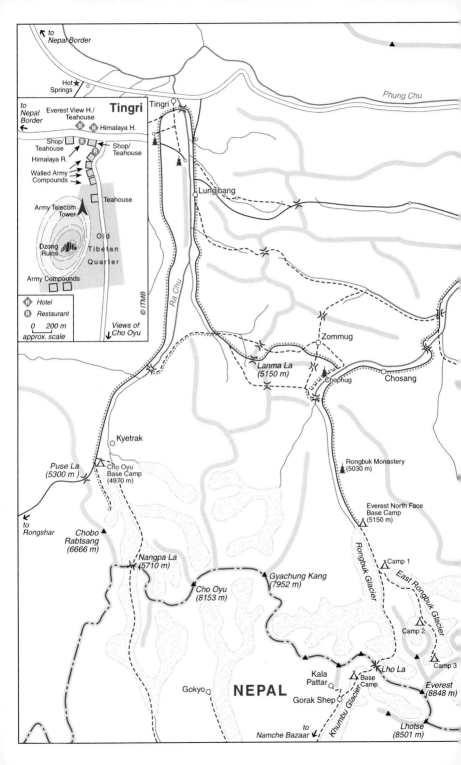

to Nepal Border

Hot Springs ★

Phung Chu

Tingri ○

to Nepal Border ←

Tingri

Everest View H./ Teahouse Ⓗ Ⓗ Himalaya H.

Shop/ Teahouse Ⓡ Ⓡ Shop/ Teahouse

Himalaya R.

Walled Army Compounds

Teahouse

Army Telecom Tower

Dzong Ruins

Old Tibetan Quarter

Army Compounds

Ⓗ *Hotel*
Ⓡ *Restaurant*

0   200 m
approx. scale

© ITMB

Views of Cho Oyu ↓

Lungjhang ○

Ra Chu

Zommug ○

Lanma La (5150 m)

Chophug

Chosang ○

Kyetrak ○

Puse La (5300 m)

Cho Oyu Base Camp (4970 m)

Rongbuk Monastery (5030 m)

to Rongshar

Chobo Rabtsang (6666 m)

Everest North Face Base Camp (5150 m)

Nangpa La (5710 m)

Gyachung Kang (7952 m)

Cho Oyu (8153 m)

Camp 1

Rongbuk Glacier

East Rongbuk Glacier

Camp 2

Camp 3

NEPAL

Gokyo ○

Kala Pattar ○

Gorak Shep

Base Camp

Lho La

Everest (8848 m)

Khumbu Glacier

to Namche Bazaar ←

Lhotse (8501 m)

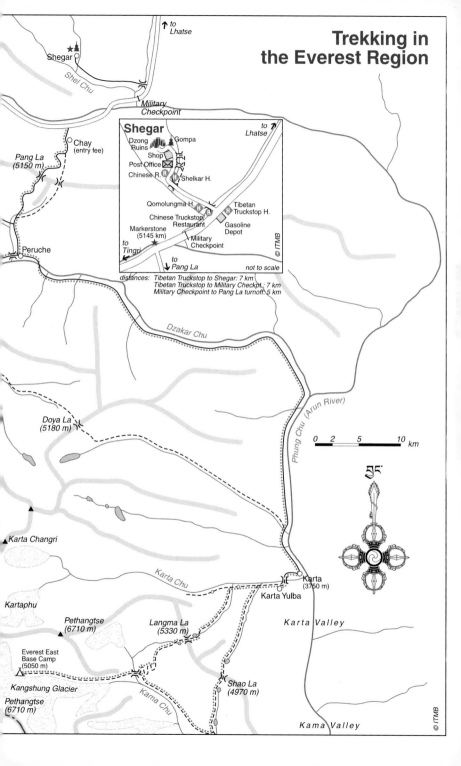

Trekking in
the Everest Region

↑ to
Lhatse

★★ Shegar

Shel Chu

Military
Checkpoint

○ Chay
(entry fee)

Pang La
_(5150 m)_

Peruche

Shegar

Dzong
Ruins Gompa

Post Office Shop

Chinese R. Shelkar H.

Qomolungma H.

Chinese Truckstop/
Restaurant

Markerstone
(5145 km)

to
Tingri

Tibetan
Truckstop H.

Gasoline
Depot

Military
Checkpoint

to
↑ Lhatse

↓ to
Pang La

not to scale

© ITMB

distances: Tibetan Truckstop to Shegar: 7 km
Tibetan Truckstop to Military Checkpt.: 7 km
Military Checkpoint to Pang La turnoff: 5 km

Dzakar Chu

Doya La
_(5180 m)_

Phung Chu (Arun River)

0   2   5   10 km

▲ Karta Changri

Karta Chu

Karta
(3760 m)

Karta Yulba

Kartaphu

Pethangtse
_(6710 m)_

Langma La
_(5330 m)_

Karta Valley

Everest East
Base Camp
(5050 m)
△

Kangshung Glacier

Pethangtse
_(6710 m)_

Kama Chu

Shao La
_(4970 m)_

Kama Valley

© ITMB

At higher elevations, Everest is scoured by 60-kph winds: the constant threat of avalanche, being crushed by an ice serac, falling down a crevasse, or succumbing to altitude make it a deadly peak to climb.

In 1921, the Tibetan government opened the Himalayas to the British—the first nine expedition attempts on Everest were made from the Tibetan side in the 1920s and 1930s, because Nepal was inaccessible to Europeans at the time. Although several English expeditions tackled the peak from Tibetan side, none succeeded. Early expeditions wore woollens, thick tweeds, Norfolk jackets and studded leather boots. The only hardware was ice axes and primitive crampons, but oxygen tanks were lugged along. On the third expedition attempt, in 1924, George Mallory and Andrew Irvine were making good time for the summit when they were enveloped in cloud and never seen again. Whether they succeeded in gaining the summit remains one of mountaineering's great mysteries. Another mystery: Eric Shipton, connected with these British attempts, photographed footprints left by the Yeti (known as *migyu* in Tibetan: Shipton was given to practical jokes). Failing to summit Everest, Shipton and his climbing cronies set about bagging a host of first ascents of lesser peaks around Everest.

Since the 19th century, Tibet has attracted more than its fair share of visionaries and eccentric travellers: with Everest, spectacularly so. In 1934, British ex-army officer Maurice Wilson announced that he was going to crash-land a Tiger Moth on the slopes of the mountain and climb from there to plant the Union Jack on the summit. Incredible but true, Wilson got financial backing, learned how to fly—and flew all the way to India, where officials promptly seized his plane. Spurred on by his megalomaniacal brand of divine faith, Wilson found his way through Tibet disguised as a deaf and dumb monk. At Rongbuk, he got on famously with the head lama. Wilson apparently believed that earlier British expeditions had cut an ice stairway straight up the mountain—he thought he would simply climb this staircase and pray his way to the top. He had little equipment, no warm clothing and no mountaineering experience. Another British expedition of 1935 found his frozen body at around 6700 metres.

In 1947, Canadian climber Earl Denman sneaked into Rongbuk to assault the mountain: he got above Camp 3, but turned back. This was the last attempt from the Tibetan side for some time—the Tibetans banned issue of travel permits to Tibet. In 1950, after the Chinese invasion, no foreign climbers were allowed in. Western attention had already shifted to Nepal, which had become accessible after 1949. In May 1953, New Zealander Edmund Hillary and Sherpa Tenzing Norgay "knocked the bastard off" (as Hillary put it), summiting from Nepal as part of a British expedition.

Meanwhile, from the Tibetan side, the Chinese would not allow climbers to attempt the route until they had succeeded in putting Chinese mountaineers on top first. In 1959, the Chinese and the Russians undertook a joint reconnaissance. With the rift between China and Russia in 1960, China carried on the work alone, and then stepped into the Everest spotlight in a big way. In March 1960, the Chinese claimed that all of Everest, as well as an 8-km stretch south to Namche Bazaar, belonged to China. At the time, China was busy testing the limits of Indian and Nepalese patience in border disputes. The Everest claim did not sit well with the Nepalese Prime Minister, who made a counter-claim that all of Everest belonged to Nepal, including parts of Rongbuk Glacier. The same month, a 214-man Chinese expedition arrived at Rongbuk base camp for a summit attempt. A Chinese and Tibetan climbing team reached the summit, but there were no photos as the summit took place at night. Another expedition took place in 1963. In 1975 (by which time the border between Tibet and Nepal had been firmly delineated as running across the summit) the Chinese mounted another huge expedition. One Chinese and eight Tibetans gained the summit and left a tripod there—definite proof of their ascent.

In 1980, the Chinese, satisfied that their claim had been accepted, opened the north side again to foreigners. In August, 1980, in contrast to the huge Chinese teams, came a team of two—Italian climber Reinhold Messner and his girlfriend. In one of mountaineering's most extraordinary feats, he made it to the top of Everest, solo and without oxygen, by a route first pioneered by Mallory and Irvine. This ascent stands as the only complete solo ascent made on Everest where the climber survived. Two years earlier, climbing from the South Col, Messner and Habeler were the first to climb the mountain without oxygen. Until they attempted this feat, it was unknown if a climber would survive reaching the top without oxygen, as once past 7000 metres is known as the Zone of Death (no further acclimatisation is possible). At Everest's peak, a climber without oxygen could suffer debilitating physical and mental problems. Messner did not go in entirely blind—he was a passenger on a plane flying at high altitudes, and tested himself out without oxygen for a short period.

In 1986 Messner claimed another record—the ascent of all 14 peaks over 8000 metres, including ascents of Everest and Shishapangma in Tibet. To date, a handful of climbers have repeated the feat. Messner narrowly missed being first in the race to bag the highest peak on all seven continents. This record fell to Canadian Patrick Morrow. New Zealander Rob Hall raised the bar by bagging the Seven Summits in seven months. Others have gone on to bag the Seven Summits plus the two poles. Where will it end? Well, there's still the snowboarding record up for grabs: climb the Seven Summits and snowboard down. Some other Everest descent records: in September 1988, French climber Jean Marc Boivin paraglided from the summit, landing at Camp II (Nepalese side) in 11 minutes. Four years later, Pierre Tardivel skied down the Nepalese side from the South Summit in three hours—the highest ski run ever.

At last count, close on 700 climbers had summited Everest—the majority from the Nepalese side. Over 150 deaths have been recorded in climbing attempts on Everest—about a third of those deaths being Sherpas. Many of the Sherpas act as porters, but others have developed reputations as fine climbers—Ang Rita Sherpa has summited Everest a record ten times. Politics at the top: Everest is the only place in Tibet where the Tibetan flag can be flown without interference. Sherpa climbers tackling Everest from the Nepalese side are prone to leaving small Tibetan flags fluttering from the summit; they also leave an image of the Dalai Lama in the snow at the summit. When he summited in 1996, Jamling Norgay (son of Tenzing Norgay, who summited in 1953) left an ice-axe with the flags of Tibet, Nepal, India, the USA and the UN flying from it.

KARTA

Everest East Base Camp, elevation 5050m

This arduous 10-day loop takes you through the Kama and Karta valleys with views of Everest's Kangshung Face. Of the three faces of Everest, this is the one rated the most daunting to climb, and the one rarely viewed by Westerners. The 1921 British expedition, exploring the Karta Valley on its reconnaissance of Everest, decided the approach was out of the question. It was not until 1981 that an American team tried to summit the Kangshung Face. They failed, but another expedition with some of the same members succeeded in 1983.

Of the treks described so far, the Karta loop is the most taxing, requiring considerable logistical support. Several outfitters such as World Expeditions (Australia) and Himalayan Kingdoms Expeditions (UK) arrange trips—starting from Kathmandu, stopping to trek at Karta and moving on to Lhasa. If you are very determined and well-supplied with food and camping gear, you should be able to put together your own trek.

Caveat: Porters and yak-handlers in the Karta area have a notorious reputation for being unreliable and reluctant companions. On group tours, histrionic scenes have included porters getting drunk on chang at breakfast—and not getting under way with the yaks until mid-day, thus throwing out the daily trekking targets. Furious arguments can erupt over what loads are to be carried on the yaks, porters can be rough in handling duffle bags, yak handlers may stop and demand extra money before continuing. So it goes on. They are also known to be fond of pilfering loose items.

Kangshung Trek

To save time and conserve energy, it would be advisable to get a ride to the trailhead village of Karta. The approach by road is initially the same as for Rongbuk, with a turn-off at Peruche. From Peruche to Karta is about six bone-jarring hours by Landcruiser, with repeated river fords. You could trek in—the scenic 90 km from Peruche to Karta would take three or four days (a donkey and guide can be hired in Peruche to assist).

Everest East Face base camp can be reached by several routes: a 10-day loop takes in several of these. There are two high passes en route: trekkers pick the lower one (Shao La, 4970m) to go over first as this allows more chance to acclimatise. At the base of Shao La are two glacial lakes, where good campsites are found. If the weather is clear, there are good views of Everest, Makalu and Lhotse from the top of Shao La. Shao La leads into the beautiful Kama Valley which is surprisingly coated with meadows full of rhododendrons, and, further on, forests of pine and fir. Westward along the Kama Valley there are many streams to cross, and meadows with wildflowers. From this vantage point, there may be views of Chomo Lonzo. The trek continues to Everest East base camp—at a site called Pethang Ringmo by British climber George Mallory. If the weather is co-operative, there

MOUNTAIN BURIAL

One of Everest's less salubrious records is highest rubbish dump in the world. Some expeditions have been undertaken solely to clear out the hundreds of oxygen bottles and canisters strewn at the highest camp, about 900 metres below the summit. Something that cannot be so easily removed: the bodies of dead climbers. Because of the weight, carrying back dead alpinists from this zone—at these high altitudes—is exceedingly difficult. Instead, if possible, bodies of climbers are simply pushed into crevasses—a dispatch known as "mountain burial."

That's indeed if there's still a body left. Macabre sightings at high elevations include partial cadavers. These act as grim landmarks, and reminders of how thin the line is between life and death up here. The area above 7000 metres is called the Zone of Death because the body cannot acclimatise here. Climbers have to move quickly in this zone before their strength is sapped by dehydration, cold and high altitude.

It is said there is no morality above 7000 metres. If climbers stop to help another climber at this elevation, they will most likely have to abandon their own summit attempt. In a 1996 summit attempt, two Japanese climbers on the Tibetan side were heading for the top when they came across three Ladakhi climbers from an Indian expedition. The Ladakhis had summited but had been forced to spend the night out—though horribly frostbitten they were still alive, and moaning unintelligibly. Not wanting to jeopardise their ascent, the Japanese climbers simply sidestepped the Ladakhis—not offering food, water or oxygen—and carried on to the summit. On the way down from the summit they again passed two of the Ladakhis, who were left to die where they had fallen. Interviewed soon after their descent, one Japanese climber explained that the Ladakhis looked "dangerous"; the other Japanese climber said, "We were were too tired to help. Above 8000 metres is not a place where people can afford morality."

are unparalleled views of the Kangshung Face and Kangshung Glacier.

The return trek is made via Langma La, 5330m, with steep rocky sections giving way to more gentle pastures. At the Kama River is the medieval village of Lundrubling, with solid houses of stone and timber. With a few hours' trekking to the east, you return to Karta Yulba.

Lesser-known than Everest—but no less spectacular—is Cho Oyu, an 8153-metre behemoth. You can see the peak quite clearly from Tingri. The walk out (or drive) to base camp crosses the plains of Tingri in the same direction as the Rongbuk trail. Cho Oyu base camp is nestled at 4970m. You can take a day-hike from here toward Puse La for good views. Near Cho Oyu base camp is Kyetrak, with the ruins of a salt depot on the old trading route from Nepal, crossing Nangpa La. The glaciated route is still used by the odd Nepali trader—and used as an escape route by Tibetan refugees, which might explain Chinese military manoeuvres in the area.

SHISHAPANGMA
BASE-CAMP TREK

Shishapangma is the only 8000-metre peak totally within Tibet (the others—Everest, Lhotse, Cho Oyu and Makalu—lie on the Tibet-Nepal border). For a long time it was not a question of climbing Shishapangma, but getting to see it. It was not until 1951 that Peter Aufschnaiter (the Austrian who escaped with Heinrich Harrer to Tibet) was able to get within 10 km of Shishapangma to photograph it. This was only the second photo taken of the mountain—the first being an aerial one taken in 1950. Shishapangma was the last of the 8000-metre giants to fall to climbers.

The first ascent of Shishapangma (Xixabangma) was achieved in 1964. In March that year, an army of over 200 Chinese support personnel and climbers gathered at the north base camp. Climbers swore to plant the five-starred red flag on the summit "for the honour of the party and the socialist construction of the Motherland" (as described in the magazine *China's Sports*). The climbers not only put the red flag on the summit, they also deposited a bust of Chairman Mao. The summit was reached by four Tibetan and six Chinese climbers—one of whom, Wang Fuchou, had climbed Everest four years earlier. In 1980, a German climbing team summited the peak; in 1982, British climbers Doug Scott and Alex MacIntyre reached the top via the southwest face. French climber Didier Givois and two companions not only summited Shishapangma, they telemark-skied back down it.

Ironically, since the Lhasa-to-Kathmandu-route opened to tourism in the 1980s, Shishapangma has become the most accessible of the

8000-metre peaks. There are two approaches to Shishapangma. You can drive to Shishapangma north base camp by heading north out of Nyalam, and taking a fork to the west that leads to Lake Palku Tso. Heading along this road is another fork to the south, leading to the village of Serlung. Here you can hire yaks and handlers if you want to trek in, or just motor on for the last 15 km from Serlung to the north base camp at 4900 metres.

Shishapangma south base camp, at 4980 metres, can be reached by an in-and-out trail from Nyalam, taking about 4 or 5 days for the round trip. You head out northwest of Nyalam, following a river through alpine valleys. Because Shishapangma is a conglomerate peak, it's difficult to determine where the real summit lies.

WEST TIBET

There are two main targets in West Tibet, both taking about a week to reach from Lhasa. The main focus of interest—both pilgrim and trekker—is Mount Kailash. A second spectacular site is the ruins of the Guge Kingdom near Zanda. You can visit both if you have lots of time and money—and luck on the road.

Another variable here is that you may not want to return to Lhasa, or even start from Lhasa. Kailash can also be approached or left from the road going down to Kathmandu. There is a shortcut around the south side of (Lake) Palku Tso, which skirts close to Shishapangma north base camp. Group tent-trekking tours from Kathmandu either drive up through Nyalam, or use another five-day walk-in route from Simikot (far western Nepal) to Burang. These trekking trips are Sherpa-escorted and very expensive. Indian pilgrims arrive as part of a lottery system: they come over the Lipu Lek pass to Burang, then on to Kailash. Some Western group tours have been allowed to follow this same route, trekking in through the Garhwal Himalaya and over Lipu Lek pass.

ROUTES FROM LHASA

Travel to Kailash is like one of those epic Marco Polo diary entries: "Five or six days' hard journey to the west, you come to a great snow-covered mountain which is considered very holy by the Tibetans, who leave articles of clothing as proof of their pilgrimage to it...." The pilgrimage to Kailash has long been considered the most difficult in Asia—due to sheer distance, harsh weather conditions, the high altitude and lack of any supply points. No matter which way you go, the trip is arduous and you need good planning. Timing is everything at Kailash. It's snowed in for much of the year. June and July are good. August is not good—monsoon rains can wash away roads and bridges leading in. September is possible. Treks at Kailash start and finish at Darchen, an encampment on the south side of the peak. There are half a dozen routes to Kailash, all of them arduous and time-consuming. Consult the colour map in this book for an overview of routing.

Hiring Vehicles: A Landcruiser driver would be most reluctant to travel alone on any of the Kailash routes. If he gets stuck in mud or trapped while fording a river, there's no way out. You have some options: arrange to hire two Landcruisers, or, better yet, hire a Landcruiser and a truck. The Landcruiser can seat four paying passengers plus guide and driver; the truck seats two paying passengers in the front cabin, plus driver. The truck acts as a tow vehicle if the going gets rough—it can haul the Landcruiser to the next town for repairs. In the back of the truck are all the supplies for the trip: food, gasoline, camping gear and so on. You can rotate passengers through the two vehicles. A Landcruiser and truck combination might work out at $4500 for six people for 25 days. That means about $750 a person, including permits, gasoline, driver and guide fees, but not food. Take as much food and water with you as you can manage from Lhasa: potatoes, vegetables, dried fruit, roasted walnuts—anything that will last the distance. Some take along lots of liquid supplies too.

Another good transport configuration here is one truck and two Landcruisers, if you can find enough people for the journey. This makes more efficient use of the truck by sharing it between two Landcruisers. The full circuit of Lhasa via the north route to Kailash and back to Lhasa on the south route is just over 3000 km—a major road trip.

A far cheaper way to go (about $250 a person) is with ten people in the back of a truck (guide and driver in the cabin, plus one passenger on a rotation basis). Chinese Dongfeng trucks are not known for their shock-absorbers: you'll be thrown around like a sack of potatoes, showered in dust, and have your kidneys messed with. There are periodic clamp-downs by authorities on this kind of truck transport—sometimes they turn a blind eye, other times they say foreigners can't use trucks.

Permits: Visiting the region of West Tibet requires more than usual in the way of permits. Apart from the regular ATP listing Ali,

Darchen and so on, you need special permits to visit the Guge Kingdom. This paperwork starts in Lhasa, continues in Ali or Darchen, and then requires more work in Zanda.

North Route: The longest way to Kailash is from Lhasa via Lhatse and Gertse to Ali, then south to Darchen. En route, you could make a sidetrip to Zanda and Tsaparang. Lhasa to Kailash by this route is around 1900 km (the Ali to Darchen stretch is 330 km). A return to Lhasa would probably be made on the south route via Huore and Zongba to Saga. From here you either continue onward to Lhasa, or cross the Yarlung Tsangpo by ferry at Saga, detour around the south side of Palku Tso and head for Zhangmu on the Kathmandu route. The north route—though long—has the advantage of roads that are in reasonable shape. Some parts need no roads at all—the trucks forge their own route across grassland.

There are some horrible, polluted, soul-destroying truck-stop towns en route. No-name hotels have rough and tumble facilities, if any at all—hot water supply comes in thermoses. Some towns like Tsochen and Gertse have a few small restaurants hidden away. This is the main Lhasa-Ali-Kashgar truck and military supply route, so truck-stops cater to the driving crews. Among the truck-stops are Sangsang (4520m), Raga (4800m), Tsochen (4650m), Dongco (4400m), Gertse (4400m), Tsaka (Yanhu) and Gakyi (4450m). There are some high passes of 5000 and 5200 metres north of Tsochen. The wild terrain in between truck-stops makes the journey more than worthwhile: you might see wild asses, antelopes and even black-necked cranes. There are a few hot springs along the way, too.

Kashgar Route: Connecting from Ali through Yecheng to Kashgar is this route, the wildest of all. Some have managed to hitch from Kashgar to Ali—the stumbling block is Yecheng, 250 km south of Kashgar, where PSB men are prone to sending travellers back to where they came from. The route crosses some very high passes and there are no supply points along it. Kashgar is in a remote corner of the PRC, but the Karakoram Highway to Islamabad provides a convenient exit or entry (open May to November, with valid Pakistan visa).

South Route: Although the south route to Kailash from Lhasa, via Lhatse and Paryang, is more direct (a total of 1200 km), it is also more prone to flooding, washed-out roads and downed bridges. There are some high passes on the south route: Paryang and Huore both sit at 4500 metres—between them is a pass of 5100 metres. Some travellers take the south route up to Darchen and retrace their passage the same way, perhaps detouring from Saga (4500m) around the south side of Palku Tso to the Tong La pass, and on to Nyalam on the Kathmandu route (see the Lhasa to Kathmandu Route map in this book for visual details).

ALI
Shiquanhe, elevation 4220m

Ali is a Chinese concrete monstrosity of a town, with some of the ugliest post-Mao proletarian-monolithic socialist-realist architecture in Tibet. It's composed of concrete cubicles and wooden kiosks, with garbage all over the place. At least there's a Lion statue in the middle, not a Mao statue. The town is Chinese to its rotten core—no Tibetan towns existed out this way except for the old capital of Gartok (a nomad tent encampment which has disappeared without trace). Although it is commonly called Ali, the town is also referred to by the river it is located along—the Indus, which the Chinese refer to as Shiquanhe and the Tibetans call Sengghe Tsangpo ("River issuing from the Lion's Mouth"; hence Sengghe Drong, or "Lion Village," is the Tibetan name for Ali).

Ali is easily the largest town in western Tibet, with the largest military garrison of the region. Army platoons jog around the streets in formation at six in the morning, and again around sunset. After sunset the top brass head for the karaoke bars and help themselves to the women. Otherwise, there's not a whole lot to see in Ali, apart from a place called the Cultural Relics Bureau, which has a display centre. The main reason for visiting Ali is shopping—for food and for permits.

Basics

Ali Hotel at the east end of town is a concrete wasteland where little seems to work. Rooms downstairs are cheaper than the ones upstairs—you might be able to get a hot water thermos and basin together to clean up. A cleaner place to stay is the Government Guesthouse, opposite the PSB office; the price difference is minimal. To the southwest side of the Lion statue is a Chinese restaurant with quite palatable Sichuan food. There are also eateries on the road to the south. Food kiosks in this vicinity may have little nuggets hidden away, including chocolate bars, pineapple in jars, crackers and candles.

Facilities

You can stock up on supplies like shampoo. The kiosks around town are the best bet; there's not much in the "department stores". Facili-

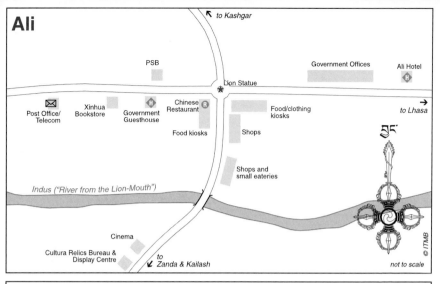

Ali

to Kashgar

PSB

Lion Statue

Government Offices

Ali Hotel

Post Office/ Telecom

Xinhua Bookstore

Government Guesthouse

Chinese Restaurant

Food/clothing kiosks

to Lhasa

Food kiosks

Shops

Shops and small eateries

Indus ("River from the Lion-Mouth")

Cinema

Cultura Relics Bureau & Display Centre

to Zanda & Kailash

not to scale

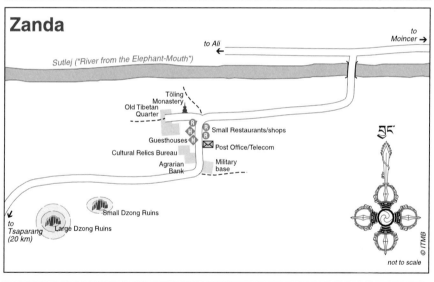

Zanda

to Ali

to Moincer

Sutlej ("River from the Elephant-Mouth")

Töling Monastery

Old Tibetan Quarter

Small Restaurants/shops

Guesthouses

Post Office/Telecom

Cultural Relics Bureau

Agrarian Bank

Military base

Small Dzong Ruins

to Tsaparang (20 km)

Large Dzong Ruins

not to scale

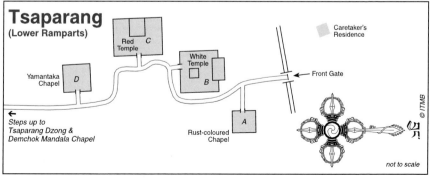

Tsaparang
(Lower Ramparts)

Caretaker's Residence

Red Temple

C

White Temple

B

Front Gate

Yamantaka Chapel

D

A

Steps up to Tsaparang Dzong & Demchok Mandala Chapel

Rust-coloured Chapel

not to scale

ties to the western side of town include a small Xinhua bookstore, a PO/telecom office, and just west of this, a bank. There's also a hospital in Ali.

Mobility

A glance at the map will show Ali is strategically sited at the junction of the north route from Lhasa, the south route from Kashgar, and onward routes to Zanda and Kailash. PSB men will be on the lookout for travellers who don't have their papers in order: the PSB office will most likely want to check your permits if you are spotted. Some backpackers who have hitched out this far have been able to turn themselves in at Ali, pay a fine, and be issued with permits for Kailash. This policy can easily change. If you want to finalise paperwork for visiting Zanda, you must visit both the PSB office and the Cultural Relics Bureau, to the south end of town, to get the right papers.

ZANDA
Tsanda, Tsada, Zada, Thöling, Toling; elevation 3660m

From Ali, the road to Zanda traverses an entire mountain range—a breathtaking trip, with snowy passes as high as 5200m and 5500m—before dropping down to a canyon with ghostly shapes. You drive through this canyon along a dry riverbed to reach Zanda. With such a spectacular route, allow an entire day to motor by Landcruiser from Ali to Zanda, with frequent stops en route. The canyons, with hues of yellow, red and copper, are extraordinary for their phantasmagoric sculpted forms, which appear at times to be like the outlines of dream castles or cathedrals, at other times like gigantic guardian statues or mythical animals.

Zanda is the Chinese name for an ancient Tibetan town of Toling, once the capital of Ngari (west Tibet). Remnants of this capital are scattered around town and the surrounding hills; there are dozens of chorten-like structures toward the Sutlej River.

Toling Gompa

The main sight in town is largely-abandoned Toling Gompa. Toling dates back to the 11th century when a structure was built by Yeshe O, the king of Guge. Assisted by scholar Rinchen Zangpo, he led a revival of Buddhism in western Tibet. Buddhism was snuffed out in a few short years in central Tibet by King Langdarma (who ruled 838–842), a staunch supporter of the Bon faith: upon the assassination of Langdarma, Tibet was broken up into lay and monastic pockets of influence. The Guge Kingdom became an enclave that was vital for

the survival of Buddhism. King Yeshe O and Rinchen Zangpo pro-
moted cultural exchanges with Indian Buddhists. Although over a
hundred monasteries were built in the western region (which at that
time encompassed Ladakh), Toling became the most important
centre of Buddhist study, and its reputation grew with the arrival of
11th-century scholar Atisha from India. Eventually the kingdom was
sacked in the 17th century. In the mid-1960s, Red Guards trashed
Toling Gompa.

The main draw at Toling today are the fine murals in the few
chapels remaining. In addition to destruction by Red Guards, murals
in the White Temple have suffered water damage. Similar to those at
Tsaparang, the murals are in early Newari and Kashmiri styles—
rarely seen in Tibet. You need a powerful flashlight to view them, and
considerable perseverance to persuade the caretaker-monk to open
chapels in the first place. You may have to bribe your way through
the place, even if you've already paid up through the Cultural Relics
Bureau.

Out of Town

On ridge-tops to the southwest of Zanda are two dzongs (citadels)
made of clay. This is the most peculiar hiking you'll ever do: scram-
bling over sand, dealing with crevasses of clay. Access to the larger
dzong (the one to the west) is via a steep trail, and then through a
sloping tunnel carved out of clay. Above the tunnel are former cave-
dwellings—and dangerous crevasses. From here you continue climbing, and reach a vantage point with a magnificent view of the Sutlej
valley.

Permits

If you want to visit Toling Gompa in Zanda or the ruins of the Guge
Kingdom in Tsaparang, you need permits from the Cultural Relics
Bureau, located near the bank. Tsaparang requires separate permits
from Lhasa, Ali and Zanda—put them all together and you are allowed to visit. With one of those permits missing, there could be
problems.

Nuts & Bolts

Zanda is a glorified army garrison—facilities are for the military, not
for the stray tourist. There's a big army base at the southern end of
town, and an old Tibetan quarter at the northwest end. In between is
a main drag with two guesthouses—one of which belongs to military.
The one near Toling Gompa is preferable—there are balcony rooms

upstairs, and there's a tap in the courtyard with running water. Several small Chinese restaurants line the main strip, and some tent-shops (selling supplies out of tents); there's also a post office (with telephone) and the Agrarian Bank.

TSAPARANG

Located 26 km west of Zanda (a one-hour drive) are the extensive ruins of Tsaparang, the once-powerful capital of the 10th-century Guge Kingdom (pronounced Goo-gay). The main building material is not stone, but clay—with walls, buildings, secret tunnels and escape exits all fashioned from this material. Thousands of people lived here in cave-dwellings in this kingdom of clay, which appears to have been operational in the 10th and 11th centuries. Little is known of the history of the Guge Kingdom, but some of the exceptional murals at Tsaparang portray realistic scenes with courtiers and visiting dignitaries—and give some idea of how people lived.

To access temples at Tsaparang, you need the caretaker to open the doors. The Tibetan caretaker lives in a small house near the main gate: if he's not at home, he's probably in the tiny village visible not far away from the ruins. The caretaker may want to see your paperwork, and may insist that no photos be taken inside the temple structures. Interior photography of the site is a very sensitive point; official permits for photography are complex to obtain, and expensive if you do manage to get them.

Tsaparang is built tier on tier up a clay ridge. The best-preserved parts are the lower ramparts; at the very top are excellent views of the area from the dzong. As you go through the gate into Tsaparang, the first thing you see is the Rust-coloured Chapel (A), thus designated because its function is not clear—it bears murals of Tsongkhapa, Sakyamuni and Atisha. The White Temple (B) suffered extensive damage to its statuary, but its murals remain intact. Some murals portray Avalokitesvara—the 11-headed, thousand-armed bodhisattva of compassion The mural style is Kashmiri The Red Temple (C) was destroyed and left open to water damage, but even so, its murals are striking—with beautiful large Tara frescoes. Engrossing here are murals apparently depicting scenes from daily life at Guge—in one section envoys arriving by donkey at the court; another part shows a high lama giving teachings. The Yamantaka Chapel (D) is named after its resident tantric deity Dorje Jigje: the walls bear murals of deities locked in *yabyum* embraces with their consorts.

From here, wend your way up clay steps, passing through a fantastic winding tunnel to the top-most ruins. There's an entire ruined citadel at the top. Once past the tunnel, there is a complex of chambers and passageways: the citadel had its own water supply in times of siege, and the king had an escape route tunnel that lead off the rear of the ridge.

At the top, the most impressive structure is Tsaparang Dzong—the king's simple summer palace—with expansive views over the valley. There are several temple complexes at the top: the most important is the tiny Demchok Mandala Chapel. This chapel is usually locked—if you manage to get in, you can view the remains of a large 3-D mandala, which was smashed in the Cultural Revolution. The chapel is a *gonkhang* or protector temple, and the site of initiation rites. It is thought that in times of crisis, the king and ministers would come to this chapel to ask for protection or direction. The chapel is dedicated to the protector deity Demchok, who is depicted in murals with his consort Dorje Phagmo. Fascinating tantric murals cover the walls: a flashlight is needed to view them. Depicted are rows of dancing dakinis, the female deities who personify the wisdom of enlightenment; below these are gory scenes of disembodiment from hell realms.

TIRTAPURI

While Kailash is the main sacred site of western Tibet, there are a number of others on the pilgrim's "wish-list." After Lake Manasarovar, the most revered site is Tirtapuri, a yellow-streaked rocky landscape with hot springs. After encircling Kailash and Manasarovar, Tibetan pilgrims come to Tirtapuri for a *relaxing* circuit—the kora is only an hour, and there are grassy meadows for picnicking as well as hot water for soothing tired limbs. Tirtapuri lies 10 km southwest of Moincer (which has a basic guesthouse), approachable by Landcruiser or truck. There is a short circuit in the Tirtapuri region—you can follow the pilgrims as they walk past elaborate mani walls and sacred caves, and pay their respects at a small monastery. The entire Tirtapuri circuit takes an hour, but you should allow several hours to stop and drink in the atmosphere and the landscape. At the site, pilgrims bathe—or dip their feet—in several sulphurous hot-spring pools, which can accommodate three or four people. The hot springs are reputed to have healing powers—and Tibetans search the waters for pellets of lime, for medicinal purposes. Just being able to feel hot water is therapeutic enough for Western visitors.

THE KAILASH REGION

Kailash is the centre of the universe—or at least the Tibetan Buddhist universe. In the Tibetan worldview, at the cosmic axis of the universe

POWERING UP AT KAILASH

In Darchen, you can stock up on last-minute supplies—and get your pilgrim supplies too. At tents and shops at the northeast side of Darchen, pilgrims purchase prayer-flags (to drape at the passes), small squares of paper with windhorses embossed on them (to fling around at the main pass), and for good measure, prayer-beads (to mumble mantras with, to get over the high passes). The windhorse (lungta) is a beautiful steed that brings good fortune (symbolised by the jewel on its back) wherever it goes. It is also painted on prayer-flags—the wind sets the horse in motion, carrying good fortune in all directions.

In their lifetime, all Tibetans aspire to make the sacred pilgrimage to Kailash—some travel enormous distances in the backs of open trucks to get there. Pilgrimage is considered healthy and holy—the most popular time to attempt Kailash is after the annual harvest. When it comes to the Kailash kora, there's a kind of merit point system involved: the more you suffer, the greater the merit earned. Some pilgrims attempt not one circuit, but three (often on consecutive days in one season) or thirteen circuits, or 108 circuits (spread over a number of years), which assures entry into nirvana. Prostrators, who proceed with inchworm-like motions, flinging themselves to the ground, take 15 to 25 days to complete the Kailash circuit, and must prostrate through anything in their path—be it snow, mud, slush, whatever. If you see a prostrator going in an anticlockwise direction, it must be a Bon adherent. For Bon believers, Kailash is the spiritual centre of the Shang-Shung ancient Bon empire of western Tibet.

Punctuating the Kailash circuit are sacred markers in stone—carved chortens, carved mani-stones, cairns with prayer-flags. Offerings made by pilgrims at these sites might include pins (said to sharpen mental faculties), discarded clothing (as proof the pilgrim has been there) or tsampa (thrown in the air as protection against evil).

lies Mount Meru, the abode of the gods. Mount Kailash is thought to be an earthly manifestation of the mythical Meru. Things are not as simple as this, however, as the Tibetan worldview incorporates existence in multiple dimensions. The Tibetan name for Kailash is "Kang Rinpoche"—Precious Jewel of Snows: the dome-shaped peak is symmetrical like an uncut diamond, with a permanent cap of ice and snow. At 6714 metres, the mountain is modest by Himalayan standards, but nevertheless impressive to view. The peak is sacred to Tibetan Buddhist and Bon adherents, and to the Hindus and Jains of India.

In the late 19th century and early 20th century, Kailash assumed mythical dimensions among western geographers and explorers. For the longest time, there was reputed to be a high mountain that was the source of the great rivers of India. But Tibet was inaccessible, so geographers were unsure if this was myth or fact. Finding the source of India's great rivers was a prime geographer's puzzle, on a par to finding the source of the Nile. The British employed Indian pundits, who, disguised as pilgrims, measured distances with prayer-beads, and tossed marked logs into rivers to find out where they would pop up further down the line in India.

Eventually, it was discovered that the headwaters of four of Asia's mightiest rivers lay within 100 km of Kailash—the Indus, the Yarlung Tsangpo (which later emerges in India as the Brahmaputra), the Karnali (a major tributary of the Ganges), and the Sutlej. Remarkably, the mouths of the same rivers end up as far as 3000 km apart. The Tibetans know the rivers by more prosaic names, identified with the four cardinal directions and four legendary animals. Thus the Indus becomes the "River issuing from the Lion's Mouth" (Sengghe Tsangpo or Sengghe Khambab, at the north), the Yarlung Tsangpo becomes the "River from the Horse-Mouth" (Tamchok Khambab, to the east), the Karnali becomes the "River from the Peacock-Mouth" (Mabchu Khambab, to the south), and the Sutlej is the "River from the Elephant-Mouth" (Langchan Khambab, situated in the west).

Darchen

Also known as Tarchen or Dharchen (elevation 4620m), Darchen can best be described as a cross between a Tibetan tent encampment and a Chinese truck-stop depot. A few tents and adobe hutches dispense noodles and tea, and there are some shops by the river on the eastern side of Darchen. Not a lot of choices when it comes to places to stay—most travellers opt for a room at a Chinese-run Gangdishi Guest-house, a truck-stop compound with a large parking area. Prices tend to be high for what you get (which is little more than a rock-hard bed)—you may have to bargain. Useful to know: you can leave your gear here when trekking, in a locked storeroom. There's similar-priced lodging at another compound run by the PSB. It's a good idea to hang around Darchen for a day or two to acclimatise—perhaps taking a day hike up to Serlung Gompa.

Kailash Kora

The circuit around the sacred mountain is known as the Kailash *kora.* Tibetans complete the circuit in one long day, starting before dawn, and finishing after nightfall. Unless you are super-humanoid, don't attempt this at altitude. The minimum time for a Westerner to complete the circuit would be two days. Most allow three to four days. If you have a tent and want to dawdle, taking in the landscape at a leisurely pace, plan on five days or more.

You can head out of Darchen carrying your own backpack with food supplies, or you can hire a local porter in Darchen to carry gear. Group tours often hire yaks in Darchen to carry camping gear and duffle bags on the kora. As an individual, you probably won't need to camp out (you can stay at two monastery guesthouses along the route), but if planning a more leisurely kora, you'll need camping gear so you can stop where you want. Don't expect much in the way of food on the circuit—there may be some teahouse tents along the way, if you're lucky. Sometimes the gompa guesthouses sell noodles. A clean water supply is essential—take along water bottles and filtering devices (water can also be boiled). It is not advisable to trek around Kailash alone—there are too many variables at stake. Walk with at least one companion.

Fellow hikers at Kailash are mainly Indian and Tibetan pilgrims. The Tibetans come from as far away as Kham, usually arriving by "pilgrim truck". Tibetan pilgrims comprise many different nomad groups with a fascinating array of costumes—particularly the women. Women coat their faces in *tocha*—a cosmetic made of concentrated buttermilk or roots—to protect the skin from dryness and UV rays. Indian pilgrims come as part of a lottery system run by the Delhi government, in operation since the early 1980s. Each year, up to 10,000 Hindus from all parts of India apply. About 700 finalists are chosen: after fitness tests, this number is whittled down to about 400. Hindu pilgrims are allowed ten days in Tibet. Travelling in groups of around 35, the lucky lottery winners walk across Lipu Lek Pass where they are met by Chinese guides—and the sacred circuit of their dreams gets under way.

Acclimatisation Hike: Strongly recommended is a day trip up to Gyangdrak and Serlung gompas, due north of Darchen. These gompas are situated at 5000 metres: you can complete a triangular loop in about six or seven hours, returning to Darchen by nightfall. This hike serves several functions: you can adapt to the altitude somewhat (by hiking high but sleeping low) and you can find out how to pace yourself at altitude. If intending to trek around Kailash with your own backpack, you might want to take the full load with you on the day hike to find out just how heavy it is.

Day One: The target of the first day's walk is usually Drira Phuk Gompa, about 8 to 10 hours from Darchen, including stops. Leaving Darchen, you head west: you'll know you're on the right trail when you come across a cairn adorned with prayer-flags, and with discarded clothing left by pilgrims—tattered shirts, sweaters, worn-out runners, old socks, yak head and goat horns. Further on is Tarboche, a large flagpole from which flutter long lines of prayer-flags. Every year, at Saka Dawa (full moon day in May or June), thousands of Tibetans gather to celebrate: the flagpole is taken down, and new prayer-flags are placed on it, replacing the tattered ones from the previous year. If the pole tilts after it is raised again, it is considered a very bad omen. Pilgrim trucks can reach this site by dirt track, so this is often where Tibetans start the kora.

Beyond Tarboche, high on a ridge—a 20-minute climb up from the trail—is Choku Gompa, which was originally set up in the 13th century as a shrine. The current building was reconstructed after the Cultural Revolution, and is looked after by monks from the Drukpa Kagyu sect (as are the other two monasteries on the kora route). Shiny-eyed pilgrims crowd in to see the monastery's famed treasures: a white stone statue of the Buddha Opame, and a sacred silver-embossed conch shell, said to have been Milarepa's. From Choku, there's a choice of hiking up either side of Lha Chu (River of the gods), though a canyon with impressive rock peaks, such as Nyanri. At Drira Phuk Gompa, there is simple concrete building with a few rooms where you can stay—or you can camp out in the grassy fields nearby.

Day Two: This is a rest day, with a possible half-day hike up to Ghangjam Glacier and back. Building in a rest day at Drira Phuk gives your body a chance to recover, and will help you acclimatise for the arduous walk over Drolma La. Drira Phuk offers the chance to get quite close to Kailash, on a half-day hike to the toe of Ghangjam Glacier at 5270 metres. Assuming clear conditions, there are awesome views of the glistening icy walls of Kailash's north face from this vantage point. You begin to understand why the Tibetans call the peak Kang Rinpoche (Precious Jewel of Snows), and why it is said that a wish made in front of the north face will definitely come true—one day.

Day Three: Heading out of Drira Phuk, you begin the tough ascent to Drolma La. This is the longest haul on the circuit—it takes about 10 to 12 hours to walk to Zutrul Phuk. Out of Drira Phuk is a bizarre sight: a field littered with discarded clothing. The place is

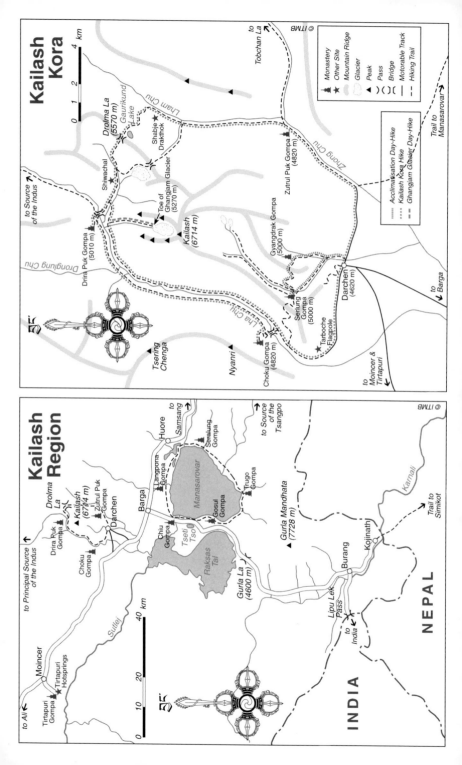

Kailash Kora

Legend:
- Monastery
- Other Site
- Mountain Ridge
- Glacier
- Peak
- Pass
- Bridge
- Motorable Track
- Hiking Trail

- Acclimatisation Day-Hike
- Kailash Kora Hike
- Ghangjam Glacier Day-Hike

Labels (Kailash Kora map):
- to Tobchan La
- Drolma La (5570 m)
- Gaurikund Lake
- Lham Chu
- Shabje Drakthok
- Shiwachal
- Toe of Ghangjam Glacier (5270 m)
- Drira Puk Gompa (5010 m)
- to Source of the Indus
- Dronglung Chu
- Kailash (6714 m)
- Tsering Chenga
- Lha Chu
- Nyanri
- Choku Gompa (4820 m)
- Zutrul Puk Gompa (4820 m)
- Zhong Chu
- Gyangdrak Gompa (5000 m)
- Serlung Gompa (5000 m)
- Tarboche Flagpole
- Darchen (4620 m)
- to Barga
- to Moincer & Tirtapuri
- Trail to Manasarovar
- © ITMB

Kailash Region

Labels (Kailash Region map):
- to Ali
- Moincer
- Tirtapuri Gompa
- Tirtapuri Hotsprings
- to Principal Source of the Indus
- Drolma La
- Kailash (6714 m)
- Zutrul Puk Gompa
- Drira Puk Gompa
- Choku Gompa
- Darchen
- Barga
- Sutlej
- Huore
- to Samsang
- Langpona Gompa
- Serlung Gompa
- to Source of the Tsangpo
- Manasarovar
- Chiu Gompa
- Tseti Tso
- Gosul Gompa
- Trugo Gompa
- Raksas Tal
- Gurla La (4600 m)
- Gurla Mandhata (7728 m)
- Lipu Lek Pass
- to India
- Burang
- Kojinath
- Karnali
- Trail to Simikot
- NEPAL
- INDIA
- © ITMB

Shiwachal, named after a cremation ground in Bodhgaya, India (Shiva-tsal). In this symbolic field of death, pilgrims must leave behind a personal item—clothing, a lock of hair, or even a few drops of blood—as proof of being there. A rock pillar in the middle of Siwachal is covered with scraps of cloth and bracelets.

Toiling upward, you reach Drolma La, which is the focus of the entire kora. Drolma La means "Pass of Tara": a large boulder depicting Tara is festooned with prayer flags. Tibetans attach their own prayer flag, and leave coins, locks of hair or other mementoes of their passage; they fling windhorse squares into the air and shout *Tso tso tso! Lha Gyalo!* (Victory to the gods!). Down the other side of the pass is a beautiful greenish tarn, Gaurikund Lake—Hindus are supposed to take a dip here, but ice skating might be more appropriate. You continue down, down, down—on a descent that is taxing on the knees—to meadows where Tibetans picnic. Eventually, you reach Zutrul Phuk Gompa, which has a basic concrete guesthouse attached.

Day Four: Around the Kailash kora are relics left by the great cave-dwelling ascetic Milarepa, who engaged in a competition with sorcerer Naro Bon Chun. At Zutrul Puk Gompa, the reconstructed monastery encloses a cave that Milarepa fashioned with his bare hands—there's a statue of him within. The caretaker monk will show you around—you may need a flashlight. The final showdown between Milarepa and Naro Bon Chun is said to have taken place on the peak of Kailash: in the ensuing duel, Naro Bon Chun fell, and in so doing, is said to have carved a long vertical cleft in the mountain's south face.

And so, totally wasted, totally knackered, you head back to Darchen to complete the Kailash circuit. Fortunately it's a level or downhill walk to Darchen, and it doesn't take that long to dribble back into town.

Chiu Gompa

South of Darchen is a scene that frequently appears in photographs of Kailash: a monastery crowning a hill in the foreground and Kailash poking up in the background. The monastery is Chiu Gompa—the most impressive of the gompas encircling Lake Manasarovar. It's an easy drive from Darchen. The ancient monastery is thought to have been the lasting resting place of sage Padmasambhava. You can work your way up to the top chapel, with views of the entire area. A family-run guesthouse is located near Chiu Gompa, and close to this are some sulphurous hot springs channelled into a pool, where it's possible to wash your hair.

Tibetans undertake several koras in the Kailash region: the first of Kailash itself, the second of Lake Manasarovar, and then a visit to Tirtapuri (some pilgrims tackle Lake Manasarovar first). Lake Manasarovar draws Hindu pilgrims who come for ritual bathing in the icy waters: full submersion in the waters is claimed to ensure enlightenment (Tibetan Buddhists, by contrast, settle for a sip and a splash over the head). Indian pilgrims pick up pebbles from the lakeside and fill containers with holy water when returning home. A 90-km walking circuit around the lake takes about four to five days. The route is perfectly flat and lies at 4560 metres in altitude.

Eight monasteries encircling the shores of the lake were once so sited to represent the Dharma wheel with its eightfold path. They were destroyed during the Cultural Revolution, but some have been partially restored and remain active. Even if you don't attempt a circuit of Manasarovar, it's well worth driving past Chiu Gompa as far as Gurla La for a glimpse of magnificent Gurla Mandhata. If you can, try and continue as far as Burang.

If contemplating the Manasarovar circuit, you would probably need a pony or donkey assistant to carry camping gear and food; bring sunscreen and insect repellent. You can start and end the circuit at Chiu Gompa, where there are places to stay. An alternate starting point is from the town of Huore (where horses can be hired), ending at Chiu Gompa again (not a complete circuit, but close)—this will cut down the walking time. Foreigners rarely undertake the Manasarovar circuit (usually they are spent after the Kailash trek) but the lake offers pristine hiking, with bird-life visible at certain parts, and a slew of monasteries or ruins along the way. The route usually proceeds from Chiu Gompa past Langpona and Serlung gompas to Trugo and Gosul gompas, passing by the small lake of Tseti Tso, and continuing north back to Chiu Gompa.

Raksas Tal: While Manasarovar is identified with the positive forces of light (the sun), the lake next door, Raksas Tal, is aligned with the forces of darkness (the moon). For this reason, Raksas Tal is shunned by pilgrims—its waters are rumoured to be poisonous (actually, they're not), as opposed to the healing waters of Manasarovar.

THE ROAD TO BURANG

Right down south, close to the Nepal-India borders, is the old trading town of Burang—also known as Purang or Taklakot. Burang lies at 3900 metres in elevation. The distance from Darchen to Burang is around 110 km, or a three-hour drive. Indian pilgrims enter via Lipu

Lek Pass and Burang to get to Darchen; Western trekkers are permitted to take a five-day hike from Simikot (in Nepal) to Burang (or over the Lipu Lek Pass), and take a Landcruiser to Kailash. As an individual, you won't be able to cross here, but regardless of this, Burang makes a great drive—passing between Lake Manasarovar and Lake Raksas Tal, and driving right by Mount Gurla Mandhata.

Gurla Mandhata, though 7728 metres, appears to be quite low from this perspective, and the summit appears so close you almost imagine you could get out and start walking up it. Which is exactly what a couple of American climbers once did (unofficially)—telling their startled driver to come and fetch them in a few weeks, after they'd bagged the peak! Gurla La, a pass of 4600 metres, offers spectacular vistas, as does Ara La (4200m): continuing southward are the pretty villages of Garu and Topa, with handsome handcrafted houses.

Burang is an old caravan stop on the banks of the Karnali River. Today it functions as a military outpost, with lots of men in green running around. It is aligned along a north-south road: at the north side is a military checkpost (your documents will be scrutinised); toward the southern side are some small restaurants and shops, an expensive guesthouse, and the post office, bank and PSB office. Staying in Burang is a problem as the sanctioned guesthouse is an overpriced dump. It's difficult to find an alternative. While "restaurants" are mediocre, you may be able to buy fresh vegetables at a street market and take them to a restaurant to be stirfried. Stocks of canned fruit and other items are quite good.

There's good hiking and a few things to see in Burang—you can combine several options by taking a western fork out of town. Head toward a bridge that spans the Karnali at the northern end of Burang. There's a small bazaar selling clothing, and some food (a small eatery here) with a few snooker tables. Continue west on a trail that leads up a steep hillside. Set into the cliff face is a remarkable cave-temple, Gokung Gompa. The caretaker monk will show you around for a token fee—the monastery ranges over three storeys, set within caves. Cave-dwellings are used as houses in this area. If you carry on over the top of a crest, you'll come to the Nepalese Bazaar, where Nepalese goods are sold in exchange for Tibetan wool, which is rolled into huge balls. Concrete shopfronts offer Nepalese and Indian goods, portered in from the Nepalese town of Darchula.

To the northwest of Burang, on a hilltop, you can make out the ruins of Shembaling Gompa. Once the largest monastery in the region, it housed several hundred monks—and was completely destroyed in the Cultural Revolution. Today the biggest active monastery in the region is at the pretty village of Kojinath (Korja or Kojarnath), situated 15 km southeast of Burang, on the Karnali River right near the Nepalese border.

SHAMBHALA AND SHANGRI-LA

As earthly paradises go, Tibet's vision is a bit different. Most Tibetans haven't heard of Shangri-La, but James Hilton (the author of *Lost Horizons*, 1933) probably based his story about Shangri-La on the Tibetan legend of Shambhala, which most Westerners haven't heard about.

The Shambhala legend was first heard by Jesuit and Capuchin missionaries who stumbled into Tibet, and who probably served as models for Hilton's characters. In Lost Horizon, a Capuchin monk called Perrault had made his way into the valley of Shangri-La and attempted to convert the residents. Instead, he was converted to Buddhism, and some 200 years later, as High Lama, this wizened gentleman was still alive to tell new recruits the rules. The main luxury at Shangri-La was Time—that slippery gift that often eludes Westerners. Shangri-La was a repository of the best of eastern and western knowledge, preserved for:

> a time when men, exultant in the technique of homicide, would rage so hotly over the world that every precious thing would be in danger, every book and picture and harmony, every treasure gathered through two millenniums, the small, the delicate, the defenseless—all would be lost...

Hilton set his story in a Tibetan monastery high in the mountains. The location is not revealed—the Western visitors arrive in a plane that crash-landed. This world has led Westerners to confuse Tibet with a mythical realm and not a real place. The phenomenon has been dubbed "The Shangri-La Syndrome" by Tibetan intellectuals.

There are several Tibetan versions of the legend of Shambhala, but they run in the same pattern. Somewhere to the north of Tibet is a kingdom ringed by impenetrable snowcapped mountains and cloaked in mist. In this sanctuary, poverty, hunger, crime and sickness are unknown, and people live a hundred years. In the city of Kalapa there is a glittering palace where the sacred Kalachakra teachings are kept. According to the legend, about 300 years from now, when Lhasa lies under water, the world will erupt in chaotic warfare. When the last barbarian thinks he has conquered the world, the mists will lift from Shambhala and the King of Shambhala will ride forth to destroy the forces of evil. The King will establish a new Golden age of a thousand years.

The Shambhala theme is often depicted in Tibetan temple murals—sometimes in mandalic form. There are large Shambhala murals in the Potala and the Norbulingka in Lhasa, and also at Samye. Many other monastic frescoes portray the Kalachakra deity. Tsongkhapa and other great Tibetan wizards and sages are thought to have visited Shambhala in the past. When the Golden Age dawns, it is said that the tomb of Tsongkhapa at Ganden will open up, and he will live again to teach true wisdom. A number of ancient, surrealistic Tibetan texts have been written on how to get to Shambhala. Some say Shambhala lies in west Tibet, near the Guge Kingdom; others think it is in the north, in Changtang, or much further north in the Kunlun range, or even in Mongolia. Yet others think it lies at the North Pole. Some Tibetans believe Shambhala is a mystical nirvana of the gods; others believe it is real, but that the journey is not external but internal—and that the war with ignorance is in your own heart.

THE TIBETAN WORLD
Tibet outside the TAR, Tibet in exile, Tibetan kingdoms & fiefdoms

A prophecy attributed to the great sage Padmasambhava says: "When the iron bird flies and horses run on wheels, the Tibetan people will be scattered like ants across the face of the earth, and the Dharma will come to the land of the redskins." Whether this is what he actually said, or whether somebody made it up later to suit the situation, the Tibetans are certainly widely scattered—but not across the face of the earth. They are mostly scattered across the Himalayas. In the old Tibetan flat-earth worldview, however, they would be at the edges of the earth as the Tibetans knew it (which did not much extend beyond the Asian/Indian continent). Of the following destinations, the most rewarding trips are those to the high Himalayan regions inhabited by Tibetans. Journeys to these places can be stymied by formidable obstacles—both physical and bureaucratic. But if you make it, you are rewarded with glimpses of the traditional way of life and festivals no longer seen in Tibet itself.

Probably the most surprising thing you learn as you visit different parts of the Tibetan world is the fact that the Tibetans are not really unified, except in their common beliefs. Tibetans are a very tribal people. Historically, different groups, while they recognised the power of the Dalai Lama (centred in Lhasa), were never obligated to the central Tibetan government—and were beyond its control. Centuries ago, rivalry between sects of Tibetan Buddhism openly took place, with, in some cases, battles fought. Tension between "clans" and rival sects is on-going, even in exile.

TIBET OUTSIDE THE TAR: KHAM & AMDO

Tibetans are today found scattered through areas of western China bordering the TAR. In fact, according to Chinese statistics, there are more Tibetans in the Chinese provinces adjoining the TAR than there are within the TAR itself.

Vast tracts of what were formerly the Tibetan territories of Kham (east of Lhasa) and Amdo (northeast of Lhasa) were carved off by the Chinese into four neighbouring provinces of the TAR. Tibetans referred to this area as "Four Rivers, Six Ranges"—later used as the name of a Khampa guerrilla resistance movement. The Chinese christened the new slabs of territory "Tibetan autonomous prefectures". The process started under the Chinese KMT regime before 1949, and continued under the communist government from 1950 into the 1980s. Kham falls into present-day western Yunnan and Sichuan provinces, while Amdo falls into western Gansu and Qinghai provinces. Some areas are occupied by Tibetan-related minority groups, such as the Qiang people of northern Sichuan. The ethnic Tibetan area can be roughly correlated with the Tibetan plateau. On the plateau, the Tibetan nomad culture still is present: where the plateau drops off, the descent is made to Chinese towns. However, there has been lots of Chinese infiltration since the 1950s.

Few foreigners visit the Tibetan communities in these parts, but travel is easy enough because these areas are not classed as "Tibet", so stringent travel restrictions imposed by the Chinese don't apply here. However, deeper in, toward the TAR borders, the policies of PSB offices vary—some turn a blind eye, while others jump on travellers and turn them back if they appear to be headed overland toward Lhasa (which they invariably are).

Following up: There are 2700 pages of further reading, along with photos, maps, charts and other data on the CD-ROM *Tibet Outside the TAR* (produced 1997, available through ICT, Washington).

Key Destinations

Key destinations in Kham and Amdo are the larger monasteries, the object of pilgrims who travel great distances to see them: Kumbum, Labrang, Tongren, Derge and Jyekundo.

Kumbum in Amdo: Kumbum (Taersi) lies 26 km southwest of Xining in Qinghai province. Built in 1577, Kumbum is one of the Big Six—the six great lamaseries of the Geluk sect. Tsongkhapa was born close to this place, and the present Dalai Lama was born in the nearby village of Takster (although there are few Tibetan families remaining in Takster, pilgrims make the trip to the village as a form of homage). In its prime, Kumbum once housed 3000 monks, but under Chinese rule it was closed down and turned into an agricultural commune until it reopened in 1979. Currently, the monastery houses about 400 monks, with half the buildings functioning in museum mode.

Inside a spectacular green-tiled building at Kumbum is a silver pagoda containing the earthly belongings of Tsongkhapa. The monastery is said to have been built around a legendary pipal tree, said to bear a Buddha-like image on every leaf. The lamasery contains a wealth of Chinese and Tibetan styles of architecture, statuary and art. It is famed for its elaborate yak-butter sculptures—in the shapes of animals, landscapes and religious figures—which can reach 15 metres in length. Festivals at Kumbum attract large numbers of Tibetan pilgrims. Because Kumbum is easily accessed (being so close to Xining) it unfortunately also attracts hordes of Chinese tourists, who stand next to chortens or cardboard cutouts to have pictures taken. The monastery has a disturbingly commercialised air about it.

Labrang Monastery, Xiahe: Starting from either Xining or Lanzhou, you can follow a great route southward via the Aba grasslands to Chengdu, passing through ethnic Tibetan areas (travel through Gansu and Sichuan is far more pleasant than travel through barren Qinghai province, which is known as the black hole of China—with many prison camps). The highlight of the trip is a visit to Labrang Monastery in Xiahe, which is wide open to foreign tourists.

From Xining, you can travel by bus to Tongren, a small town with a large monastery constructed in the modern era, with new murals and sculpture. There's a rough road from Tongren over a high pass to reach Xiahe (or you can reach Xiahe from Lanzhou).

Xiahe (Sangchu) is a fascinating town with three distinct populations: Tibetan, Hui Moslem and Chinese. Labrang Monastery in Xiahe is a sprawling monastic walled compound with over a thousand monks—easily the largest and most important monastery outside the TAR. The monastery was built in the early 18th century and contains numerous temples, living quarters, and instructional institutes. From about 1960 to 1980, it was closed down completely, but was miraculously revived in the early 1980s. It is a Buddhist university of sorts—with monks studying logic, medicine and astrology among other disciplines.

From a distance, the lamasery looks to be on the same scale as Tashilhunpo Monastery at Shigatse. With such a large contingent of monks, you can be sure that the Chinese keep a close eye on proceedings. Strangely enough, Tibetan devotional items like prayer wheels and katas are mostly sold here by Hui Moslems (who are Chinese except for their Moslem religion). At a cool 2900 metres, Xiahe is surrounded by hills—it makes an excellent place for hiking, and for following pilgrim circuits.

From Xiahe, heading south across the Aba grasslands, you cross the Gansu border into Sichuan province and on to Zoige, elevation 3400 metres. The town of Zoige, about halfway from Labrang to Chengdu, looks like the perfect set for a Luis Bunuel movie. I saw yaks and cows roaming the streets, dusty Tibetan horsemen (with sheepskin coats trimmed in leopard skin) coming down the main street, and in the middle of it all, Tibetan monks calmly playing billiards on open-air tables. The monks were from a monastery on the outskirts of town—you have to wonder what kind of curriculum they follow. The town also boasts a disco, where the bar dispenses glasses of green tea to the needy, poured from large kettles.

Motoring southward, you reach Songpan, an ancient Chinese garrison town with drum towers and walls. Qiang Tibetan women visiting the market wear elaborate headdresses of amber and coral. Tibetans in this area are Bon: a little way out of Songpan is a Bon monastery, which is rare to find in present-day TAR. You can detect a Bon monastery by the fact that pilgrims circle it anti-clockwise. From Songpan, there's a rough road leading 100 km east to Jiuzhaigou National Park, with superb hiking. Heading south from Songpan, the road drops right off the Tibetan plateau through forested zones, following the banks of the fast-flowing Minjiang River—rolling toward Chengdu, the bustling capital of Sichuan.

Kham Monasteries: These places are extremely difficult to reach, being in obscure locations, and are most likely off-limits to foreign devils. Your progress may be stymied by officialdom. On the Chengdu to Lhasa northern route lies Derge Monastery, just east of Chamdo, near the Yangtse. Derge is the largest woodblock printing monastery left in the Tibetan world. There are two kinds of ink used here—black for religious texts and red for medical text. Some 300 workers under the direction of the abbot assemble texts by hand for shipment to temples in Qinghai, Gansu or Sichuan provinces, as well as to the TAR itself. The monastery possesses several hundred thousand woodblock plates, and a library with rare Sanskrit editions.

Linked to the former kingdom of Derge are two other obscure monasteries to the southeast of Derge. Only reached by horseback (about six hours from the nearest road) is Palpung Gompa, a fortress-style monastery with a complex design, like a mini Potala. The monastery is a base of the Kagyu sect; the gompa has been adopted by the New York-based World Monuments Fund, and placed on its highly endangered list. Four hours away is the Sakya-sect monastery of Baiya, with rare murals.

Precisely in the middle of nowhere (actually near the convergence of the TAR-Sichuan-Qinghai borders) is Jiegu Monastery at the town of Jyekundo (known in Chinese as Yushu). The town was once a busy trading centre for wool and tea; its rich grasslands supported great herds of yaks and sheep. Jiegu temple complex was totally destroyed during the Cultural Revolution, and then totally rebuilt. An unusual feature is the grey-walled cell-like housing of the monks. The town lies at 3700 metres by a river in a pretty valley surrounded by high peaks, with dzong ruins occupying one hilltop.

TIBET IN EXILE

Until the mid-20th century, there was little motivation for Tibetans to leave the sanctuary of Tibet: some Buddhist masters travelled back and forth to India, and certain groups like the Sherpas migrated southward over the Himalayas. The exodus of Tibetans from their homeland really began in earnest with the escape of the Dalai Lama in 1959, who was soon followed by some 60,000 of his people. Today, Tibetan refugees continue to escape, dodging Chinese bullets and biting snowstorms to negotiate high passes when crossing from Tibet into Nepal.

In exile, the Dalai Lama has established nearly 200 monasteries, with over 15,000 monks. There are estimated to be about 140,000 Tibetan refugees living in exile, mostly in India (100,000) and Nepal (perhaps 20,000). The West has been very reluctant to accept Tibetan refugees—occasionally the doors have opened a crack, allowing 2000 to settle in Switzerland, 2500 in the US, and 700 in Canada. In pockets of the Himalayas in India and Nepal, you can see Tibetan culture in a more pristine environment—without Chinese troops and police. Traditions disrupted in Tibet, or festivals that are no longer permitted in the TAR, can be seen in places like Dharamsala. The main Tibetan exile location is India. A rough breakdown of where they live: in northwest India, about 21,000 in Himachal Pradesh, 6500 in Uttar Pradesh, and 5000 in Ladakh; in central India, about 8000; in south India, approximately 30,000; in northeast India, an estimated 8000; while 14,300 live in West Bengal and Sikkim.

India's relations with China are cool, perhaps even cold—as in Cold War. Although India was quick to recognize the PRC when it came to power in 1949, tempers flared over border disputes, with a major showdown in 1962. China considers parts of Sikkim and Arunachal Pradesh to be its territory, as it has never recognized the India-China border drawn up by the colonial British in 1914. China lays claim to 90,000 sq. km of territory in Arunachal Pradesh. In late 1962, the PLA invaded, humiliating the Indian defenders: their artillery and trucks failed to work in the high-altitude conditions and many Indian soldiers fled. Thousands of Indian soldiers were killed. The PLA were within a few days' march of Calcutta when the US airlifted military supplies to India, at which point the PLA abruptly turned around and left, withdrawing to the old border-line. A few months later, Pakistan ceded 25,000 sq. km of disputed Kashmiri territory under its control to China, which enabled the Chinese to build a strategic mountain road connecting Xinjiang to Tibet through the zone (known as Aksai Chin).

In the late 1960s and 1970s China openly armed and trained separatist militants in northeastern India. Since the 1970s, China has given military support to Pakistan, and is believed to be the source of Pakistan's supply of Silkworm missiles—capable of striking Indian cities—and there are strong suspicions that China provided critical expertise and components to enable Pakistan's nuclear testing in 1998. China has given military support and training to three nations surrounding India: to Pakistan, Burma and Bangladesh.

India sees both Pakistan and China as border threats. In 1998, India's Defense Minister, George Fernandes, accused Beijing of stockpiling nuclear weapons in Tibet and extended military airfields in Tibet. In May 1998, India went nuclear: it shocked the world by conducting a series of nuclear tests in Rajasthan. This resulted in economic sanctions by the US, which are hypocritical considering America's nuclear arsenal. Beijing got the message loud and clear: China is not the only nuclear power in the region. A few weeks later, Pakistan exploded a series of nuclear devices, raising the stakes of destabilisation dramatically.

Dharamsala

Arriving in India in 1959, exiled Tibetans did not fare well in hot and humid conditions, and were susceptible to diseases and viruses not found on the Tibetan plateau. Where they could, Tibetans gravitated to mountain zones with cooler climates—to places like Manali and Mussoorie.

The base of the Tibetan government-in-exile is Dharamsala, a former British hill station in Himachal Pradesh, 380 km north of Delhi. India tolerates this government-in-exile, but does not officially recognise it: India does not allow Tibetans to engage in political work, but as one exile put it, "everything we do here is political." Tibetans do not belong to India either. They do not take out Indian citizenship: they remain stateless, so they don't lose their identity. Most have Indian registration certificates. Even Tibetans born in India—who have never been to Tibet—choose to remain stateless.

Dharamsala is the lifeline for Tibetan culture. The Dalai Lama resides here, along with the ministers and cabinet of the government-in-exile, and the oracle of Tibet. At Gangchen Kyishong are the offices of the Central Tibetan Administration, with various ministries and information centres, as well as the Tibetan Computer Resource Centre and the Library of Tibetan Works & Archives. The LTWA acts as a repository for ancient books and manuscripts from Tibet; a team of Tibetan scholars is engaged in translation, research, and publication of books. Among other educational centres around Dharamsala is the Amnye Machen Institute, a small centre for advanced Tibetan studies; the institute also endeavours to expose Tibetans to western literature and culture through translations. Among their publications is a fine map of Lhasa City.

Knowledge of Tibetan medicine is continued through the Tibetan Medical & Astro Institute, the only one of its kind in the world. It dispenses herbal medicines and trains students in Tibetan medical practices; research on new herbal medicines is also carried out here. The Tibetan arts have been revived through the Norbulingka Institute (for Tibetan artisans) and TIPA (Tibetan Institute of Performing Arts). The Tibetan Children's Village, looking after orphans, is operated by the Dalai Lama's sister Jetsun Pema. In Dharamsala you can see festivals celebrated in full fashion, and Tibetan Buddhist ceremonies that carry real meaning (not restricted as they are in Tibet itself). Among the bigger celebrations are Losar (new year) and Monlam.

The Tibetan community-in-exile is not as cohesive as you might think. There are various points-of-view on Tibetan independence—some believe in full independence, others in limited autonomy. Some favour the use of force, fighting a guerrilla war. When it comes to the government-in-exile, the Dalai Lama has tried to establish a quasi-democratic set-up, but this doesn't always work as few would like to oppose him in public. This is where people get confused: opposing a point-of-view of the Dalai Lama is taken as a mark of disrespect. Educated Tibetans say not enough steps have been taken for ushering the Tibetan community into the modern world—for example, translating modern literature into the Tibetan language.

Nor is the faith of Tibetan Buddhism unified. Apart from the four main schools of Tibetan Buddhism, there are a number of off-shoots or sub-sects. A major rift in the community developed in 1997 over a wrathful spirit with three bloodshot eyes, wreathed in the smoke of burning human flesh. Known as Dorje Shugden (Powerful Thunderbolt), this spirit seems to have originated in the 17th century: he is regarded by some as a protector deity, and by others as a murderous demon. The Dalai Lama, beginning in 1976, discouraged the propitiation of Shugden worship on the advice of the state oracle. In 1996, the Dalai Lama prohibited Shugden services in state offices and in government-in-exile-run monasteries, on the grounds that it is damaging to Buddhism. The subject is arcane and complex: several Dalai Lamas—the 5th and 13th in particular—tried to stop the practice and teaching of Dorje Shugden worship. The controversy is on-going: the Chinese, happy at any exile strife, have seized upon the rift to restore Shugden temples in occupied Tibet.

High points: Dharamsala is divided into two very different parts: Kotwali Bazaar and lower Dharamsala, and McLeod Ganj in upper Dharamsala. The centre of activity for the Tibetan exile community is McLeod Ganj, set in forested mountain slopes. This laid-back town of perhaps 6000 has lots of small restaurants and cafés where travellers hang out. Apart from the temples and Tibetan-type attractions of McLeod Ganj, and the opportunity to take meditation classes, there is excellent trekking in the area—with camping trips of up to a week possible. Other excursions include rafting and horseriding.

Hazards/downers: During peak tourist seasons (June and November), the tiny town of McLeod Ganj gets so crowded that it's difficult to find a room in a hotel or guesthouse. People find the place so relaxing they just stay on: there's a very real danger of lingering over apple pie or chocolate cake in the cafés of McLeod Ganj, and completely losing track of time.

Bizarre notes: Nechung Monastery—the former Lhasa seat of the state oracle—was rebuilt in Dharamsala, with 70 monks studying the sacred rituals surrounding the oracle. The oracle is a man who acts as a medium to convey messages to the Dalai Lama from Dorje Drakten, a protector-deity. The messages are used in important decision-making. Ceremonies where the oracle goes into a trance are secret: the oracle is dressed in a traditional brocade costume and a heavy headdress of precious metals. The ceremonial headdress is thought to weigh 20 kilograms: normally it is too heavy to be worn without support. However, when in a trance, the oracle's strength increases considerably, and attendants quickly strap on the headdress. During the trance, the oracle is said to dance around as if the headdress weighs nothing.

Getting there: You can reach McLeod Ganj by day or overnight bus from Delhi, taking about 12 to 15 hours for the 380-km drive. The closest railway station is Pathankot. There's an airfield at Gaggal, connecting to Delhi, Kulu and Simla.

Getting in: Indian visas are valid up to six months; multiple-entry visas are available.

Best time to go: March to the end of June, plus October to November. Watch out for the monsoon (July to mid-September). Winters can be very cold in Dharamsala, but February is when Losar (new year) is usually celebrated.

Following up: *www.tibet.com* is the official website of the government-in-exile: it's maintained by the Office of Tibet in London.

Bodhgaya, Sarnath & South India

Bodhgaya, in Bihar state (in north-central India, due south of Kathmandu), is the place where the Buddha attained enlightenment under a Bodhi tree. The original Bodhi tree was destroyed, but a sapling taken from it was introduced back from Sri Lanka—this exercise was repeated half a dozen times. The present tree is part of the grounds of Mahabodhi Temple. Bodhgaya is today a site of special significance because the Dalai Lama has conducted Kalachakra initiations there. These esoteric initiations were once highly secret and exclusive, only conducted in Tibet. In the ceremony, the initiator would harmonise inner elements of the body and min to bring about harmony and peace in the outer world. In an attempt to counter humankind's destructive forces, the Dalai Lama has dispensed with exclusivity, conducting

Kalachakra initiations around the world: up to 150,000 devotees have attended initiations in Bodhgaya.

Another Kalachakra empowerment site and Indian pilgrimage site visited by the Dalai Lama is Sarnath, 10 km from Varanasi. Sarnath is the site of the Buddha's first sermon at Deer Park, "Setting in Motion the Wheel of the Law." Symbolising this sermon is the golden sculpture of the wheel with two deer that sits over the entrance of most temples in Tibet and is the national emblem of Tibet.

Like neighbouring countries, the Indians are not keen on large groups of Tibetans amassing, which will explain scattered settlements in central India (8000 Tibetans) and south India (30,000 Tibetans) where frontier-type settlements were hacked out of humid jungle, and the temples of Sera, Ganden, Drepung and Tashilhunpo were built anew at Mundgod, Mysore and Byllakuppe.

TIBETAN KINGDOMS & FIEFDOMS

Apart from the three Tibetan realms already mentioned (Tibet proper, Tibet outside the TAR, Tibet in exile), there is another realm: a fourth Tibet. It is largely composed of kingdoms and fiefdoms that broke away from Tibet centuries ago, when Tibet itself still had ruling kings. The people in these places speak and read Tibetan, and follow Tibetan cultural practices, but otherwise have developed their own worlds. They do not identify with Tibetan exiles, nor particularly want to attract them.

INDIA

Ladakh & Zanskar

The kingdoms of Ladakh and Zanskar (northwest India) originally splintered from West Tibet. Tibetans settled in Ladakh between 500 and 600 AD. Upon the death of the King of Ngari (western Tibet) around 930 AD, his kingdom was split between his three sons: one taking Guge and Burang, another Ladakh, and the third Zanskar and Spiti. The kingdoms of Ladakh and Zanskar changed hands numerous times. The most famous king of Ladakh, Senge Namgyal (1616–1642), overran the kingdom of Guge in west Tibet, and even threatened central Tibet. By the end of the 17th century, Ladakh's power was declined, leaving it vulnerable to Muslim incursions.

Due to its strategic location, Leh once hosted a busy trading bazaar, attracting caravans from Kashgar, Khotan, Yarkand, Lhasa and Rawalpindi. With India's independence in 1947, Ladakh was absorbed into the Indian state of Jammu and Kashmir. Pakistan contested the borders and seized Baltistan, plus a part of Ladakh and part of Kashmir. In 1962, the Chinese attacked Ladakh and took over the region east of Nubra, effectively ending any trade. There's a heavy Indian military presence in Ladakh, to counter potential threats from Pakistan and China.

High Points: Dominating Leh is a derelict palace, built in the same monumental style as the Potala. There are many monasteries within easy driving range of Leh: some, such as Hemis Gompa, host traditional festivals and monastic dances. Most imposing of the lamaseries is Tikse Gompa, a fantastic complex that occupies a whole hillside 17 km upstream from Leh; the main hall houses a 15-metre-high seated gold image of Maitreya. There are excellent trekking and mountaineering opportunities in Ladakh and Zanskar—you can put your own small group together and head out with a guide and donkey to carry gear.

Hazards/downers: In snow-blocked months, the only way in is to fly to Leh from Delhi—flights are often overbooked or cancelled, or both. Travellers have experienced the opposite—made it into remote Zanskar but then been unable to get out due to heavy snowfall. Facing the prospect of being locked into Shangri-La for six months till summer, there are two ways out: radio for an Indian helicopter airlift (expensive), or hike out along the ice on the frozen Zanskar River (slippery).

Bizarre notes: Although royalty has largely disappeared from Ladakh, Zanskar still has two kings. The King of Zanskar lives in Padam, and the King of Zangla controls one castle and four villages.

Routes/logistics: Due to sporadic fighting between the Indian army and Kashmiri militants, the Srinagar to Leh route is not recommended (although you can travel from Leh to Lamayuru and back to Leh). Travellers use the Manali to Leh route to enter or exit Ladakh and Zanskar (you should be also aware that foreigners have gone missing in the Kulu Valley near Manali under mysterious circumstances—do not trek alone in this region). Although buses have been known to wheeze over the high passes on the 475-km Manali-Leh route, it is best negotiated by a 4WD vehicle, like a jeep. Along the route lies Tanglang La—at 5330 metres, one of the highest road crossings in the world. The Manali-Leh road is generally open July to October.

Getting In: No special permits are required to visit—an Indian visa suffices. However, certain areas are out of bounds to tourists.

Following up: Andrew Harvey's *A Journey in Ladakh* (1983) is the classic travelogue about the region based on his 1981 trip. On the net, you can access a chunk of the Rough Guide to India (*www.hotwired.com/rough/india/himachal/regions/index.html*)

Darjeeling, Kalimpong & Sikkim

Darjeeling and Kalimpong in northeast India was once controlled by Sikkim, but in the 18th century, Kalimpong was lost to the Bhutanese while Darjeeling fell to the Nepalese. Eventually, the lands fell into the hands of the British East India Company, which developed the region as a tea-growing centre. Darjeeling is a former British hill station—a cool place at 2100 metres, and the base for trekking in the area. From Darjeeling there are views of Kanchenjunga—at 8595m, the third highest peak in the world. There are several Tibetan monasteries around Darjeeling. Apart from being a resort, Darjeeling is a major educational centre—attracting the children of wealthy Sikkimese and Bhutanese.

From Darjeeling you can take a bus, jeep or taxi to Kalimpong. In the days of British Raj, the main wool-trade route to Lhasa was via Kalimpong and Sikkim through Yadong to Gyantse. This trading route has been closed since 1962 as a result of border clashes between China and India, but there is talk of opening it up again. Kalimpong is a pleasant trading town—famed for its cheese—with several Tibetan monasteries. The town attracts Indian tourism.

Sikkim used to be a Tibetan kingdom—a kind of vassal state. Later, it was run by the Rajas of Sikkim; in 1975, it was annexed by India (China also claims the whole of Sikkim). The story of the demise of Sikkim has all the elements of a fairytale—with a bad ending. In Darjeeling in 1959 the crown prince of Sikkim, Palden Thondup Namgyal, met Hope Cooke, an American on a study trip of India. He married her in 1963 at a ceremony at Gangtok Monastery; two years later he became king and she was given the title of queen. But the match did not sit well with the people of Sikkim. Hope Cooke remained distant: she never converted to Buddhism and she made frequent trips to Europe and America with the couple's two children. In 1973 there was a wave of unrest in Sikkim, and Indian troops took advantage of the situation to place the royal family under house arrest. Hope Cooke eventually left the king, returned to New York with her children, and filed for divorce. In 1975, the Sikkim National Congress voted to incorporate Sikkim into India. The monarchy was abolished, and Sikkim was annexed as the 22nd federal state of India. The deposed king died in 1982 in a New York cancer clinic.

Gangtok, elevation 1500 metres, is the capital of Sikkim. Here you can find the former royal palace, the royal chapel, and the Institute of Tibetology, with a fine collection of Buddhist literature. About 25 km from Gangtok is Rumtek Monastery, built as a replica of Tsurphu Monastery (near Lhasa—see *Exploring Central Tibet* chapter for more about Tsurphu) by the exiled head of the Kagyu sect, who fled Tibet in 1959. There are excellent treks north of Gangtok—usually arranged in small groups with permits.

Routes/logistics: Half the thrill is getting there: the "toy train"—a narrow gauge railway completed in 1881—winds up from Siliguri for the 80 km to Darjeeling, passing tea plantations and misty mountains. The closest airport to Darjeeling and Kalimpong is Bagdogra. You can overland from Darjeeling via the border town of Kakarbhitta to Kathmandu.

Getting In: Darjeeling is open without permit. You can obtain a 7-day permit for Sikkim in either Darjeeling or Siliguri. Longer permits for Sikkim may require booking a trek with an agency in advance.

When to Go: Best months are April–May (spring flowers in bloom) and October–November (post-monsoon). Winters are cold, with occasional snowfalls.

NEPAL

Nepal is a small country sitting on a border shared with an up-and-coming super-power. The Nepalese have no desire to confront the PLA, so the Nepalese government has worked closely with the Chinese since their invasion of Tibet, and fully supports the Chinese position in Tibet. There are frequent visits from both sides: King Birendra has visited Lhasa.

In the late 1960s the Chinese requested help in snuffing out Khampa resistance, operating from Nepalese territory, in the region of Mustang. After the Dalai Lama appealed to the Khampas to lay down their arms, the Nepalese Army surrounded the last guerrillas in Mustang and ambushed them. Most were killed.

Nepal is the main conduit for refugees escaping Tibet. They hike over high passes to the south of Tingri and Sakya. Refugees run a gauntlet through Nepal—Nepalese police routinely rob Tibetans and there have been cases of them raping Tibetan women. The Nepalese have in the past co-operated with the Chinese in handing over escaping Tibetans: this policy seems to vary. Escaping Tibetans usually try to reach the safe haven of India, although there are refugee camps for Tibetans in Nepal.

About 20,000 Tibetans exiles living in Nepal. But no politicking is allowed—Nepali officials have sworn to cooperate with Chinese and swear they will not allow any demonstrations by Tibetans in Nepal. In fact, demonstrations have taken place—on March 10, 1998, some 5000 Tibetan refugees gathered at Bodnath Stupa to voice their protest, but were barred from walking to the Chinese Embassy by Nepali police in riot gear.

The Nepalese press is blatantly pro-Chinese, muzzling voices that support the Tibetan cause. Oddly, however, Kathmandu is the best place in Asia or the Indian sub-continent to buy materials on Tibet—Free Tibet stickers, Free Tibet T-shirts, books, magazines, tapes. It is this material that roadblock searches in Tibet are directed at, if you head toward Lhasa by road from Kathmandu.

Two of Nepal's major foreign exchange earners centre around Tibetans: carpets and tourism. The flourishing Tibetan carpet industry—centred in Kathmandu—was initially set up by exiled Tibetans in the early 1960s as part of a Swiss aid project to benefit Tibetan refugees in Nepal. The venture became wildly successful and is a major foreign income earner in Nepal. Tourism in Nepal is largely connected with Tibetans: Kathmandu's most popular temples are Tibetan; the commonest trekking routes are through Sherpa or ethnic Tibetan regions.

Sherpas, a group that migrated from Tibet centuries ago, are directly involved in the tourist, trekking and mountaineering cottage industries. They are often wealthy business people who run lodges, guide groups and so on. Sherpas speak a language similar to Tibetan—they can converse with Tibetans, but have no written language. They are followers of Tibetan Buddhism. Sherpas have been sympathetic to the Tibetan cause, and have formed a kind of "underground" to help arriving refugees in Nepal. There are probably around 20,000 Sherpas living in Nepal—with the strongest base around the Khumbu area. Sherpas are identified by the last name "Sherpa" as in Jangbu Sherpa or Tashi Sherpa. Other Tibetan-related groups in Nepal are the Lhobas from Mustang, the Dolpopas from Dolpo.

High points: In Kathmandu, Bodnath Stupa is the main Tibetan temple area, surrounded by Tibetan-run shops and businesses; further out from Kathmandu is the Monkey Temple in Swayambunath. Nepal is the most "developed" of any of the trekking destinations in the Himalayas. Teahouse trekking is the easiest way to visit regions with Sherpa or Tibetan-related populations—places like Solo Khumbu, Langtang, and Annapurna. A visit to the restricted Mustang or Dolpo regions requires self-sufficient camping trips: usually only in groups, with a liaison officer, and special permits worth $700 per trekker. Both Dolpo and Mustang used to lie on old salt-trading routes from Tibet: Tibetans took salt and wool south to exchange for grains from India.

Hazards/downers: In peak seasons—October especially—popular trails can be jammed with trekkers, and lodges can be full. Near Namche Bazaar, Lukla Airstrip waiting-room can get pretty wild as trekkers and mountaineers duke it out to get on overbooked light aircraft back to Kathmandu. Failure to make it onto a flight may mean a meaningless 10-day walk back.

Bizarre notes: Mustang is a Himalayan kingdom with a real king—King Jigme Parbal Bista, who is the 24th monarch in a line stretching back to the 14th century. His wife, the queen of Mustang, is originally from Shigatse in Tibet. Trekkers take a week to reach the walled citadel of Lo Manthang, where the king lives. If the king is around, trekkers can most likely drop in for a quick audience over a cup of butter tea. Not having the time or the stamina to trek for a week, Nepalese dignitaries have been known to drop in for tea by helicopter—landing in a wheatfield next door to the king's humble palace. The king himself, if he goes out to Jomosom, relies on neither of these transport options. He rides one of his horses out, escorted by a mounted bodyguard. The king breeds the best horses in Mustang: one of his horses can fetch several thousand dollars.

Routes/logistics: Most trips have a start or end point (or both) in Kathmandu. Good trekking equipment can be bought in Kathmandu—a lot is left behind by expeditions.

Getting in: One-month visas are available on arrival at Kathmandu airport, or when coming in by road from Tibet. Visas are easily extendable. If you go trekking, you need a permit for each region to be visited—these are obtained in Kathmandu.

Best time to go: Go in the October–early December or March–April trekking seasons. Avoid the mid-June to late-September monsoon season—trails are slippery, and roads can be washed out, with frequent landslides and mudslides.

Inspiration: *The Snow Leopard* (1987) by Peter Matthiessen, is a finely wrought account of a journey to Dolpo. Matthiessen also wrote text for *East of Lo Monthang* (1995), a photobook featuring pictures of Mustang by Thomas Laird. In the fiction line, *Escape from Kathmandu* (1989) by Kim Stanley Robinson takes the reader on a wild ride, with some hilarious excursions to the Tibetan side. Taking a mystical tack on snowboarding is *Surfing the Himalayas* (1995) by Frederick Lenz.

On the net, an excellent website with many links is run by Amaa Consultants at *www.catmando.com/nepal.htm*. If you go to the news section you can access *Travellers' Nepal* (magazine) and the *Kathmandu Post* (newspaper).

BHUTAN

In the Himalayas, of the vast area that was once the spirited domain of the Tibetan religion and culture—stretching from Ladakh to Yunnan—only the tiny enclave of Bhutan survives as a self-governing entity, with Tibetan Buddhism as its state religion (Outer Mongolia, far to the north, is also independent and follows Tibetan Buddhism, but its people and language are Mongolian). With an area of 47,000 sq. km., Bhutan is roughly the size of Switzerland, and seeks to be as neutral. It allows India to control its foreign policy in exchange for military protection from China. To protect itself from a take-over by India, Bhutan has held a seat at the UN since 1971.

Although Bhutan was self-governing since the 17th century in a kind of theocracy, the Bhutanese monarchy is a hereditary dynasty started in the early 20th century. Ugyen Wangchuk, previously the governor of Bhutan, was crowned hereditary monarch of Bhutan in 1907 with British support, after his role as intermediary between the British and the Tibetans during the Younghusband expedition of 1903.

The present monarch, King Jigme Singye Wangchuk, has been in power since 1972. He is married to four daughters of a Bhutanese nobleman. Through his efforts, Bhutan has entered the international community, establishing diplomatic relations with many countries. King Jigme Wangchuk has fostered the traditional culture of Bhutan to the point of strong-arming other ethnic cultures. The predominant ethnic groups in Bhutan—the Drukpas and Monbas—migrated from Tibet centuries ago. Bhutan, however, is not a safe haven for refugee Tibetans, whom the Bhutanese fear will build up in greater numbers and power (there are several thousand currently living in Bhutan). Nor are they keen on a large Nepalese presence. The southern lowlands are mostly occupied by people of Nepali origin.

Figures on population in Bhutan vary wildly from 600,000 to 1.8 million. How you can lose a million people on a census is hard to fathom, but it seems that in a 1988 census ethnic Nepalis may have actually outnumbered Drukpas in Bhutan, so the government could have rearranged the population figures to suit. The government banned the speaking of Nepalese, and has an on-going program to boot as many ethnic Nepalis as possible back to Nepal, citing their failure to assimilate to Bhutanese culture and learn the language as the reason for marching orders. Numbers of these people languish in refugee camps in southeast Nepal.

The official faith of Bhutan is Drukya Kagyu, a tantric form of Tibetan Buddhism (and a subsect of the Kagyu order); also practiced is Buddhism of the Nyingma school; in Nepali areas, the faith is Indian and Nepali-influenced Hinduism. Bhutan's national language, called Dzongkha, is related to Tibetan but quite different from Lhasa dialect. Dzongkha is a compulsory subject at school—although the medium of instruction is English.

High points: Bhutan has a pristine environment—untouched by industrial development, or in fact any kind of development. The best way to see this beautiful land is by trekking or jeep safari; more recently, whitewater rafting and mountain-biking have been introduced. Top treks include the one north toward Mount Chomolhari on the Tibetan border. Bhutan is famed for its traditional festivals—elaborate affairs with parades, Cham sacred dances and archery contests.

Hazards/downers: The crippling cost of getting into Bhutan—hazardous to your wallet, but the factor that keeps the tourist masses at bay.

Bizarre notes: The king is so intent on preserving the traditional way of life that it is an offence not to wear the wear the national robe (*kho* for men, and *kira* for women)—a fine can be levied. In addition to the national dress, men or women may wear a ceremonial scarf, and men often wear argyle socks.

Getting in: Access is restricted—only in a group-tour or by personal invitation from a party in Bhutan. This policy keeps the numbers down to around 4000 visitors a year. They either fly into the Paro (west of the capital of Thimpu), or come overland through Phuntsoling. With advance clearance, visas are issued on arrival at either location. On group tours a set fee of $120–230 a day is levied on each visitor, depending on the kind of trip. This may sound very high, but it includes all the bills (accommodation, food, trekking equipment, transport). Paperwork can take several months to complete if going through an agent outside Asia; in Kathmandu, the red tape can be completed in a week.

Best time to go: Best seasons are the fall (November) or the spring (April/May). Avoid the June–October monsoon.

Following up: Barbara Crossette's book *So Close to Heaven* (1996) explores the vanishing Buddhist kingdoms of the Himalayas.

For up-to-date information and news snippets on Bhutan, check these websites: *www.bhutan-info.org* (government tourism homepage) and *www.kuensel.com* (national weekly English newspaper online).

OUTER MONGOLIA

Apart from a few monastic visitors, there is no Tibetan presence in Outer Mongolia. It is not a Tibetan kingdom or fiefdom, but the country is mentioned here because it preserves Tibetan Buddhist practices: the national faith of Outer Mongolia is Tibetan Buddhism. Outer Mongolia makes an interesting case study: it was a Tibetan Buddhist nation under Communist (Russian) domination and then regained its independence soon after the collapse of the Soviet Union in 1990. In the 1996 election, the Mongolian Democratic Coalition garnered most of the seats, ending 75 years of communist rule. This is the scenario that intrigues Tibetans most—the Fall of the Chinese Empire (with breakaway slabs being Tibet, Xinjiang and Inner Mongolia).

In the Stalin era, 700 larger and 1000 smaller monasteries were destroyed in Outer Mongolia, and thousands of monks were executed by the Russians in an attempt to wipe out Tibetan Buddhism, the predominant faith in Mongolia. A handful of larger monasteries survived (such as the one at Karakorum), and now, out on the grasslands, felt tents (gers) are converted for use as temples as Tibetan Buddhism enjoys a comeback. Also staging a comeback is Mongolian military hero Genghis Khan. After the last Russian troops left in 1992, Genghis rode back in, appearing larger than life—on the screen in a four-hour epic movie, playing at cinemas in Ulaan Baatar. Genghis' fat bearded face also popped up on banknotes, and on the label of Chinggis Khan Vodka, a twist for the national Russian beverage.

All of which makes the Chinese very nervous—they're not keen on Genghis nationalism spilling over the border into their zone of Inner Mongolia (Genghis Khan's tomb is located in Inner Mongolia). Genghis brings back bad ancestral memories for the Chinese—in the early 13th century his hordes of horsemen surged with ease over the Great Wall, which was designed to keep them out. The Mongols weren't in any hurry to leave, either—the sons and grandsons of Genghis (particularly Kublai Khan) hung around China for the rest of the 13th century. Thus relations with Chinese-controlled Inner Mongolia are testy. There are hardly any Mongolians left in Inner Mongolia anyhow—out of a population of 20 million, perhaps only two million are reckoned to be Mongolians (the rest are Han Chinese settlers). This is what the Dalai Lama points his finger at: Inner Mongolia has been swamped by Han Chinese and has totally lost its identity.

Relations between Tibetans and Outer Mongolians, by contrast, are good. The Sakya sect established relations with the court of Go-dan Khan in the 1240s—an on-going link. At the court of Kublai Khan in the 13th century, a great contest took place to see which philosophy had the greatest power—Islam, Nestorian Christianity, Confucianism, Taoism or Tibetan Buddhism. The latter prevailed, but it was not until the 16th century, under Altan Khan, that Tibetan Buddhism really took hold in Mongolia. Altan Khan conferred the Mongolian title Dalai Lama (meaning "Ocean of Wisdom") on Sonam Gyatso (the third Dalai Lama).

Despite Chinese protests, the current Dalai Lama has visited Outer Mongolia a number of times since 1990, drawing huge crowds. He has established teachings there through his own monks. With the revival of Tibetan Buddhism in Mongolia, the Dalai Lama has a new ally: Buddhism is also rejuvenating in the Mongolian-populated areas of Russia, Buryatia and Tuva, on China's sensitive border zones.

High points: Ulaan Baatar is a dump, with Soviet-style apartment blocks blotting the skyline, but it has an incredible Fine Arts Museum, with intricate bronze statuary and stunning woven or painted tankas, some showing scenes of Lhasa and the Potala. The beautiful statuary in this museum is largely the work of 17th-century master sculptor Zanabazar, who studied in Tibet and returned to Mongolia to spread Tibetan Buddhism.

There are more animals in Outer Mongolia than people—many more—with animal husbandry the mainstay of the economy. With a population of 2.3 million spread over an area of 1.56 million sq. km., Mongolia is very sparsely inhabited and largely untouched—it's one big wildlife sanctuary in a sense, with herds of gazelles, wild camels, wild asses and bighorn sheep roaming the wilderness. That's what is most surprising about a visit to the Gobi Desert—the unexpected amount of wildlife. This is probably the way Tibet used to be. To see this kind of pure environment, go to the mountainous Lake Hovsgol region in the northwest, or to the Gobi in the southwest.

Hazards/downers: Food in Mongolia is hard to find—and inedible when you do find it. Bring your own in the form of freeze-dried soups or meals to supplement the Mongolian meat-based staples.

Bizarre notes: Large, whimsical postage stamps feature subjects like a Mongolian cosmonaut (sent into space on a Russian craft), Mickey Mouse, and Fred Flintstone riding a dinosaur past some *gers*. Also featured on stamps are Taras, and tantric deities locked in *yabyum* embraces. On the 1-tugrig banknote, the snow lion appears—

as it used to on pre-1950 Tibetan money (the watermark on this bill is Genghis Khan).

Routes/logistics: Journeys to Mongolia invariably start and end in Ulaan Baatar. A single passenger rail-line traverses the country from north to south, linking Moscow to Beijing via Ulaan Baatar. There are few roads in Mongolia, but a jeep can go anywhere on the grasslands in the summer—no road is required. As an individual, you'll most likely have to get together with other travellers to rent a jeep. The trick is to find a jeep that has gasoline—there's a severe shortage of the precious stuff. Mongolia is one of the few countries left where ancient Russian turboprop jets are still in use—on domestic runs.

Getting in: Individual travel restrictions have eased up since 1991. The easiest way to get into Mongolia is to extend your stay off the TransMongolian Express. Some longterm visas available direct from embassies from places like London (UK) or Vientiane (Laos). It's hit-and-miss: some embassies issue them, others don't. Monkey Business (aka Monkey Star), a Belgian travel agent with temporary offices in Hong Kong and Beijing, seems adept at getting these visas on short notice—they run tours to Outer Mongolia. You can also get Outer Mongolian visas in Ulan Ude (on the TransMongolian, near Lake Baikal), and in Hohhot, the capital of Inner Mongolia.

Best time to go: Winter is severe with possible heavy snowfall and sub-zero temperatures, made even more subzero by howling winds. In other words, go in the summer—from June to September. The Nadam Fair—featuring horse racing, wrestling and archery— takes place in July.

Inspiration: Tim Severin's book *In Search of Genghis Khan* (1991); on the net, *www.mongoliaonline.mn* has lots of links.

CONTEXT, SUBTEXT
the forces shaping Tibet: facts, arguments, issues

There are so many things wrong with Tibet that it's hard to know where to start. Tibetans experience great frustration that their country is being destroyed and their people persecuted—and the world does nothing about it. In part, this is due to ignorance: the world does not know enough about Tibet or what the contentious issues are. One thing is certain, though: Tibetan culture in Tibet is in dire danger of disappearing altogether.

Long-winded explanations about Tibetan history and culture—and the severe problems that the Tibetans face—tend to flounder because of the complexity of the situation. The following section offers a more concise approach by limiting the scope to 10 issues, raised in 10 simple questions—a kind of "Tibet Top 10." This approach has been adapted from the Tintin Travel Diaries series' *Tibet,* which throws out 30 questions to introduce Tibet to young readers. While this tack may appear simplistic, it narrows the focus and is a lot easier to digest. And hopefully more thought-provoking—maybe it will get you thinking about other simple questions. What have the Chinese got to lose by leaving Tibet? What would happen if the Dalai Lama went back to Lhasa for a visit? There are lots of questions here, but few answers…

History and Culture:
Was Tibet independent?
Can communism and Buddhism co-exist?
What do Tibetan Buddhists believe in?
How do Tibetan nomads survive?
The Trouble with Tibet:
Why do they cut all the trees down?
What rights are the Tibetans fighting for?
How are reincarnate lamas found today?
The Campaign for Tibet:
Who is the Dalai Lama exactly?
How did rock stars get involved in this?
Why did Hollywood lock horns with Beijing?

WAS TIBET INDEPENDENT?

According to China, definitely no. According to the Tibetans, definitely yes. In medieval times, as in Europe and the Americas, boundaries between China and Tibet shifted with political fortunes. At one point, Tibetans were a warrior group that threatened China. At another point, Chinese troops occupied parts of Tibet. So did the Mongols. So did the Nepalese. At various points of Chinese history, the Chinese have been conquered the Mongols and the Manchus, and China has been occupied by the powers of England, France, Germany and Japan.

Tibetan recorded history dates back over 2000 years. The emergence of Tibet as a geopolitical entity dates to the 7th century, when warrior-king Songsten Gampo unified the clans of Tibet. At this time, Tibet was a great military power that expanded its boundaries south into India and east into China. At the centre of Lhasa, outside the Jokhang Temple, stands a stone obelisk that affirms in Tibetan and Chinese the terms of a peace treaty concluded between Tibetan king Ralpachen and Chinese emperor Wangti in the year 823. It is written in stone: "Tibet and China shall abide by the frontiers of which they are now in occupation. All to the east is the country of Great China; and all to the west is, without question, the country of Great Tibet." If Tibet really were part of China, it's odd that the Chinese would wait over a thousand years before staking their claim. A better explanation would be that the Tibetans successfully defended themselves against the Chinese for more than a thousand years.

The snowcapped peaks and high deserts of the Tibetan Plateau served as natural defense barriers to entering Tibet—and increased Tibet's isolation. Curiously, the main Chinese claim to Tibet goes back to an era when China itself was occupied by a foreign power—the Mongols. In the 13th century, the Mongol Khans ruled an empire that stretched as far as Europe. Tibet fell under Mongol domination—and the Mongols took a great interest in Tibetan Buddhism. In 1350, Tibet resumed its independent ways, but enjoyed a special patron-priest relationship with Mongolia over the next few centuries. Invited to educate the Mongols in spiritual matters, the Tibetans in turn accepted Mongolian guarantees to stave off would-be invaders.

By the 17th century, Mongol power was waning, and another set of invaders stormed the Great Wall to occupy China: the Manchus. By this time, Tibet had largely demilitarised—perhaps the first nation in history ever to do so. The national priorities lay in spiritual matters. The Manchus recognised Tibet as an independent nation under the authority of the Dalai Lama, and agreed to protect the peace of the demilitarised nation. Over the next 300 years, Tibet's fortunes fluctuated, with various incursions across its borders by the forces of Nepal, China—and Great Britain.

In 1911, with China weakened by civil war, the Tibetans seized the opportunity to formally announce Tibetan independence, expelling all Chinese from Tibetan soil. Between 1913 and 1950, Tibet asserted its independent status by controlling its own affairs, signing treaties with neighbouring nations, patrolling its own borders, bearing its own flag, and by issuing its own currency, passports and stamps. In this regard, it was actually ahead of its neighbours: India and China shook off the yoke of colonial rule only after World War II.

Pre-1950 Tibet operated under one of the most unusual forms of government in the world: a theocracy, or a Buddhocracy. The people lived in a unique environment—a land situated on the world's highest plateau. Over the last two thousand years, Tibet has nurtured a culture that is very different from that of China—with a separate language and literature, separate form of religion, separate economy and central government, and distinct forms of art and architecture. Out of this rare society—based on the tenets of Tibetan Buddhism— emerged a distinct "Tibetan-ness." It is this Tibetan-ness that forms the basis for their claim to independence.

CAN COMMUNISM AND BUDDHISM CO-EXIST?
No reason why not. Both are rational, non-theistic (no belief in a superior god) and altruistic philosophies. The problem is communist intolerance of Buddhism, not the reverse. In the early years after the

Chinese invasion, the Dalai Lama claimed that he liked some of Mao Zedong's ideas—even going so far as saying he considered himself half-Marxist, half-Buddhist. And Buddhism had long been practiced in China itself. But Mao Zedong told the Dalai Lama "religion is poison."

One of the main reasons the Chinese claimed they set out to "liberate" Tibet was to free it from "feudalism," which, it transpired, meant not only Tibetan aristocrats but also the entire monastic system. The communists lumped Tibetan Buddhism in with the old "feudal" ways of Tibet. The monks did nothing: they just sat around the monasteries and exploited the people—which prevented Tibet from modernising. The question remains: what would've happened if the Chinese had not invaded in 1950? The Dalai Lama—not of age to rule at the time—was most certainly a progressive person who intended to introduce modern ways. He was—and is—fascinated by the West and by modern inventions.

Communist countries have historically replaced Buddhist teachings with communist ideology—weakening the power of the monasteries, eliminating the privileges of monks and discrediting the monastic leadership. Persecution of Buddhists in Russia and Mongolia nearly wiped their numbers out. What does the Chinese communist leadership do about a region that is overwhelmingly Tibetan Buddhist in faith? Well, they set up the Chinese Religious Affairs Bureau to oversee what is happening in the monasteries, to introduce Marxism into the curriculum and to demand allegiance to Beijing. During the Cultural Revolution, statuary at main altars in some Lhasa temples was replaced with portraits of Mao Zedong. Karl Marx believed religion to be the opiate of the masses, employed by repressive regimes to divert the attention of the people from their true enemies. In a true communist society, religion does not exist—it is replaced by loyalty to the Party. A modified version of this is that religious practices that do not harm political rule can be tolerated. In Tibet, however, monks and nuns often spearhead political protest.

WHAT DO TIBETAN BUDDHISTS BELIEVE IN?
Tibetan Buddhism has all the trappings of a religion—temples, abbots, monks, monasteries, sermons, holy texts—but is actually not a religion. With no belief in a superior God, Buddhism does not qualify: in fact, it can be equated with agnosticism.

Buddhism is primarily a philosophical belief system based around respect for all living things, and the concept of compassion—providing a code of ethics to live by. Tibetans are an extremely devout people—Tibetan Buddhism forms a significant part of their lives and their identity. Material gain is not high on the list of priorities for Tibetans: spiritual fulfilment is.

At the core of Buddhism is the concern with suffering—how to overcome that suffering and achieve a full life. The higher goal of Buddhism is to attain enlightenment—which means to be fully awake to the reality of life, to have an understanding of suffering and how it may be overcome. The Buddha is the "enlightened one" or "he who is fully awake." Buddhism is fairly easy-going: it does not require (or expect) converts, or people to spread its message. Neither does it demand sole faith in Buddhism: you can be Jewish, or Christian, or atheist—or communist, for that matter. Except for monks, Buddhism does not require attendance at a fixed place of worship, nor does it have stringent rules or vows to follow.

There are a number of branches of Buddhism—the three major ones are Zen (mainly identified with Japan), Mahayana (identified with Tibet), and Theravada (identified with Thailand and Cambodia). Tibetan Buddhism is unique because it is a blend of Mahayana Buddhism (originally from India) and the ancient Tibetan shamanist cult of Bon, heavily associated with magic and sorcery.

In contrast to the stripped-down tenets of Zen, Tibetan Buddhism hosts a vast pantheon of animist spirits, protectors, tantric deities shown in blissful union with their consorts, and an array of bodhisattvas and Buddhas; other icons are real figures—founders of the various sects and past Dalai Lamas. There are few female deities in the Tibetan Buddhist pantheon; women have a low profile in the leadership of Tibetan Buddhist sects. This is a contentious area of Tibetan Buddhism—and one difficult for Western women to accept. Compared with men, women are considered to be a lower form of incarnation.

Most Tibetan Buddhists believe in reincarnation—on a higher plane, a person is reincarnated as a human, on a lower plane as an animal or an insect. But there is, in addition, belief in the concept of different realms after death. Similar to Christian beliefs in Heaven and Hell (which may have derived from Buddhism), there is belief in an earthly realm, a heavenly realm, a hell realm, and limbo zones like the realm of hungry ghosts. For reincarnation, rebirth in the human world is far preferable to that of hell or hungry ghosts. Only high lamas are said to be able to direct a specific rebirth in their next incarnation.

A related concept is karma—Tibetans believe that they may have inherited some bad karma from previous lives—a situation that must be corrected by doing good deeds in the present life. Many Buddhist practices hinge on accruing merit—doing good deeds. Merit can be accrued by making donations to temples; by assisting in the building or repair of temples, Buddha images or shrines; or by going on pilgrimage to sacred Buddhist sites. In their lifetime, many Tibetans want to undertake a pilgrimage to Lhasa and to Mount Kailash, among other holy places. Karma is cause and effect: good deeds have good effects, bad deeds have bad effects. By following the right path in this life, a person can accrue merit, with karmic carry-over to the next life. A tree drops a seed that becomes a tree—but this tree is not the same as the original one.

One of the ultimate forms of merit-making is to become a monk or a nun. In old Tibet, it was an honour for a family to be able to send a son to a monastery—this was seen as an opportunity to gain a proper education, since monasteries in old Tibet were the only schools. The bulk of Tibetan literature is based on its religion—texts were printed with inked woodblocks at certain monasteries. Unlike Theravadan Buddhist traditions, monks at Tibetan Buddhist monasteries are actively involved in the creation of artwork. Apart from nomad-folk themes, most Tibetan art has a religious function. Inspiration is the goal of the artwork—helping the viewer to spiritual realisation—and thus the creation becomes far more important than the creator: most Tibetan art is anonymous. Tibetan Buddhism is the source of most of Tibet's statuary, tankas and murals, as well as sacred dance and music at festivals—and the temple and shrine architecture that dominated the landscape in old Tibet. A unique Tibetan monastic art-form is the creation of sand mandalas—circular sand paintings made by monks from coloured sand over a period of several weeks. Elaborate ceremonies take place at the monastery during and after completion of the sand mandala: it is then destroyed—to indicate the impermanence of all things.

Since 1959, Tibetan Buddhism has been in a state of flux because traditions were severely disrupted by Chinese takeover, and lineage holders fled into exile. The Tibetans in exile say that real Tibetan Buddhism continues in freedom outside Tibet, but not inside Tibet. The Dalai Lama has attempted to draw the four main schools of Tibetan Buddhism together: the differences between them being more of a political nature than a religious one.

The oldest school is the Nyingma sect, founded around the 7th century by Indian master Padmasambhava. The tradition is carried on through reincarnates of great teachers. The Sakya sect, founded in the 11th century, is not as prominent as the other three schools. At its head is the Sakya Trizin, who fled Tibet in 1959 and established his base in Dehra Dun, India. The Kagyu sect also emerged in the 11th century; the lineage holder is the Karmapa. The 16th Karmapa fled Tibet in 1959 and founded Rumtek monastery in Sikkim; on his death in 1981 a search was conducted for the 17th Karmapa—eventually a boy from east Tibet was installed at the traditional seat of Tsurphu Monastery near Lhasa in 1992. The Geluk sect, founded in the 14th century by Tsongkhapa, is closely associated with the Dalai Lama. The lineage holder is the Ganden Tripa, who is elected every seven years in Dharamsala.

A number of new schools, sub-sects and offshoots have been founded in exile by various masters. Some very strange permutations have taken place in the West. Exiled Tibetan Kagyu lama Chogyam Trungpa (1939–1987) established training centres and retreat communities where he promulgated his "crazy wisdom" visionary approach. In 1970 he shocked his students in Scotland by marrying a young English woman and flying to North America, where he went on to establish a series of dharma centres under the banner of Shambhala International. Chogyam Trungpa was dubbed "the cocktail lama" due to his scandalous predilection for women and wine, and his highly unconventional personality.

One thing that Tibetans in exile have attempted to do is cut down the amount of ritual involved in Tibetan Buddhist ceremonies, and concentrate on the pure elements of Buddhism. In its "purist form", Buddhism has gained wide appeal in the West. But how can the ancient faith of Tibetan Buddhism be in tune with the modern world? Buddhism appeals to the rational, scientific world because the Buddha did not insist that followers accept what he said: he told them to question everything, and test his words for their veracity. Attributed to the Buddha is this disclaimer: "Like analyzing gold through scorching, cutting, and rubbing it, monks and scholars are to adopt my word not for the sake of respecting me, but upon analyzing it well."

HOW DO TIBETAN NOMADS SURVIVE?
Early travellers to Tibet remarked on how cheery Tibetan nomads were in the face of one of the harshest environments in Asia—a high treeless windswept plateau. Maybe its their ribald sense of humour that sustains them in subzero temperatures and howling gales. Whatever the case, the nomads are part of the romance of Tibet—with their yaks, yak-hair tents, their elaborate costumes and jewellery, their raucous folksongs.

It is thought up to a quarter of Tibetans in the TAR—perhaps half a million people—are *drokpas* (pastoral nomads), moving households in search of pasture for their animals. Other traditional occupations for Tibetans were trader, farmer, merchant or monk. Livestock—yaks, goats, sheep, donkeys and ponies—are central to the livelihood of the nomad, and the basis of their culture. Their movements are seasonal, linked to weather conditions and availability of forage for their animals. Tibetans are among the last nomads in Asia—other pastoral nomads include the Mongols (mostly in Outer Mongolia) and the Turkic tribes of China's far northwest, such as the Kazaks. Tibetan nomads face a great battle to retain their way of life as the Chinese are suspicious of those on the move, and attempt to make them settle: the nomad way of life is fast disappearing. True nomads are found in the grasslands of northern Tibet, and at the peripheral zones of Kham and Amdo. Hastening the demise of the nomads are occasional bitterly cold winters. The winter of 1997–98 was particularly savage, with a long snowfall and temperatures of −30 C to −40 C, which wiped out large herds of yaks and sheep. The death toll for nomads was unspecified, but it is certain that a number died.

Playing a key role in the survival of the nomads is the yak—a comical creature best described as a cow with a skirt. The yak is the male animal: the female is called a *dri*, while a yak-cow hybrid is called a *dzo* (a very useful word to remember when you are playing Scrabble). Wild yaks can weigh up to a ton—double the size of domestic yaks. Yaks are superbly adapted to high- altitude living and cold conditions, and are sure-footed on mountain slopes. Tibetans use all parts of the yak. With a harsh climate and a lack of vegetables, meat-eating is a necessity in Tibet. Yak-meat is the principal meat eaten—preserved in dried or semi-dried form. The hair and hide of the yak are used for making thread, blankets, ropes, bags, clothing and boots. Yak milk, yoghurt, butter and cheese provide sustenance. Yak-dung is collected and stacked—it is the main fuel source on the treeless plateau. Yaks are also used for riding (though they hate the idea), as a pack animal, and in farm work (for ploughing). Yak-hide is even used to make ingenious small boats.

Nomads live in thick heavy tents woven from the hair of the yak. These tents can be dismantled piece by piece, rolled up, and loaded onto yaks or donkeys. Upon arrival at a new site, the tent is quickly reassembled. At the centre of the tent is usually a stove, fuelled by yak-dung; one corner of the tent always has a little altar. To beat the cold, Tibetan nomads cocoon themselves in long sheepskin jackets— the top and sleeves can be shuffled off when temperatures rise. Much warmer than sheepwool is foxfur—often used in hats. Cashmere goats provide a particularly fine wool—highly valued in the West. After several valiant efforts to obtain breeding stock for cashmere (wrong animals, two of same sex) the British finally procured some cashmere goats and took them to the far north of Scotland, leaving them out in the freezing cold. However, it clearly wasn't cold enough—or windy enough—for the goats, who refused to grow their cashmere undercoat.

Tibetans are among the few people in Asia who thrive on dairy products—mostly yak and goat derivatives (milk, butter, yoghurt, cheese). The Mongols and the Kazaks eat similar fare. You might have trouble recognising these dairy products: yak-butter floating in the tea—or tooth-breaking pieces of dried cheese, strung together like a necklace. Large amounts of tea are consumed: three to five cups of tea are considered necessary for everyone in the morning, and some people might drink 40 cups a day. Chinese brick tea was once considered so valuable it was a form of currency. Instead of milk, yak-butter is used, and since sugar is hard to come by in Tibet, nomads just use salt! (there are copious salt deposits found near lakes). Tea is made in a wooden churn—a long cylindrical object.

Often mixed with tea and rolled into balls is the great staple of the nomads—*tsampa*. This flour is usually made by roasting barley, but can also be made from corn, wheat, millet or oats. Tsampa is a tasteless flour, but highly sustaining—it is obtained through bartering, and held in cloth bags. It stores very well. Often eaten raw from the bag, tsampa can be consumed in cakes or soup. Pardon the pun, but tsampa is so ingrained in Tibetan nomad life that it is virtually synonymous with Tibet. An American Tibetologist claims one of the key factors for determining if a person is Tibetan or not is whether he or she eats tsampa—and actually enjoys it. Another barley derivative is *chang*, a milky fermented beer that is brewed on special occasions, and frequently offered to guests. Chang can also be made from rice, wheat, corn, oats or millet. Since chang is home- brewed, the alcohol strength varies wildly.

WHY DO THEY CUT ALL THE TREES DOWN?

The Dalai Lama once said that he could understand Chinese anger with Tibetan "separatists", but what did they have against the trees? Why do they cut all the trees down? This raises the essential issue of what the Chinese are doing in Tibet in the first place. The answer is: they're doing what every colonial power has done throughout recorded history—they are exploiting the colony's resources. They are cutting down all the trees because China proper has run out of trees. It is estimated that over 50 percent of Tibet's forests have been cut down since 1959—mostly in eastern, northeastern and southeastern Tibet. If massive clear-cutting takes place on the slopes of the Tibetan plateau, there will be nothing to stop landslides and mudslides cascading down during monsoon season into neighbouring nations like Burma or India. There could be unbridled erosion and flooding in these areas; the monsoon patterns themselves could be affected by change in the ecological balance in Tibet.

Pre-Chinese-occupied Tibet was not a paradise. It was a medieval society that was out of synch with the rest of the world, and which paid dearly for its isolationist policy and its failure to keep abreast of the times. This has led to the conception that Tibet was "backward" or "primitive." In fact, in some ways, the Tibetans were more advanced than their Western counterparts. Though they had no sewage systems or concept of garbage disposal, in the realm of conservation, they were light years ahead of the West. The Buddhist compassion for all life—human, animal or insect—protected Tibet's wildlife, and in a sense, made Tibet one great wildlife preserve. Because Tibet was isolated from the rest of the world for so long, it sheltered rare species: even in the 1990s, species thought long extinct have been discovered in Tibet (a breed of small forest pony was found in Kham, and the Tibetan red deer was found in the Shannan district). Huge herds of wild gazelles, antelopes, wild asses and yaks used to graze the grasslands of Central Tibet. If animals were culled, the Tibetans only took what they needed, so impact on the wildlife was minimal.

With the coming of the Chinese, that all changed rapidly. Chinese soldiers machine-gunned wildlife not only for food, but for export to China—and for sport. Some of Tibet's once-plentiful wildlife now faces extinction: in the last 40 years, large mammals have gone the way of the bison in North America. Apart from supplying China with meat, there is a demand for rare animals in Chinese restaurants and for Chinese traditional medicine. This has decimated numbers of the snow leopard, for instance.

Tibetan Buddhists have a sense of sacred landscape. Larger lakes and mountains were sacred—left untouched—and mining was rare. With its harsh environment, Tibet has a delicate ecological balance—one with which the Chinese are interfering. Such interference can have disastrous consequences, leading to increased desertification at Qinghai Lake—or destruction of an entire ecosystem. This may be happening with the building of a hydroelectric project at Lake Yamdrok Tso—a highly controversial project that the Chinese have rushed, with uncertain results. Another dam is being constructed in

Kham. The Chinese have made a priority of exploiting Tibet's untapped oil and mineral wealth. Oil fields in Amdo produce over a million tons of crude oil a year; in 1997, more oil fields were discovered in the Changtang region of northern Tibet.

Apart from exploitation of natural resources comes the threat of pollution of existing ones. Although Chinese officials have shied away from the topic, there is evidence that remote parts of Tibet have been used for the dumping of nuclear waste. China is interested in using Tibet as a missile-launching site, targeting Indian cities. There are a number of missile bases and military airfields scattered around Tibet. Far more progressive is the Dalai Lama's vision. He calls for complete demilitarisation of the region of Tibet, to serve as a buffer between the nations of India and China. He envisages the transformation of Tibet into a sanctuary, a zone of peace—as it once used to be.

WHAT RIGHTS ARE THE TIBETANS FIGHTING FOR?

December 10, 1998 marks the 50th anniversary of the United Nations' adoption of the Universal Declaration of Human Rights (UDHR). This document was principally crafted by Canadian law professor John Humphrey as the UN response to atrocities committed during WWII—ostensibly to ensure that horrors like the Jewish Holocaust would never happen again. In Tibet, they happened again—within a scant 15 years of that declaration: 1998 also marks the 48th year in a row that the UN has turned a blind eye to the devastation China has wreaked in Tibet, violating the majority of the 30 articles of the UDHR. True, in 1959, 1961 and 1965, resolutions were passed at the UN demanding that China respect the UDHR in Tibet, but there was no punch behind the resolutions. They were promulgated before the PRC became one of the five permanent members of the UN Security Council, with full veto power.

Why Are We Silent? This is the title of a 60-second cinema ad about Tibet, marking the 50th anniversary of the UDHR. The clip features six movie and rock stars reading extracts from the UDHR against a background of Tibetan imagery. In early 1998, members of the Tibetan Youth Congress staged a hunger strike in Delhi. Six hunger strikers, representing the six million people of Tibet, demanded that the UN resume its debate on the question of Tibet; that the UN appoint a Special Rapporteur to investigate the situation of human rights in Tibet; and that the UN appoint a Special Envoy to promote a peaceful settlement of the question of Tibet and initiate a UN-supervised plebiscite to ascertain the wishes of the Tibetan people. The lengthy strike was broken up by the Indian police.

China has one of the worst human-rights violation records in the world. The US Department of State's 1997 report on Tibet slams China for "serious human rights abuses in Tibet" and for imposing "intensified controls on fundamental freedoms." Evidence for reports like this is drawn from interviews with credible Tibetan refugees, who tell of forced sterilisations and abortions, as well as arbitrary arrest, torture in prisons, and cases of summary execution. Despite mounting evidence, China vigorously denies any transgressions, says that torture has been completely abolished, and claims that Tibetan people have gained real democracy and equality after 1959 "democratic reforms". Beijing blithely churns out glossy brochures in English that quote the UDHR to back up the Chinese claim that rights are better now than they were under the Dalai Lamas. This won't explain why Tibetan monks have been given long prison sentences for translating the UDHR into the Tibetan language. Meanwhile, Clinton, who in 1992 delighted in mocking George Bush for consorting with Chinese communists "despite their undisguised contempt for democracy and human rights" has done an about-face. The Clinton administration has delinked human-rights issues from trade, and continues to affirm China's Most Favoured Nation trading status.

What human rights do the Tibetans want? The basic ones: the right to freedom of speech, freedom of thought, and freedom to follow Tibetan Buddhist beliefs. The right to a proper education, the right to use the Tibetan language. The rights of the child. Even the most fundamental of human rights are denied to Tibetans. These include the rights to clean water, sufficient food, a home, health care, proper education, employment, protection from violence, equality of opportunity, and a say in their future. In Tibet, Chinese violations of the UDHR are so blatant that they have led scholar Robert Thurman to say "Tibetans are the baby seals of the human rights movement." The Dalai Lama puts it this way: "the Chinese are entitled to their happiness, but not at the expense of another nation or people." He accuses the Chinese of pursuing a deliberate policy of cultural genocide in Tibet. By the government-in-exile count, over a million Tibetans have perished—either directly or indirectly—at the hands of the Chinese since the 1950s.

Population Transfer

Before 1950, there were no Chinese settlers in the TAR. Accurate figures on current Chinese population in Tibet are hard to come by: Chinese figures do not include the sizeable military contingent. However, it is certain that China is providing incentives to bring settlers into Tibet—higher salaries, more benefits and tax breaks. In the provinces at the edge of the TAR, Han Chinese settlers outnumber the Tibetans. The Chinese do not integrate with the Tibetans, nor bother to learn the language. Not only are they starting to outnumber the Tibetans, they are reducing them to second-class citizens in their own land. For doing the same job, Chinese workers are usually paid a higher salary than Tibetans.

In Inner Mongolia, after 1949, when the communists took control, millions of Han Chinese flooded onto the steppes—with government encouragement and incentives. The Mongols are now a minority in their own land—there are now 20 million Han versus four million Mongolians. Mongol nomad livelihood has been severely disrupted by Han Chinese turning pasture into irrigated farmland. All this is in contravention of the Geneva Convention. A similar situation appears to be developing in Tibet.

Political Prisoners

Numbers of political prisoners held in prisons in Tibet range from an estimated 1210 (government-in-exile figure) to 50 (Chinese figure). The Chinese figure is skewed because Chinese officials maintain that prisoners in Tibet are common criminals, not political prisoners. If a prisoner is convicted for holding up a Tibetan flag, this is noted as "prisoner trying to incite public disorder" so somehow it becomes a criminal offense, not a political one. Conditions in prison are poor, with beatings and torture routine. Across China, about 6000 prisoners a year are executed (this figure is only an estimate, but one which outstrips all other countries in the world combined). Prisoners are usually executed with a bullet to the back of the head: the bill for the bullet is often sent to the family of the executed, as further humiliation. There is some evidence that body parts of executed prisoners are sold on the international market. Chinese spokespeople blithely deny that any of this ever takes place.

Prisoners of Conscience

Believed to be the world's youngest political prisoner is Gedhun Choekyi Nyima, the Dalai Lama's choice for 11th Panchen Lama. His whereabouts are unknown: he has not been seen in public since May 1995. In August 1995, Ngawang Choephel disappeared in Tibet. Choephel is a Fulbright scholar who was researching traditional music in Tibet and videotaping dance and song performances. It was not for another 14 months that his mother discovered that he was still alive—and in prison. He was charged with spying for the Tibetan government-in-exile—a sentence of 18 years was handed down.

Ngawang Sangdrol is a nun who was 13 years old when she was first jailed for demonstrating for a free Tibet. After her release, she was forbidden to rejoin her monastery. In 1992, she was arrested again for demonstrating and sentenced to three years in jail. In 1993, while in prison, Ngawang and 13 other nuns recorded Tibetan protest songs—the tape was smuggled out by a sympathiser and taken to the West. When they learned of this, the Chinese increased the nuns' sentences a further six years. In 1996, Ngawang's sentence was increased a further nine years: she is not due for release until the year 2010. In a rare protest from the UN, in 1995 the UN Working Group on Arbitrary Detentions ruled the nun had been punished for exercising her rights to freedom of opinion. The group called on China to release her, in line with the principles of the UDHR—a call that was ignored by the Chinese. In 1998, as part of a campaign commemorating the 50th anniversary of the Universal Declaration, Ngawang Sangdrol was featured in a joint campaign by the Body Shop and Amnesty International, putting some pressure on the Chinese.

Religious Freedom

It is estimated that up to 70 percent of political prisoners in Tibet are monks and nuns. The reason they are imprisoned is a combination of their political attitudes and their fight for religious freedom. In the past, monks and nuns have spearheaded the Tibetan independence movement: their vows may empower them to act politically. Celibacy puts them in a better position to sacrifice their lives as opposed to those with families. And dying for Tibetan independence is a selfless act guaranteeing a human rebirth in the next life.

Since April 1996, Chinese officials have conducted a "Strike Hard" campaign, deliberately directed at monks and nuns. Chinese work-teams have been dispatched to all monasteries and nunneries in Tibet for "patriotic re-education" (an on-going process). Dalai Lama pictures have been banned in all temples and public places, and Tibetan monks and nuns are required to sign a five-point agreement—pledging to oppose the idea of an independent Tibet, to denounce the Dalai Lama, to recognise the Chinese-appointed Panchen Lama, to oppose those advocating independence for Tibet, and to work for the unity of "the motherland". According to China's own statements, the majority of Tibet's 46,000 monks and nuns in 1700 monasteries and nunneries have come under the program. As a result, in the first two years of the program, it is estimated that 14 monks and nuns died, upwards of 300 were arrested, and over 3000 were expelled from their monasteries or nunneries. In addition, seven monasteries and nunneries were completely closed down.

HOW ARE REINCARNATE LAMAS FOUND TODAY?

One of the major rights that Tibetans are fighting for is freedom to follow Tibetan Buddhist beliefs. Tibetans in exile maintain that they are the last refuge for Tibetan Buddhist practices, and that its survival lies with Tibet in exile. However, there are quite a number of obstacles to that survival. One of them is how and where to find incarnates.

In Tibetan Buddhism, a high lama is said to be able to redirect his soul into the body of another. The reincarnate is known as a *tulku*, or Living Buddha, and is usually found in a one- to three-year-old boy (if the search takes longer, the boy could be up to six or older). Most tulkus are officially instated at four or five years old. Finding the incarnation of a high lama upon his death is a complicated matter for the Tibetans—it involves the assessing of omens and portents, consulting the state oracle, performing divinations for clues, and perhaps visiting Tibet's sacred oracle lake, Lhamo Latso. Potential candidates are screened through extensive interviews; the final confirmation of a reincarnate is made by the Dalai Lama himself.

After the Dalai Lama's flight to India in 1959, the process of finding and verifying reincarnate lamas has become even more complicated because it must be determined if the incarnate has been born inside or outside Tibet. Most are now found outside Tibet: tulkus have been found among the Tibetan exile community in India and in Switzerland. If a tulku is discovered inside Tibet, it is difficult for the Dalai Lama's emissaries to carry out the selection process. This puzzles the Tibetan community-in-exile: where are the reincarnates to be found? And if one is discovered inside Tibet, what should be done about it? Can a reincarnate be a Westerner?

Asked about his own incarnation, the Dalai Lama has said that logically if he is in exile, his reincarnate can only be found in exile. But he has wavered on the question of whether the method of finding the Dalai Lama should be altered—whether the Dalai Lama should be chosen democratically, like the Pope. In the case of the Geluk Sect throneholder, the process has been altered: the leader is elected in Dharamsala every seven years. The Dalai Lama has also taken the unusual step of saying in an interview that in future the Dalai Lama could be a woman (all 14 Dalai Lamas thus far have been men). The stories behind three controversial tulkus are briefly described here.

The Spanish Lama

Dharamsala, March 1987: a two-year-old boy, Osel Torres, is enthroned with much pomp and ceremony as the reincarnation of renowned teacher Lama Thubten Yeshe. Lama Yeshe was the founder of the Foundation for the Preservation of the Mahayana Tradition (FPMT), an international organisation with over 80 dharma centres worldwide. Osel ("Clear Light") was discovered through oracles and dreams by Lama Zopa Rinpoche, who took over directing the FPMT after the death of Lama Yeshe. Subjected to traditional tests, Osel passed with flying colours, and at the age of two was recognised by the Dalai Lama. One major difference: Osel is Western. Since globe-trotting Lama Yeshe was one of the biggest transmitters of Tibetan Buddhism in the West, it was reasoned his reincarnate was Western also. Lama Osel is the son of Paco and Maria Torres, who were devoted followers of Lama Yeshe in Spain; the couple have five other children. Lama Osel went on to receive a formal Tibetan education at Sera Monastery in South India. Reincarnate lamas undergo severe training: without special qualities, most would collapse under the strain. The strain is greater on Osel because he is Western, thus making him a celebrity lama—one scrutinised by Western media.

The Karmapa Returns

Officially, the Chinese are atheist, and have ignored the selection of reincarnate lamas as "feudal superstition." This attitude, however, has changed: in 1992, the Chinese recognised an incarnate in the 17th Karmapa of the Kagyu sect, enthroned at Tsurphu Monastery, assisted by the Chinese Religious Affairs Bureau. This is the first time since 1959 that the Chinese have recognised an incarnate, although it appears in this case they wanted to direct the choice of the incarnate. The choice of the 17th Karmapa, a boy from eastern Tibet, has caused a rift among Kagyu sect followers at Rumtek Monastery in Sikkim, where the 16th Karmapa lived in exile until his death. However, it appeared from the choice of the 17th Karmapa that was possible for an incarnate to be found within Tibet and approved by both the Dalai Lama and the Chinese. That is, until the events of early 1995.

The Case of the Missing Lama

In January 1989, when the 10th Panchen Lama died of a heart attack at Tashilhunpo Monastery in Shigatse, the Dalai Lama's government-in-exile started collecting names of potential candidates. In 1991, a divination was performed that determined the reincarnate had been born inside Tibet. Approaches to Beijing to co-operate in a search for the incarnate were rejected, but in 1993, a message was sent to India by Chatral Rinpoche, the head abbot of Tashilhunpo Monastery, explaining that the proper rituals were being carried out. The search by a committee from the monastery (sanctioned by the Chinese) had whittled down the number of candidates. A six-year-old boy from Nagqu (northern Tibet), named Gedhun Choekyi Nyima, looked most promising.

Several divinations were performed in Dharamsala, India, in early 1995 to determine if the boy was the right candidate, and these proved positive. On this basis, in May 1995, the Dalai Lama declared the child the official 11th Panchen Lama. At this point, all the Chinese had to do was go along with the Dalai Lama's choice—the boy was, after all, one of their own sanctioned candidates. But Chinese officials were apparently infuriated that the choice of candidates had been "leaked" to the Dalai Lama's government-in-exile.

This time, for the first time since taking over Tibet, the Chinese stepped in—in a big way. They condemned the Dalai Lama's choice, detained Chatral Rinpoche (the abbot responsible for the search), and took the six-year-old in question into custody—making him the world's youngest political prisoner. Neither the boy nor his parents have been seen in public since, leading to fears for their safety.

In the meantime, Tashilhunpo Monastery split into pro-Dalai Lama and pro-Chinese factions—an estimated 50 Tibetans were detained following the fallout. In July 1995 the leading lamas at Tashilhunpo were sacked, and replaced with pro-Chinese head lamas. In November that year, 75 Tibetan Buddhist leaders were rushed to Beijing, lectured by President Jiang Zemin, told to reject the Dalai Lama's choice, and asked to prepare another list of candidates. The new candidate would be selected by drawing a ball from the Golden Urn—a lottery system from the 18th century, from an outdated Mongolian treaty.

In November 1995, another six-year-old boy from Nagqu, named Gyaltsen Norbu, was virtually hand-picked by the Chinese as the new Panchen Lama. Ten days later, at a highly-publicized enthronement ceremony, security was tight, with hundreds of PLA troops deployed at Tashilhunpo Monastery. In January 1996, Gyaltsen Norbu was in Beijing, shown being greeted by President Jiang Zemin. The Chinese choice for Panchen Lama does not seem to spend much time in Shigatse—the reason given is safety concerns (that he will be threatened by Tibetans).

The interference of atheist China in Tibetan Buddhist ritual is hard to fathom. Did it really matter to the Chinese which six-year-old boy from Nagqu was chosen? To the Tibetans it does—no Tibetan will accept a Panchen Lama who is not verified and sanctioned by the Dalai Lama. The only way the Tibetans will accept such a choice is under duress—and this is apparently the next step, as Chinese force monks in major monasteries to swear that the Chinese choice is the only legitimate one, and to renounce the Dalai Lama. A deluge of Panchen Lama posters, pictures, books and videos spreads the word of the Chinese choice. As for the Dalai Lama's choice: blackmarket pictures of the missing lama are sold in Lhasa—despite the risk of a jail sentence if found in possession of such a picture.

In the aftermath of these events, the abbot of Tashilhunpo Monastery, Chatral Rinpoche, was sentenced to six years in jail for "leaking state secrets". The head of the Tantric University at Tashilhunpo, Kachen Lobsang Choedrak, was detained; and the secretary of Tashilhunpo, Gyatrul Rinpoche, was fined and expelled for refusing to endorse the Chinese-chosen candidate. Chinese work-teams moved into Tashilhunpo Monastery to force monks to pledge their loyalty to the communist party—those refusing to do so were expelled or imprisoned.

Conflicting reports have been given by the Chinese concerning the whereabouts of Gedhun Choekyi Nyima, the Dalai Lama's choice. Chinese officials have variously said the boy is living in Beijing, or in a town in the north of Tibet. In February 1996, in the aftermath of the Panchen Lama run-in, an intense anti-Dalai Lama campaign was launched—with the removal of all Dalai Lama pictures, including those from the Potala. Monks were told to sign pledges denouncing the Dalai Lama and approving the Chinese choice of Panchen Lama.

WHO IS THE DALAI LAMA EXACTLY?
He's funny, he's charismatic, he has a deep booming voice. He's a thorn in the side of the Chinese, who vigorously protested the award of the Nobel Peace Prize to him in 1989. He cracks jokes on the Larry King show. He's been a guest editor at French *Vogue*, and has written introductions to scores of books about Tibet. He's been featured on the cover of numerous magazines, and in billboard ads by Apple Computers as one of the great thinkers of the 20th century—in the same league as Einstein and Picasso (the Dalai Lama's picture, however, did not appear in billboards in Hong Kong).

Who is he? The title is synonymous with Tibet: the Dalai Lama is Tibet's greatest campaigner. Revered as the living incarnation of the bodhisattva of Compassion, Tenzin Gyatso is the spiritual leader of all the Tibetan Buddhist sects. The Dalai Lama claims he is a simple monk ("a naughty Buddhist monk") but he's much more than that: his upper arm bears vaccination scars, revealing how well-travelled he is. He is a fighter for Tibetan rights, the foremost proponent of world peace—and tireless promotor of what he calls his real religion: kindness and compassion.

The Dalai Lama is an international icon, and inspiration to millions of Buddhists—and to millions of advocates of nonviolence and right living. On a global basis, he has no equal (the Pope comes to mind, but the Pope is a proselytiser, seeking converts—the Dalai Lama doesn't). He cuts across barriers of race, religion and creed. All this is even more remarkable when you consider that the Dalai Lama's first language is not English, and that no government is willing to recognise him as a political leader—they accept him as a Nobel laureate or as leader of Tibetan Buddhism. The Dalai Lama has significantly raised awareness about Tibet, and the countries of Costa Rica, Poland and Norway have voiced support for Tibet in international forums.

The Dalai Lama's life has undergone fantastic twists and turns: the stuff that legends—and Hollywood movies—are made of. The Tibetan system of finding reincarnates, based on oracles and visions, dates back to the 15th century. Since lamas in the Geluk sect were celibate, a method of selecting the leader had to be arrived at. The system of choosing a reincarnate worked beautifully—no king's sons fighting each other for the throne, no dispute over who would reign. It was, in addition, egalitarian—the reincarnate could come from an impoverished nomad family. The 14th Dalai Lama was born in a cowshed in Amdo Province, of a very poor family. At age two, he was identified by disguised lamas as the reincarnation of the 13th Dalai Lama—and the spiritual leader of four million Tibetans. His family were informed they would be moving to Lhasa. The boy was installed at the age of four upon the Lion Throne in Lhasa, and embarked upon a formidable course of monastic studies—training in Tibetan Buddhist metaphysics that would continue for the next 18 years. His new home was the dark, thousand-room Potala Palace.

In 1950, the Chinese invaded Tibet; a month after the attack, the Dalai Lama was rushed through an enthronement ceremony to give him his majority—and assume the leadership of Tibet in the face of Chinese aggression. He was just 15 at the time. At age 18, he was negotiating face-to-face with Mao Zedong and Zhou Enlai over the fate of Tibet. In 1959, at the age of 23, the Dalai Lama escaped from Lhasa—ironically disguised as a soldier—and fled into exile in India, losing his country and his people. He issued a statement condemning the Chinese. He was just a Tibetan refugee, and a humble monk—no passport, no country, no status.

The Dalai Lama still travels on a refugee's yellow identity certificate. If anyone had told the Dalai Lama back in 1959 that he would still be in exile 40 years later, he wouldn't have believed it. Other Dalai Lamas had fled Tibet during political crises—to Mongolia, to India—but only for a period of a few years. Tibetans going into exile in 1959 all believed they would soon return, and have not tried to take out Indian citizenship because it would mean a loss of their Tibetan identity.

The Dalai Lama's idol is Mahatma Gandhi—from whom he learned the path of nonviolence. But this path has produced no concrete results: the Dalai Lama is in a dilemma because nothing has become of his peaceful approaches in the last 40 years. The Chinese pre-condition for discussion about Tibet is that the Dalai Lama abandon any thought of independence. The Dalai Lama has in fact abandoned his position of asking for full independence, and is asking for autonomy within the PRC, similar to what existed in Tibet from 1950 to 1959, and similar to the system guaranteed for 50 years in Hong Kong SAR (Special Administrative Region), whereby Hong Kong continues its free ways but cedes military power to the PRC. But even this has not brought the Chinese to the negotiating table, because the Chinese claim that Tibet already is autonomous and that what the Dalai Lama is really after is independence. What keeps the Dalai Lama going? "A belief in the rights that we have," he says. It is the Tibetan struggle in a nutshell.

After his dramatic escape in 1959, the Dalai Lama kept a low profile through the 1960s, engaging in personal retreats. In 1974, he took his first trip to the West. Since then he has globe-trotted at an astounding rate, spreading the message about Tibet and his ideas on world peace. Dalai Lama's most endearing quality is what he calls a "radical informality"—his uncanny skill at cutting to the heart of the matter, and being on the same wavelength as ordinary people. He is one of Tibet's most accomplished philosophers, trained in a traditional Tibetan system—and yet he comes across as a kind of jovial uncle.

HOW DID ROCK STARS GET INVOLVED IN THIS?

Having largely failed to interest politicians in his agenda, the Dalai Lama has been looking elsewhere, and found new avenues to broadcast his message—in movies and in rock music. Rock stars helped many causes—rainforests, Biafra—but none as on-going as Tibet. Tibetan Freedom Concerts are organised by Adam Yauch of the Beastie Boys, who swore off punk lifestyle excesses and drugs after trekking in Nepal. In 1992, on the trail in Nepal, Yauch encountered a group of Tibetan refugees fleeing over the Himalayas. He travelled with them to a refugee community in Kathmandu, where he ran into Erin Potts.

Later, when the Beastie Boys were recording an album, Yauch contacted Erin Potts and asked how he could donate royalties from the songs. Potts suggested Yauch give the money to small groups to raise awareness about Tibet. Yauch talked about Potts doing the work, and "it just kept expanding from there." Potts and Yauch co-founded the Milarepa Fund, a non-profit organisation protesting human-rights abuses in Tibet. It is named after the 11th century Tibetan sage who enlightened his students through music and poetry.

In 1996 Yauch and the Beastie Boys organised the first Tibetan Freedom Concert, held in Golden Gate Park, San Francisco—where it attracted 100,000 people. Appearing were a mixture of international artists—U2, Radiohead, Alanis Morissette—as well as Tibetan musicians like Nawang Khechog. Although most came for the music, and the musicians did not perform songs specifically about Tibet, there were brief on-stage presentations about Tibet—a mix of monks and punks. Guest speakers at the 1996 Tibetan Freedom Concert included monk Palden Gyatso (imprisoned in Tibet for over 30 years) and Tibetan scholar Robert Thurman; opening and closing the day's music were monks offering prayers. The concerts were cybercast live on the net, drawing a huge following; 1998 saw the release of a "rockumentary" about the concerts, called *Free Tibet*. Yauch plans to hold a Tibetan Freedom Concert every year—and he's kept the momentum up. At the 1997 concert, held in New York, Tibetan monks recited Buddhist chants to bless the concert area before rock royalty took the stage. The June 1998 Tibetan Freedom Concert, held in Washington, DC, attracted a crowd of 120,000 and featured performers like REM, Sean Lennon and Jakob Dylan; Adam Yauch and the Beastie Boys performed a set of hip-hop and instrumental funk. There are plans afoot for Tibetan Freedom Concerts in other countries, such as Australia.

Proceeds from the concerts and CDs goes to funding the Milarepa Fund, which supports Tibetan refugee programs in India and Nepal, and other projects like awareness campaigns conducted by Students for a Free Tibet on college campuses. In fact, the growth of SFT was spurred largely by the 1996 Tibetan Freedom Concert: SFT is the fastest-growing movement in US colleges today, with over 350 chapters in schools, colleges and universities.

As part of the concerts, vendors and suppliers agree not to sell anything made in China or involved with the US-China Business Council. This puts Coke, Pepsi and Budweiser out of the picture—

and Reebok is out too. So is Motorola, but concessions had to be made—at the 1997 concert, security guards used walkie-talkies made by Motorola. It's hard, it seems, to completely avoid products made or assembled in China (the Tibetan government-in-exile does not support a boycott like this). A kind of reverse embargo: in 1998, an official at the Chinese Embassy in London said that China would not welcome the music of those artists taking part in the concert, and they would not be allowed to visit China. Since China is one of the world's worst copyright transgressors (there are factories in China that copy CDs and cassettes and distribute them in Asia) the first restriction is hardly a threat. The official further stated that Western artists had no right to interfere in China's internal affairs.

WHY DID HOLLYWOOD LOCK HORNS WITH BEIJING?

Gyantse, November, 1987: a young British tourist, Kris Tait, is accosted by a Chinese soldier on a bicycle, who tries to tear off her T-shirt. She at first assumes he's trying to assault her, but when a Tibetan crowd gathers—chanting "Dalai Lama!"—it occurs to her that the soldier is after the T-shirt, which appears to bear an image of the Dalai Lama printed on it. Actually the T-shirt is embossed with the mug of the late Phil Silvers, a cult figure from late night BBC reruns of the 1950s American TV series, Sergeant Bilko. The woman manages to wrench free from the soldier, and flees to her guesthouse to change clothes. Kris Tait, an avid Bilko fan, later says there is a resemblance between Silvers and the Dalai Lama—the same quizzical eyebrows, the same thick glasses. Hollywood's dust-up with the Chinese over the Dalai Lama has just begun.

Dissolve to 1997, when the sleeves are rolled up, and the big brawls begin, as Hollywood takes on China in earnest, with full-length movies about the Dalai Lama in the works. Disney's Touchstone Pictures is faced with the most momentous decision of its corporate career—sell Mickey Mouse in China, or humour director Martin Scorsese? Which goes? Whose wrath will be greater to face—that of surly Chinese officials, or of Scorsese without his morning coffee? Scorsese is filming a movie about the early life of the Dalai Lama—one which has raised the hackles of the Chinese, who threatened to halt work on the creation of a Disneyland near Shanghai. The clash of the Titans has begun.

Flashback to 1937: Frank Capra's epic, *Lost Horizon*, is released by Columbia TriStar. The film, based on the book of the same name, is the first big budget movie to use a Tibetan setting: a Tibetan monastery high in the snowcapped mountains where the wisdom of the ages is preserved by wizened lamas. The film cost four times the amount of any Columbia TriStar film at the time, using a set considered the largest ever built in Hollywood. During WWII, Tibet remained neutral—a kind of Switzerland in High Asia (although the British Mission remained in Lhasa, without official diplomatic status). *Lost Horizon* was widely circulated among the armed forces during WWII—it bolstered the hope that there was a place during mankind's darkest days where the values of civilisation were preserved. Sixty years later, Columbia TriStar released *Seven Years in Tibet*, quite a different version of Shangri-La—one man's vision of the last years before Tibet itself was engulfed in war and chaos.

Why the sudden Hollywood interest in Tibet after a 60-year silence on the subject? Why did the 1990s produce a rash of Tibet films? And why is Beijing upset about them? In part, Hollywood's interest in Tibet is attributable to the collapse of the USSR and the demise of the Cold War: China provides a new "evil empire" to crusade against, in the vacuum left by the demise of Russia. China is the world's most populous nation, with expanding economic clout and a world-class nuclear arsenal. China is an up-and-coming superpower with a ruthless leadership: a change of Western attitude to China definitely occurred after the Tiananmen Massacre in 1989. Suddenly, what the Dalai Lama had been saying all along—that the Chinese were killing Tibetans—was blatantly demonstrated at Tiananmen when the Chinese opened fire on their own people. An indicator of this shift of evil empires was the plot of the 1997 James Bond flick, *Tomorrow Never Dies*. No KGB here: the movie was originally slated to be about the handover of Hong Kong, but missed its timing so the script was changed to a stand-off between China and Britain, with the two teetering on the brink of war because of the ambitions of an out-of-control media megalomaniac (modelled on Rupert Murdoch).

In part, Hollywood's interest in Tibet is related to new-found interest in Buddhism in the US, and to celebrity actors like Richard Gere, Harrison Ford and Uma Thurman supporting the Tibetan cause. Tibet has become chic following the popularity of the Dalai Lama after his 1989 Nobel Peace Prize award. The man has become Hollywood's favourite underdog—a nonviolent rebel with a cause. The Dalai Lama has mingled with Cindy Crawford and Sharon Stone at Los Angeles parties—and Shirley MacLaine, and Steven Seagal. Perhaps this is not so unusual: the Dalai Lama has been an avid fan of the movies from an early age. In the late 1940s, he arranged for the building of a projection room in Lhasa to view films imported from India. In the early 1990s, he fine-tuned the script for *Kundun* (in readings with Melissa Mathison and Harrison Ford) and for *Seven Years in Tibet* (with Becky Johnston).

Another reason for Tibetmania is possibly that Tibet is the ultimate in exotic locations: there's renewed Hollywood interest in exotica following the phenomenal success of movies like *The English Patient*. More than likely, however, Tibet is hot simply because controversy fuels box-office hits—and there's no shortage of controversy when it comes to Tibet.

In the case of *Kundun* and *Seven Years in Tibet*, the controversy started before shooting began. Both movies set out to portray an idyllic pre-1950 Tibet, with a smiling, soft-spoken Dalai Lama at the helm—a Dalai Lama sworn to nonviolence. The Chinese claim that pre-1950 Tibet was hell on earth—a medieval society where Tibetans had no freedom, and slaved away as serfs for the aristocracy. Both movies show the Chinese as brutal thugs. Sony, which owns Columbia TriStar, was threatened in China over *Seven Years in Tibet*, as was Disney, but no economic sanctions were applied. Both movie directors were blocked from filming in India, which was their first choice of location. One thing's for sure: films like *Kundun, Seven Years in Tibet* and *Red Corner* will never be shown in China. However, there's no reason why they can't be shown in Hong Kong, where technically the laws only empower authorities to check films for violence and sex. In fact, *Seven Years in Tibet* has been screened in Hong Kong despite stern criticism from Beijing. The movie brought out Ngapoi Ngawang Jigme on the attack in Hong Kong. He complained about the movie's portrayal of himself as a turn-coat who betrayed the Tibetan army and signed the 17-point agreement with China for its annexation of Tibet. Poetic justice of a kind. Ngawang Jigme, in his eighties, has rarely spoken to the press; he has lived in Beijing since 1967, where he and his clan hold high positions.

Seven Years in Tibet has also been screened in Moscow—again despite Chinese embassy objections. The Chinese vigorously protested a screening of the movie at a film festival in Japan (the film performed well in Japan, where Brad Pitt has a cult following—among teenage girls, anyway). Other Chinese objections were raised over *Kundun* screenings—a movie which glorifies the Dalai Lama (and in one scene portrays China's great leader, Mao Zedong, as a crass, evil chainsmoking buffoon). In May 1998, the Chinese Embassy demanded that the film *Windhorse* be removed from Washington International Film Festival because it was meant to "obviously smear China's policy toward Tibet." The festival director invited Chinese Embassy officials to come to the screening of the movie and participate in an open dialogue about the film—they did not show up. The film went on to become the festival-goers' top choice.

Words are the only weapon that Tibetans have in the fight against Chinese repression of Tibetan culture and occupation of their land—and Tibetans have found words can have great impact when they are spoken on the big screen. In the US and elsewhere, Tibetans have distributed leaflets and Tibet Action Kits outside screenings of the movies. China's problem with all of this is an issue of freedom of speech. Chinese embassies around the globe have tried to muzzle Hollywood—which thus far has only succeeded in drawing more attention to the Tibetan cause.

In a world where the international community has been spectacularly silent on the topic of Tibet, the films have pricked the Western conscience, and incurred the wrath of Chinese embassy officials. China's greatest fear: that one of these Hollywood films will become a cult hit, with TV reruns for the next 20 years—like Sergeant Bilko.

TIBET HITS THE BIG SCREEN

Hollywood's first big-budget effort on Tibet was made in the days when there was no conflict between China and Tibet—on the brink of World War II, the West looked to Tibet as a source of peace and inspiration. *Lost Horizon,* a black-and-white film directed by Frank Capra (Columbia TriStar Pictures, 1937), is based on the book by James Hilton—the movie was a major hit in the 1930s and 1940s. Ironically, the first major Hollywood film showing a Tibetan monastery is completely mythical—it has led to the widespread Western perception of Tibet as an unreal Shangri-La (there was a remake of *Lost Horizon* in 1973, also by Columbia).

Fascination with the occult and reincarnation led to two disastrous Hollywood movies—*The Golden Child* and *Little Buddha.* *The Golden Child* (Paramount Pictures, 1986) is a mixture of drama and comedy, with doses of the occult, martial arts and reincarnation thrown in for good measure. A special Tibetan child is kidnapped by evil forces and rescued by Chandler (played by Eddie Murphy). The film was a megahit at the time, but is eminently forgettable. An "art" version of the reincarnation theme—equally disastrous—was the US-produced *Little Buddha* (1993), directed by Italian master Bernardo Bertolucci. He employed much the same film crew he used to shoot the acclaimed picture *The Last Emperor* (filmed in Beijing), but seriously bombed with *Little Buddha.* In the story, Lama Norbu (a

Tibetan monk) believes a Seattle boy to be the reincarnation of his former teacher. The boy and his father are invited to travel to a monastery in India (actually shot on location in Paro, Bhutan). At this point the script falls apart as two other candidates are introduced—and all three are accepted as reincarnates. A parallel story traces events in the life of Buddha, with Keanu Reeves starring as Prince Siddhartha. Glorious camera shots, but a lousy script.

The Glut of 97

In late 1997, Hollywood released two major movies about Tibet and a third related to human rights issues in China. *Kundun*, directed by Martin Scorsese (Touchstone Pictures, 1997) tells the story of the takeover of Tibet from the Dalai Lama's point of view—the camera follows events through his eyes, from ages 2 to 24. The film is a dream-like portrayal—a very non-Hollywood treatment. The narrative is punctuated by surreal visions and dreams of the Dalai Lama: in one sequence the bewildered Dalai Lama is shown surrounded by the bodies of scores of blood-streaked monks. The movie encompasses spectacular scenic shots and dazzling costumes; it was shot on a budget of $30 million. Scorsese took some big risks here—he worked with an unknown all-Tibetan cast, drawn from India, Nepal, the USA and Europe. The musical score by Philip Glass fuses Western elements with the hypnotic deep chanting of Gyuto monks. *Kundun* was mainly filmed in Morocco, where it must've been difficult to find Chinese extras—for military scenes, Scorsese used pasty-faced Caucasians to play Chinese soldiers. Mountain sequences were shot in British Columbia, Canada.

The movie is an authorised biopic, which ultimately proves something of a drawback—it adopts a highly reverential tone that makes the Dalai Lama appear mystical and not human. By the end of the movie, it feels like something is missing—the story? What? This movie throws Western audiences with its strangeness: the shifting sand mandala, the chanting of the monks, a sky burial scene—and things which Western eyes have never seen before, like the state oracle hissing in a trance. It's not exactly Hollywood hit formula material—*Kundun* performed poorly at the box office, although it garnered four Academy Award nominations.

Seven Years in Tibet, directed by Jean-Jacques Annaud (Columbia TriStar/Mandalay, 1997), is one of Hollywood's ultimate biopics—with the subjects still alive to view it. The plot re-volves around the true story of Austrian Heinrich Harrer's es-cape to Tibet during WWII and his friendship with the young Dalai Lama. Harrer himself starred in a hokey 1957 British melodrama, *Seven Years in Tibet*, directed by Hans Nieter (79 minutes long; the story-line and music are atrocious—the sav-ing grace of this low-budget movie is the inclusion of original footage of 14th Dalai Lama, filmed in Tibet by Harrer).

In 1996, Jean-Jacques Annaud set about recreating Lhasa in the mountains of Argentina, while climbing scenes were shot in British Columbia. Annaud got *Seven Years in Tibet* on the screen with a $70-million budget—the movie turned a modest profit at the box office in the US. Some scandalous information came to light during filming about Harrer's Nazi background. Annaud was able to dub over some speaking lines to suit. Consider what Harrer left out of his story: in 1997, the German magazine *Der Stern* revealed Harrer had voluntarily become a Nazi storm trooper in 1933 and a sergeant in the SS five years later—he had his picture taken shaking hands with Hitler. Harrer neglected to come clean about this in his bestseller. When confronted, 85-year-old Harrer said he needed Nazi sponsorship to climb in the Himalayas, and that the handshake with Hitler was "purely ceremonial." Not only this, but he left a pregnant wife behind when he set off for India (this does show up in the movie). The Chinese were quick to capitalise on Harrer's background, with a headline in People's Daily proclaiming: "Dalai Lama's former Teacher was a Nazi."

The film adaptation of *Seven Years in Tibet* is certainly livelier than the book. In the role of the young 14th Dalai Lama is Jamyang Wangchuk, son of a Bhutanese diplomat. Brad Pitt, who plays Harrer, starts off well portraying a climber, but falls flat later in the piece. Thewlis is much more believable as Auf-schnaiter, Harrer's little-credited companion. The film does not exactly match the book: Aufschnaiter never married a Tibetan woman, and neither was Harrer in Lhasa when the PLA arrived.

Red Corner, directed by Jon Avnet (MGM, 1997), stars Richard Gere as an American attorney who is in China to close the first satellite communications deal sanctioned by the Chinese government. When he is a busted on a bogus murder charge—the end result of which could be his execution—his only hope is a female lawyer (Bai Ling) who risks all to represent him. The movie is not about Tibet, but it relates a lot—the Chinese judicial system comes under scrutiny, and so do the trigger-happy Chinese. A remarkable facet of this movie is that the director didn't have to be on location—he recreated Beijing in Los Angeles, through computerised imagery. Shortly after the release of this film in late 1997, Chinese dissident Wei Jingsheng was freed after 18 years in Chinese prisons and sent into exile to the US. Here, he partied at Richard Gere's in New York. After viewing *Red Corner*, he was asked if his captors really treated him like that. "That's just the beginning," shot back Wei.

Sneaking Around Tibet

Windhorse, directed by Paul Wagner (Paul Wagner Productions, 1998) is a very different film from the others mentioned because the setting is modern Tibet, and it takes on political issues head-first. The low-budget movie is a "docudrama." The lead actress is Dadon, a singer born in Tibet and now living in the US. She stars as an aspiring Tibetan pop singer, Dolkar, who wins favour with the Chinese authorities through her Chinese boyfriend, singing patriotic songs in Lhasa nightclubs. Then she reconsiders her career when her cousin Pema, a Buddhist nun, is imprisoned for shouting pro-independence slogans and is severely tortured. Everything in this powerful drama rings true—the dissolute drunken brother (Dorjee), the smiling waving Tibetans who appear on Chinese television, the Tibetan prison guard torturers, the inquisition into Dalai Lama pictures.

Although the film was mostly shot in Kathmandu and the Himalayas, the crew secretly taped in Tibet with a mini-DV handy-cam, which enabled the director, crew and actors to pose as tourists innocently filming street scenes, temples and landscapes in Lhasa and the surrounding countryside. This must have made for some very complex directing problems. The digital video was later transferred to 35mm movie film. Even in Nepal, the exact nature of the project had to be hidden from a Nepali government that often suppresses pro-Tibetan political activities (the crew managed to film anti-Chinese demonstration scene in Kathmandu and were later asked for the footage). Most of the actors and a number of the crew are Tibetans with no previous film experience: their names were mostly left out of the film's credits because of potential political repercussions.

The film is in Tibetan and Chinese with subtitles. Paul Wagner, the director, is documentarian who won an Oscar in 1985 for his film *The Stone Carvers*.

The Empire Strikes Back

The Chinese are obviously worried about Hollywood's missiles: on a global basis, Hollywood has tremendous power. So what are the Chinese going to do about it—make their own movies? Why yes. They put out a movie in 1997 called *Red River Valley*. The Chinese are not just worried about Hollywood—they muzzle their own film directors. In 1997 there was a clampdown on movie-making in China, with new regulations stating a movie must be state-approved to go into production, with script clearance and a shooting permit. Foreigners require censorship clearance prior to exporting film from China, but some have managed to get around this—like Joan Chen, who shot the movie *Xiu Xiu* without official permission on the Sichuan-Tibet border in 1997. The movie is about a young woman sent to a remote corner of Tibet for manual labour during the Cultural Revolution.

An earlier full-length film about Tibet is *Horse Thief*, directed by Tian Zhuang Zhuang (Xian Film Studios, 1986). In the story, Norbu—ostracised from his community for stealing horses—is forced into further crime to survive. There's hardly any dialogue: the movie offers sweeping views of Tibet and an ethereal soundtrack.

China's biggest-budget movie to date, *The Opium War*, directed by Jin Xie, was released in mid-1997 to celebrate the handover of Hong Kong. The $12-million movie is about China's humiliation at the hands of the colonial British during the original loss of Hong Kong in the 1830s. The great novelty here is that this is a colonial war—as told by the former colonised. The Chinese film crew hired British actors and even went to England to shoot several scenes. The hero of the hour is Qing official Lin Zexu, who sparked the Opium War of 1840 by flushing a million kilos of Western-owned opium into the sea. The movie was distributed in Southeast Asia, but did not last very long at Hong Kong cinemas.

Released around the same time—a double barrel of Brit-bashing—was *Red River Valley*, directed by Feng Xiaoning (Shanghai Film Studios, 1997). The movie is China's response to Hollywood's efforts on Tibet: a fictionalised account of the

British invasion of Tibet in 1904. It has the huge advantage of being filmed on location in Tibet, but barely shows the Potala or Jokhang. While *Kundun* used Caucasian extras to play Chinese soldiers, and *Seven Years in Tibet* presented the soldiers in silhouette form, the Chinese had a complete contingent of PLA troops—who, however, were dressed up variously as British soldiers or Tibetan troops (it appears that it might have been too dangerous to use Tibetan extras in these roles).

In the movie, Tibetan soldiers and Han advisers are shown fighting side-by-side to repel the British invaders; there are two love stories with heroines. The key roles are played by Chinese actors and actresses dressed as Tibetans. Two Hollywood actors were contracted to play the main British roles in the movie: the British colonel and a war correspondent, who both speak directly in English on the screen. The movie has lots of battle scenes. After a particularly bloody encounter, leaving 1500 Tibetans dead in 15 minutes, the British war reporter says in disgust: "Perhaps it is a blood-red sun that never sets over the British Empire."

What kind of sun rises over the Chinese Empire is not elaborated on: as a period piece set almost 50 years before the Chinese invasion, *Red River Valley* avoids the issues facing present-day Tibet. *Red River Valley* was released across China in April 1997, causing a "patriotic sensation" according to Xinhua news agency. More than this, it became compulsory viewing for Tibetans in places like Lhasa and Shigatse, "to gain valuable lessons in patriotism." The movie turned a modest profit on its $1.7-million budget through marketing in Korea and Japan. The movie was a hit in China, but Chinese filmmakers still have a long way to go if they want to compete with Hollywood on the global market.

RESOURCES

maps, phrasebooks, books, videos & internet sources

Some of the following maps, books, movies, multimedia materials and websites are frowned upon, restricted, or simply outlawed in China. Do not attempt to bring in risqué material if travelling to Tibet. Books with straight printed material should not be a problem, but visual material is different—customs and soldiers will flip through a book looking for artwork like the Tibetan flag or pictures of the Dalai Lama. Kathmandu is the best place in the sub-continent to find materials on Tibet, especially books and maps. Mention of Tibetan or Taiwanese independence or criticism of Beijing's policies are in theory forbidden in Hong Kong SAR. In practice, however, books continue to circulate freely—and anti-China protests are tolerated in the colony.

MAPS

The basic problem with maps of Tibet is that the Chinese have all the data, but treat it as a military secret—only partially revealed in Chinese-produced maps. On Western maps, there are conflicting names for destinations depending on whether the Tibetan name, the Chinese name or the old English name is referred to, and which transliteration system is used. Everest, for example (English name), is known as "Chomolungma" in Tibetan, and transliterated as "Qomolangma" in pinyin Chinese. Maps of Tibet are an ideological battleground. Tibetan-exile maps show Tibet covering the entire Tibetan Plateau, while Chinese maps show the much-reduced area of the Tibetan Autonomous Region, created in 1965 (Xizang Province). Street names in Lhasa may be referred to by a Tibetan name (such as Dekyi Shar Lam) or a Chinese name (Beijing Road). There are ongoing battles between cartography departments in China and neighbouring countries. Chinese maps continue to show Tibet extending into Arunachal Pradesh. Indian customs officials scrutinise books for any maps with these inflated borders, and handstamp over them this message: "Borders neither authentic nor correct."

The best place to find maps of Tibet is in Kathmandu. In the West, a number of maps mentioned here may be difficult to impossible to track down. Accurate German cartography of Tibet includes the RV Verlag/ GeoCenter map, *Tibet, Nepal and Bhutan;* Berndtson & Berndtson's *Tibet;* and Himalayan maps in the Nelles series. The British-issued *South-Central Tibet: Lhasa to Kathmandu Route Map* is out of print, but there's a pirated version in Kathmandu. Forthcoming is the Canadian cartographic company ITM's map of Tibet. *US Department of Defense Aerial Survey Maps* provide blanket coverage of Tibet's topography—very useful for trekkers. These maps are old: geographical features are fine, but the size and location of towns may have changed. The maps are hard to find and unwieldy: it's easier to consult Victor Chan's *Tibet Handbook*—he collated a set as basemaps.

Tibetans themselves never really needed maps, nor bothered to create them—except in artistic renditions. So Tibetan-created maps of Tibet are a recent phenomenon. Published in Dharamsala in 1994 is a *Road Map of Tibet,* with place names in English and Tibetan: this map encompasses Kham and Amdo. From Amnye Machen Institute in Dharamsala comes the finest map of Lhasa yet produced: *Lhasa City* (issued 1995) with a separate gazetteer. The map details 590 locations, including sites like educational institutions, prisons and PLA bases—which are of no interest to the casual tourist. This aside, the map provides an excellent overview of Lhasa, with contour lines usable for hiking sorties. Issued by the International Campaign for Tibet (ICT) in 1994 is a subversive piece of cartography called *On This Spot.* This off-the-wall map is backed up by a wealth of text on Lhasa's history and its tragic human rights situation, as well as travellers' tales, jokes and anecdotes.

Within China: Maps are very cheap in China, but the maps published in English are weak in detail, while the maps published in Chinese are more complete (a kind of reverse censorship—the Chinese need to find their way around their own colony but they don't want foreigners to access the material). For the traveller, maps with Chinese and English on them are best: you can point to the characters for your destination when talking to Chinese drivers. The best map of China is a joint-venture effort between the Cartographic Publishing House of China and Liber Kartor AB, Sweden (1995): it's a large wall map, but you could slice off the Tibet part to make it easy to carry. On sale in Lhasa is *China Tibet Tour Map*, a foldout map of Tibet (published by the Mapping Bureau of the TAR, 1993), and *Lhasa Tour Map* (compiled by Lhasa External Propaganda Dept, 1995). The last map is also issued in a Chinese language version, with more information on it. Significantly, there are few Tibetan-language maps for sale.

PHRASEBOOKS

Any attempts you make at speaking Tibetan, however awkward, will be greatly appreciated in a place where the language has such a low profile compared to the use of Chinese. Many Tibetans—particularly in the towns—understand some Mandarin, but will most likely not appreciate attempts to communicate with them in Chinese. However, such is the dominance of Mandarin that in order to negotiate rooms in hotels or whatever, you will need some knowledge of Chinese. It's worthwhile carrying two phrasebooks to handle situations: one Tibetan, the other Mandarin Chinese. Phrasebooks become doubly useful if they have Tibetan script: you can point to phrases if the pronunciation is not getting through (this is limited by a literacy factor, however).

Tibetan is a difficult language to speak, but at least it's not tonal like Chinese. The Tibetan language is part of the Tibeto-Burman language group, although the written form is distantly related to Sanskrit. The existence of many dialects makes it hard for Tibetans to communicate with each other. Lhasa dialect is the standard, but Lhasa court dialect is dying out. The script is more uniform throughout the Tibetan world, and although different writing styles are employed, they're more easily understood from one end of the Himalayas to the other than the spoken word. The elegant Tibetan script contains 30 consonants plus four vowels, and is easily rendered on computer in Macintosh and PC formats, though not much of this is in evidence in Lhasa.

Tibetan is an ancient language which borrows modern words like "post office," "fax machine" or "airport" from the nearest language. Within Tibet, these terms may be taken from Chinese, while in India the word might come from English or Hindi. Because of this, it's sometimes possible to use an English word (with a twisted accent) and be understood—the Tibetan for "jeep" is *jip*, and the Tibetan for "Landcruiser" is *landkrusa.* It's difficult to find Tibetans to practice with in the West. You can try attuning your ear by listening to the radio transmission Voice of Tibet at the website *www.vot.org* (programmed in RealAudio).

A few useful phrases for pidgin Tibetan speakers: *tashi delay!* means "hello," *yagodu!* or *yabadoo!* means "good!" while *yapo mindu!* means "bad!" and *nying jepo* means "beautiful."

Tujechay is "thank you." As in India, *cha* means "tea," and even if it isn't the best (flattery will get you everywhere) *kala shimpo du* means "the food is good." Also vital to your survival is *kali kali,* which means "slow down," when spoken to a maniacal driver. Etiquette when you reach the prayer flags on top of passes in Tibet requires you to shout, at the top of your lungs *Tso tso tso! Lha Gyalo!* which means "Victory to the gods!" Tibetan terms used in this book can be put to good use in speaking vocabulary. A yak is a yak, and tsampa is tsampa (nobody else in the world eats the stuff). Usable are things like *dzong* (castle), *gompa* (monastery) and *tsangpo* (river). If you add *kaba yoray* to the end of a phrase, you may get the question "Where is…" so that *gompa kaba yoray* means "Where is the monastery?" Check the glossary at the back and the geographical terms at the front for more vocabulary (some terms are Sanskrit, not Tibetan).

Cheap Tibetan/English phrasebooks can be found in Kathmandu, along with Tibetans who will give lessons. In a handy format are *Tibetan Phrasebook,* with booklet and two cassettes (Snow Lion Publications, 1987), and Lonely Planet's *Tibetan Phrasebook.* Phrasebooks are only as good as the sounds you can elicit from them. If you don't have a tape, go over the sounds with a Tibetan speaker—or have a native speaker help you record your own English/Tibetan tape.

BOOKS

For such a little-visited place, Tibet has generated an enormous amount of literature. The following list is just a sampling: there are many more Tibetan-related books covering Central Asia and Greater Tibet—further suggestions are enclosed with the *Tibetan World* chapter.

Specialist Publishers

The following US-based publishers maintain lists on Buddhism in general, and distribute titles other than those published by themselves. Some sell other media, such as videos about Tibet, as well as Tibetan artefacts. **Snow Lion Publications**, at PO Box 6483, Ithaca, NY 14851, tel. 607-2738519, fax 607-2738508, is dedicated to publishing and distributing Tibetan material—both trade and scholarly works; also sells videos. Their comprehensive catalogue is online (*www.snowlionpub.com*) as is their newsletter. **Shambhala Publications**, at PO Box 308, Boston, MA 02117, tel. 617-4240030, fax 617-2361563 (*www.shambhala.com*), stocks a wide range of books in the areas of religion, philosophy and personal transformation. **Wisdom Publications**, 199 Elm Street, Somerville, MA 02144, tel. 617-7767416, fax 617-7767841 (*www.wisdompubs.org*), is a non-profit publisher dedicated to Buddhist subjects; also sells videos. **Tricycle Books**, 92 Vandam St., New York, NY 10013 (*www.tricycle.com*), has a small book publishing list as yet, but distributes a lot more titles. Tricycle is a part of the Buddhist Ray, a not-for-profit educational corporation, and publisher of the quarterly magazine *Tricycle: The Buddhist Review* which often contains articles about Tibet. **Potala Corporation**, 9 East 36th Street, New York, NY 10016, tel 212-251-0360, fax 212-696-0431 (*www.magicoftibet. com/potala/books.html*), is part of the government-in-exile's Office of Tibet—it publishes a few titles and distributes a range of books and videos on Tibet; also sells imported artefacts, ritual items, Tibetan carpets, tankas and other items made by Tibetan artisans.

History, Political Intrigue

The history of modern Tibet often reads like a good novel. *Bayonets to Lhasa* by Peter Fleming (Oxford: OUP, 1984) focuses on the bizarre British invasion of Tibet in 1903, with a storyteller's touch. *Younghusband* by Patrick French (London: Flamingo, 1995) mixes biography with travelogue and first-class research—a highly enjoyable read. *Cavaliers of Kham* by Michel Peissel (London: Heinemann, 1972) is about the secret war in 1960s Tibet—Khampa guerrillas operating from their base in Mustang, Nepal. It was written before the collapse of the guerrilla operation in the early 1970s. Tibet's early history is covered in *A Cultural History of Tibet* by D. Snellgrove and H. Richardson (Boston: Shambhala, 1995; first publ. 1968). *A History of Modern Tibet* by Melvyn Goldstein (Berkeley: UC Press, 1989) covers the period 1913–1951; it is subtitled "The Demise of the Lamaist State"—all 900 pages of it. Based on over 100 interviews with key players and refugees in the exile community is John Avedon's classic work *In Exile from the Land of Snows* (London: Michael Joseph, 1984) covering the period 1933–1983.

Human Rights

Cutting off the Serpent's Head, edited by Robert Barnett (NY: Human Rights Watch & TIN, 1996) has a subtitle: "Tightening Control in Tibet 1994–95." It documents Chinese crackdowns in the early 1990s. *Fire Under the Snow* by Palden Gyatso (London: Harvill Press, 1997) is written by a former Drepung monk who was arrested during the 1959 Lhasa uprising and spent the next 33 years in prisons in Tibet. Released in 1992 at the age of 61, he was expected to retire to a quiet monastic life in Lhasa.

Instead, he bribed corrupt Chinese prison guards to sell him torture instruments, and carrying a bag of these, he escaped to India. He then set about writing his book, and has toured extensively in the West, talking about his harrowing experiences—a pretty active "retirement." *The Voice that Remembers* by Ama Adhe (Boston: Wisdom, 1997) is an account of 27 years in Chinese labour camps by Adhe Taponstang, a woman who was imprisoned when resistance to Chinese rule started in the 1950s. *Tibet: My Story* by Jetsun Pema (Rockport: Element Books, 1997) is written by the Dalai Lama's younger sister. She founded the Tibetan Children's Village in Dharamsala, led a fact-finding mission to Tibet in 1980, and became the first female minister in the government-in-exile. *Sky Burial* by Blake Kerr (Chicago: Noble Press, 1993) is a gripping eyewitness account of China's brutal crackdown on Tibetan demonstrators. Fresh out of medical school, American backpacker Blake Kerr found himself dodging bullets, then treating Tibetans for gunshot wounds and injuries resulting from beatings, after demonstrations turned nasty in Lhasa in 1987.

Tibetan Buddhism

There's a lot of dry scholarly writing on Tibetan Buddhism—most of it incomprehensible to the average mortal. Unfortunately, Tibetan Buddhism is a complex subject—there's no easy way in. *Inside Tibetan Buddhism,* by Robert Thurman (San Francisco: Collins, 1995) is a primer and photo-book—a lucid acount by a scholar who knows how to relate to the layperson. *Religions of Tibet in Practice,* edited by Donald Lopez (New Jersey: Princeton University Press, 1997), is a scholarly work—the largest sourcebook about Tibetan religious practices. It includes many never-before-translated texts from different sects including pilgrimage guides and accounts of visits to hell. *Buddhism without Beliefs* by Stephen Batchelor (NY: Riverhead Books, 1997) comes to grips with questions like: Can you be a Buddhist and an agnostic at the same time? Do you have to believe in reincarnation to be a Buddhist? Batchelor explains how he sees Buddhism not as a religion but as liberating agnosticism: the author is a former monk in both Zen and Tibetan traditions. Some specialist titles include the following. *Early Temples of Central Tibet,* by Roberto Vitali (NY: Weatherhill, 1991) focuses on religious architecture. Two large-format books devoted to mandalas are *The Mandala: Sacred Circle in Tibetan Buddhism* by Martin Brauen (Boston: Shambhala, 1997), and *Mandala: The Architecture of Enlightenment* by Denise Leidy and Robert Thurman (Boston: Shambhala, 1997). *The Sacred Mountain of Tibet* by Kerry Moran and Russell Johnson (Vermont: Park Street Press, 1989) follows pilgrim rituals at Mount Kailash. *Reborn in the West,* by Vicki McKenzie (NY: Marlowe & Co, 1996) delves into the phenomenon of incarnates born in Spain, France and the US. *The Awakening of the West* by Stephen Batchelor (Berkeley: Parallax Press, 1994) is an account of how Buddhism arrived in the West.

The Dalai Lama

The Dalai Lama is a one-man publishing phenomenon. If you put together the books he has written himself or been interviewed for, plus the books written about him, it would occupy an entire library shelving unit. In addition to this, the Dalai Lama has penned introductions for scores of other books on Tibet. Exactly how he manages to do all this (English not being his first language), or even finds the time to do it, is uncanny. Among the books about His Holiness is *Kundun* by Mary Craig (Washington: Counterpoint, 1997), which focuses on the First Family of 1940s Tibet—the Dalai Lama's parents, four brothers and two sisters—and their considerable roles working for the Tibetan cause since occupation by the Chinese. *The World of the Dalai Lama* by Gill Farrer-Halls (Illinois: Quest Books, 1998) puts the man in context of his many roles, his people, and his vision; also looks at the different Tibetan Buddhist sects and includes copious illustration. The Dalai Lama is the author or interviewed subject of more than 20 books. Two tomes of autobiography are: *Freedom in Exile* (London: Hodder & Stoughton, 1990) and *My Land and People* (NY: Potala Publications, 1985—first publ. 1962). The Dalai Lama has written many tracts on Tibetan Buddhist practices, such as *The World of Tibet Buddhism* (Boston: Wisdom, 1995); he has also written volumes on subjects like world peace, healing anger, and the practice of compassion.

Specialist Tomes on Tibetan Culture

Because of the small market, the following books could be difficult to find—try ordering direct from the publisher. *Wisdom & Compassion—the Sacred Art of Tibet* by Marylin Rhie and Robert Thurman (NY: Abrams, 1996) is a massive and definitive catalogue of the sacred tanka painting and sculpture of Tibet. Focusing on the nomads and their fast-disappearing way of life is the well-illustrated *Nomads of Western Tibet* by Melvyn Goldstein and Cynthia Beall (Berkeley: UC Press, 1990)—the result of a lengthy research trip to the Changtang region. *Food in Tibetan Life* by Rinjing Dorje (London: Prospect Books, 1985) is an entire book on the subject of Tibetan food. A slim volume: half of it background notes, the other half recipes for butter tea, hot toddies, tsampa-cake and momos. *Tibet's Hidden Wilderness* (NY: Abrams, 1997) focuses on the Changtang region, where naturalist George Schaller was allowed to conduct research in 1988. Schaller photographed rare animals like the wild yak, Argali bighorn sheep and Tibetan antelope—remnants of Tibet's once-bountiful wildlife. *The Tibetan Art of Healing* with text by Ian Baker and artwork by Romio

Shrestha (London: Thames & Hudson, 1997) is a remarkable work. Nepalese artist Romio Shrestha has repainted 300-year-old Tibetan medical tankas with incredible liveliness and accuracy of detail. Ian Baker explains the intricacies of this little-understood branch of the healing arts. Closely linked to the study of medicine is the study of astrology. *Tibetan Astrology* by Philippe Cornu (Boston: Shambhala, 1997) is a scholarly tome on Tibetan cosmology.

Tales for Young Readers

Tibetan Folk Tales by Frederick and Audrey Hyde-Chambers (NY: Random House, 1981) includes a long piece on legendary King Gesar: the book is intended for adults and children. *Our Journey from Tibet,* by Laurie Dolphin and Nancy Jo Johnson (NY: Dutton Children's Books, 1998), is based on the real-life adventures of Sonam, a nine-year-old Tibetan girl who escapes from Tibet—tackling the arduous trek over the Himalayas to Nepal and India, and starting a new life in Dharamsala. Suitable for ages 7 to 77 is *Tintin in Tibet,* the comic book by Belgian creator Hergé. It first appeared in 1958 (drawn before the 1959 Lhasa uprising)—and does not show a single Chinese soldier. This innocuous yarn is about a young Chinese called Chang—rescued by Tintin from the clutches of a yeti in Tibet. The comic has appeared in half a dozen languages, including Tibetan—probably the only Tintin work ever to appear in this language. By contrast, *Tibet (Tintin's Travel Diaries series),* with text by Daniel de Bruycker and Martine Noblet (NY: Barron's Educational Series, 1995), tackles modern problems in Tibet. Targeted for ages 9 to 12, it is presented in the form of 30 key questions, mixing Tintin comic frames with real photos. What do Tibetan children fear? Why are the Tibetans in revolt against China?

Foreigners in Tibet, Exploration, Adventure

For late 19th and early 20th-century explorers, Lhasa was as difficult a goal to reach as Mecca. The story of the race for Lhasa is recounted in *Trespassers on the Roof of the World* by Peter Hopkirk (Oxford: OUP, 1982). Not so well known is the saga of eccentric Japanese Zen monk Kawaguchi Ekai, who journeyed in disguise and resided in Lhasa from 1900 to 1903. His remarkable adventures have been reprised in *A Stranger in Tibet,* by Scott Berry (NY: Kodansha, 1989). After 100 British soldiers forged their way through to Lhasa in 1904, the place lost some of its lustre, but then the game became to get past the British as well as the Tibetans. The British deported a middle-aged Frenchwoman named Alexandra David-Néel from Shigatse, but in 1923 she sneaked back in and reached Lhasa disguised as a beggar—the first Western woman to reach the sacred city.

She became involved in mystical practices like telepathy and shamanism—and went on to write 25 books about her experiences: among them are *My Journey to Lhasa* and *Magic and Mystery in Tibet* (published in the 1930s).

Seven Years in Tibet, by Heinrich Harrer, was first published in 1953, and has never been out of print. This bestseller has been widely translated, but it was not until 1995 that it was issued in the Tibetan language (AMI Series, Dharamsala). The book describes one of the greatest feats of mountaineering and exploration of the 20th century. In 1944, escaped POWs Harrer and Aufschnaiter walked for two years, over scores of high passes, from Zanda in west Tibet—to reach Lhasa. This feat so impressed the Tibetans that they allowed them to stay. What should've been a four-month expedition to Mount Nanga Parbat ended up being a 12-year sojourn.

Tibet is still very much terra incognita: a fascinating account of recent exploration is given in *Barbarians at the Gate* by Michel Peissel (NY: Henry, Holt, 1997). Peissel claims discovery of the source of the Mekong in northwest Qinghai in 1995, describes the discovery of an unknown breed of primitive forest pony in Kham, and discovery of beehive-shaped dwellings in Tibet's remote Changtang region. Peissel is an unconventional explorer who has made over 20 expeditions to Greater Tibet.

Mountaineering: *Everest: the Unclimbed Ridge* by Chris Bonington and Charles Clarke (London: Pan Books, 1983) is the gripping account of two of Britain's finest climbers, Peter Boardman and Joe Tasker, who vanished while making a summit attempt on the north face in 1982. *Everest: Kangshung Face* by Stephen Venables (Toronto: General Publishing, 1989) recounts a harrowing summit climb up Everest's sheer east face in Tibet. A combination of mountaineering, biography, history and exploration is pursued in *Mountains of the Middle Kingdom* by Galen Rowell (San Francisco: Sierra Club, 1983), with excellent photography.

Modern Travel Accounts: In late 1984, backpackers were first allowed access to Tibet: some ended up in outlandish places. One of the best modern accounts is *Sky Burial* (1993) by Blake Kerr—recounting the thrills, the angst, the horrors. More sedate is *From Heaven Lake* (1983) by Vikram Seth, the Anglo-Indian writer in his early days before he hit the big time. Other accounts include: *Land of the Snow Lion* by Elaine Brook (1987); *A Winter in Tibet,* by Charles and Jill Hadfield (1988); *Cycling to Xian,* by Michael Buckley (1988), about bicycling across China and Tibet; *Inside the Treasure House,* by Catriona Bass (1990); *Journey across Tibet,* by Sorrel Wilby (1988); and *Naked Spirits,* by Adrian Abbotts (1997)—a journey to occupied Tibet.

Guidebooks

While the guide you now hold concentrates on practical advice, mapping and mobility in Tibet, I highly recommend two other guidebooks. *The Tibet Guide,* by Stephen Batchelor (Somerville: Wisdom Publications, 1998, 2nd edition) covers central and western Tibet, and is an excellent source for temple descriptions and cultural dimensions, though the practical information is dated. The tome is angled for serious Buddhists: Batchelor is a scholar fluent in Tibetan. *Trekking in Tibet* (Seattle: The Mountaineers, 1991) is written by Gary McCue, a trekking guide in Tibet and Nepal. McCue covers back-country trek routes and the environment in Tibet in great detail—this book is the best resource for trekkers. It studiously avoids politics and so is acceptable to carry in Tibet.

Tibet Handbook by Victor Chan (Chico: Moon Travel Handbooks, 1994) is a very ambitious "pilgrimage guide", detailing 60 pilgrimage and trekking itineraries, with over 200 maps. Victor Chan was born in Hong Kong and graduated as a particle physicist in Canada and the US. The result of ten years of monumental research is "Vick the Brick"—a thick book that's a liability to lug around, but worth it if you want the detail. *Tibet Handbook with Bhutan* by Gyurme Dorje (Bath: Footprint, 1996) is another hefty tome, with nuggets of information not found elsewhere— sections on Kham and Amdo, and detailed monastery plans. Good for route information through Kashgar and beyond are various guides to Central Asia, including *Asia Overland* (Trailblazer, 1998), *China: The Silk Routes* by Peter Neville-Hadley (Cadogan, 1997) and *Central Asia* by Giles Whittell (Cadogan, 1996).

Photobooks

Several large-format hardcovers depict pre-1950 Tibet in black-and-white photos. *Tibet: the Sacred Realm* (NY: Aperture, 1983) is a collection of 140 rare photos from the period 1880-1950. *A Portrait of Lost Tibet* by Rosemary Jones Tung (London: Thames & Hudson, 1980) is based on pictures from the 1940s, taken by US Army officers Ilya Tolstoy and Brooke Dolan while on a mission to Lhasa. *Lost Lhasa* by Heinrich Harrer (NY: Abrams, 1992) juxtaposes black-and-white photos with lively commentary from an eyewitness to the last days of a free Tibet. Outstanding among contemporary portrayals of Tibet is *My Tibet,* with text by the Dalai Lama and photography by Galen Rowell (Berkeley: UC Press, 1990)—it shows aspects of Tibetan life that have managed to remain unspoiled. In *Tibetan Voices* (San Francisco: Pomegranate, 1996), Tibetans tell stories in their own words, and photographer Brian Harris matches them up to images. A mesmerizing book of sepia-toned images is *Tibetan Portrait* by Phil Borges (NY: Rizzoli International, 1996). The theme of these portraits—

taken in Tibet, Nepal and India—is the power of compassion in the face of conflict. *Tibet* (Boston: Shambhala, 1997) is a book of stunning images by Japanese photographer Kazuyoshi Nomachi, with well-researched caption material and side-text. *Tibet: Journey to the Forbidden City* by Tiziana and Gianni Baldizzone (NY: Stewart, Tabori & Chang, 1996) retraces the footsteps of Alexandra David-Néel, with evocative shots of Kham and Amdo.

Novels

Lost Horizon by James Hilton (NY: William Morrow, 1933; reprinted many times since) is the classic novella that introduced the word "Shangri-La" into English and created an instant myth about a sanctuary where poverty, crime and sickness are unknown. "La" means high pass in Tibetan: there are actually a few passes in the Himalayas called Shangri-La. Hilton's setting is possibly modelled on Rongbuk Monastery at the north side of Everest (mentioned in the 1920s British expeditions). The book was made into an epic movie by Frank Capra in 1937.

The Third Eye by T. Lobsang Rampa (London: Corgi, 1956, reprinted many times) describes the painful opening of the Third Eye—the wisdom eye, the power to see things profoundly. Lama Rampa claims he was initiated at Lhasa's Chakpori Medical College. In 1958, an English newspaper revealed the bestseller was not written by a Tibetan lama but by Cyril Henry Hoskins, an Irish plumber. Bald, bearded Hoskins evidently had a fertile imagination: he spent a lot of time in the British Library in London reading up. Rampa fans conceded that he was not a Tibetan lama, but insisted a lama's spirit had possessed Hoskins' body. Hoskins cranked out more novels in the series, establishing a cult following in the 1960s. To this day, librarians and booksellers are mystified about where to file the books: under religion, mysticism, thriller, fantasy, science fiction or autobiography? The best solution yet seen: New Age.

The Rose of Tibet, by Lionel Davidson (London: Gollanz, 1962), is a page-turner set in 1950—involving the beautiful abbess of Yamdring (in her 18th incarnation), a bumbling British man, sacks of emeralds, and an advancing Chinese army. *Lama,* by Frederick Hyde-Chambers (NY: McGraw-Hill, 1985) is a novel of blockbuster proportions about the rape of Shangri-La, and Tibet's struggle in the 1950s. *Stones of the Dalai Lama,* by Ken Mitchell (Vancouver: Douglas & McIntyre, 1993), is a piece of black humour set in the late 1980s about a tourist who pockets some mani stones at Lake Namtso as souvenirs. Bad karma: he finds that terrible things befall him back home, so he resolves to put the mani stones back where they belong. Tibet, however, is hard to get into—riots have broken out in Lhasa…

The Tale of the Incomparable Prince, by Tshe Ring Dbang Rgyal (NY: HarperCollins, 1996) is a rare tome indeed—an 18th century classic revived in a translation by scholar Beth Newman. It is the only novel in the Tibetan language, and is written in a Sanskrit literary form that mixes verse and prose. The author is an 18th-century prime minister, historian and biographer. The plot revolves around political intrigue in old Tibet—two men in pursuit of one fantastic woman, and themes of adventure, spirituality, lust and romance.

CD-ROM

Tibet Outside the TAR (1997) is a remarkable condensation of a 2700-page report onto one CD-ROM disk. It exhaustively researches Tibetan areas now lying in autonomous prefectures outside the TAR; the disk is replete with photographic, demographic and political data. It's based on research trips by Steven Marshall and Susette Ternent Cooke; the CD-ROM, replicated by the authors, is available through ICT in Washington. Taking a very different tack, *The Wonders of Tibet* (1996) was released by China Pictorial Publishing House in Beijing. The disk provides text and sound in English and Mandarin—the usual Chinese hoopla and howlers about Tibet, just in CD-ROM form. Armchair touring of Tibet with lots of pictures, audio tracks (including Tibetan and Chinese music) and a couple of video clips. A bit garbled at times because the makers haven't worked out the bugs when interfacing with Windows. Otherwise, there's very little on CD-ROM about Tibet—you may unearth more under the topic "Himalayas". Peak Media's *Mount Everest, Quest for the Summit of Dreams* (1995) is about an expedition to the Tibetan side of Everest. A journey to the edge of the plateau is contained in DNA Multimedia's *Up to the Himalayas* (1997).

MUSIC

Tibetan music is quite arcane and thus more likely found in specialty stores.

Western Musicians: *Tibetan Freedom Concert* is a CD compilation, mainly featuring artists from the 1997 Tibetan Freedom Concert in New York. Another all-star rock compilation is *Long Live Tibet*, released in the UK in 1998, with tracks from many artists including David Bowie, Radiohead and Terrorvision. Among the efforts of Westerners interpreting Tibetan music, *Kundun*—the original soundtrack composed by Philip Glass for the movie of the same name—is a standout (released 1997). Henry Wolff and Nancy Jennings collaborated on a CD series called *Tibetan Bells*, released by Celestial Harmonies, San Francisco (1991). The genre is endless-journey New Age material. They also collaborated with

Mickey Hart (one-time drummer for the Grateful Dead) on the album *Ya-mantaka* (1991).

Tibetan Musicians: Two renowned Tibetan musicians are resident in Australia. Yungchen Lhamo, who studied in Dharamsala after escaping from Tibet, released her first album *Tibet Tibet* in 1996, with several songs dedicated to Tibetan refugees. Nawang Khechog, who escaped Tibet for India in 1959 with his nomad family, played the bamboo flute in his youth and went on to master a variety of unusual instruments, including the Tibetan longhorn and the aboriginal didgeridoo. His albums include *Quiet Mind* (1997) and *Sounds of Peace* (1996). He worked as Tibetan assistant director and actor in *Seven Years in Tibet*, has been a guest on Kitaro albums, and appeared at Tibetan Freedom Concerts.

Tibetan Sacred Music: Recorded at various Tibetan monasteries in India are albums with renditions like "Sacred healing chants of Tibet" or "Sacred temple music". *Tibetan Tantric Choir* (1987) and *Freedom Chants* (1989) are albums by the Gyuto Monks—also featured on the soundtracks of *Kundun* and *Seven Years in Tibet.* These dirges are not for everyone. The exiled monks have mastered the Tibetan meditation technique of chanting with a deep three-note chord, which places such a strain on the vocal chords that the singer is in danger of becoming mute if he overdoes it. *Chö* is a 1997 album from nuns at Nagi Gompa, overlooking Kathmandu Valley. For the 100 nuns here, singing and chanting are part of the practice of Chö, a system of cutting through ego-clinging and countering the four demons, based in the tradition of the Prajnaparamita. The album is arranged by a composer/guitarist with the auspicious name of Steve Tibbetts.

FILM & VIDEO DOCUMENTARIES

For details on Hollywood vs. China, see the tail end of the *Context, Subtext* chapter. The following films are documentary-style. *Lung Ta: The Forgotten Tibet,* directed by Marie Jaoul Ponchenville and Franz-Christophe Girke (France, 1990) is a film showing the beauty of the country and its fragile condition. The crew received permission to film at monasteries in Qinghai province, but the content is largely about the political situation in Tibet itself. *The Knowledge of Healing,* directed by Franz Reichle (90 minutes, T&C Films, Switzerland, 1997), starts by interviewing the greatest living authority on Tibetan medicine, Dr Tenzin Choedak, personal physician to the Dalai Lama. Dr Choedak survived 21 years in a Chinese prison before escaping to India. At the Tibetan Medical Institute, he set about making herbal medicines whose recipes were thought forgotten. The film visits a Tibetan medicine practitioner in Outer Mongolia; other parts were shot in Switzerland and the West.

Everest, directed by David Breashears (IMAX, 1998), is only 43 minutes long, but has some very big ideas—showing the world's biggest mountain on a screen seven storeys high. Altogether, four kilometres of film are run through IMAX projectors. The film was shot on a $6-million budget, mainly in Nepal. Narrated by Liam Neeson, *Everest* conveys the sheer power of the mountain from some unusual angles—perched over a ladder spanning a crevasse, and 90 seconds of views from the summit. Sherpas toiled up Everest with a specially designed IMAX camera, and portered the finished film back down. The stars of the film are the climbers: Ed Viesturs, Araceli Segarra, and Tenzing Norgay's son, Tamling, who places a Dalai Lama picture and prayer flags on the summit.

While there aren't many movies about Tibet, there is a wealth of video material. Video has given a new lease of life to historical film footage—as in restored and transferred to video. And the documentary comes to the fore in video. One very good reason why there's a lot more video documentary material around than movie-film: Tibet is one tough assignment.

Since journalists are not permitted to film in Tibet, they have taken to posing as innocuous tourists with hand-held camcorders. Orville Schell used a camcorder to get footage for the one-hour documentary *Red Flag Over Tibet* (PBS Frontline, 1994). To protect their Tibetan sources, interviewers digitally alter faces and voices, or use a strong English voice-over, as in *Tibet, a Case to Answer,* a TV documentary by Vanda Kewley. *Tibet: Survival of Spirit* (90 mins, Mystic Fire Video, 1994) was filmed by a crew who spent two months unofficially in Tibet. It includes Chinese-shot footage of Jokhang temple being stormed by the military (this footage was smuggled out of Beijing by a Chinese sympathiser and given to Western sources). Another engrossing video is *Escape from Tibet* (50 minutes, Yorkshire TV, 1996): it follows Tibetan refugees escaping over the Himalayas. The production crew walked up the Nepalese side of Nangpa La Pass and waited for Tibetans to cross over.

Videos that have incurred the wrath of Chinese embassies include *Kingdom of the Lost Boy* (75 minutes, BBC, 1996), about the missing 11th Panchen Lama; and *Missing in Tibet* (25 minutes, 1996) about Tibetan musician Ngawang Choephel—sentenced to 18 years in jail for videotaping dance performances in Tibet. There are many videos on the Dalai Lama, including *Compassion in Exile* and *Heart of Tibet.* Seeking to counter the avalanche of pro-Tibetan material, the Chinese in 1997 produced their own 90-minute video on the Dalai Lama, seen through the eyes of 20 Tibetan "witnesses": this effort was screened on TV in Hong Kong.

Video Sourcing: Try and borrow the video from your local library collection or rent from a specialist video store (some made-for-TV documentaries may not be available). Videos can also be purchased or rented direct from key distributors, including Office of Tibet (New York), Mystic Fire Video (New York), Wisdom Films (Boston), Snow Lion (Boston), Videomatica (Vancouver, Canada) and Meridian Trust (London, UK).

Surfing for inspiration on the World Wide Web can be productive. On this electronic frontier, news travels fast—faster than magazines, even faster than newspapers. And it's interactive: you may be able to pose questions. Is Tibet currently open or closed for individuals? Which doors are open? You'll find many more sites than the ones listed here by using search engines like *Yahoo!* The Tibetan government-in-exile has been quick to utilise the possibilities of the net: it's an economical way of getting out news and information on a global basis. So the Tibet vs. China propaganda wars move into cyberspace, with cyber-slander on both sides. Thus far, Tibet rules the net: suspicious of the power of the net, the Chinese have been slow to adapt.

The net operates on unstable ground: websites are notoriously unstable—chopping and changing sites, or running out of funds and packing up. The following data can easily change. The prefix for opening all websites listed below is *http://* Do not insert a full stop after a web address, or the browser may fail to find it.

Finding It

Tibet Online Resource Gathering (*www.tibet.org*) is the mother of all sites—the best place to find links to Tibet-related sites. The website is funded by the International Tibet Support Group community. To find books, videos and CDs on the net, check the websites of publishers specialising in Tibetan material (see the Specialist Publishers listing under Books). You can use the powerful search engines at virtual bookstores like the huge US outfit Amazon (*www.amazon.com*) or at Europe's biggest online bookstore, The Internet Bookshop (*www.bookshop.co.uk*). The Internet Bookshop has a search function for CDs and videos; the Amazon site will search for CD titles. Music Boulevard at *www.musicblvd.com* has search engines for CDs and audio cassettes. The site *www.tibet.com/films/html* is a government-in-exile listing of some 200 videos and films about Tibet, related regions or related issues.

Current Travel Advice

All kinds of information related to your trip—airline schedules, exchange rates, weather conditions and so on—can be gleaned from the web. Some of the news sites for Tibet carry snippets of information about travel conditions. At his Swiss site, Peter Geiser (*www.datacomm.ch/pmgeiser*) has basic data on travel in Tibet. Through the site *www.catmando.com.nepal.htm* Nepalese travel agents and their e-mail addresses can be located. For health concerns—which in Tibet means high altitude concerns—you might as well talk to the experts. Visit the Himalaya Rescue Association in Nepal (*www.nepalonline.net/hra*). They provide lots of relevant detail and the latest data. A former HRA volunteer, Thomas Dietz, maintains his own website in Oregon called High Altitude Medicine Guide

(*www.gorge.net/ hamg*). For general travel health information, consult the Centers for Disease Control and Prevention, in Atlanta, Georgia (*www.cdc.gov/travel/ travel.hml*).

General Information & News

The web is your best source of news on Tibet, with online "clipping" services. Some good all-round sources: *www.tibet.com* is the official government-in-exile site, maintained by the Office of Tibet in the UK; *www. magicoftibet.com/tibetny* is the New York Office of Tibet; *www.savetibet.org* is the site of the International Campaign for Tibet (ICT) in Washington. Tibet Information Network (TIN) (*www.tibetinfo.net*) is an independent news/research service on Tibet, established in 1987. TIN acts as a database, culling material from a wide range of sources and releasing it to journalists and organisations. The site

www.insidechina.com/china/tibet/ tibet.html is the Tibet part of Inside China, a mixed-media rundown operated by European Internet Network. BBC's East Asia Today (*www.bbc. co.uk/worldservice/eastasiatoday*) has good general coverage of Asia with RealAudio round-ups; also check out Radio Free Asia (*www.rfa.org*) and the Voice of America (*www.voa.gov*).

Regional News: On the net, foreign newspapers are often free—if you had to subscribe to the print version, it would cost a fortune. You can often bring up back-issues. To find newspapers for any region of Asia, India or Central Asia, consult the Yahoo!

www.yahoo.com/News_and_Media/ newspapers/regional/countries site. This will allow you to tap into gems like the *Kathmandu Post,* in Nepal (*www.south-asia.com/ktmpost.html*), *The Times of India,* in Delhi (*www.timesofindia.com*), the *South China Morning Post,* in Hong Kong, (*www.scmp.com*) or *China Daily,* the official English paper from Beijing (*www.chinadaily.net*). A host of Asia-related magazines (such as *Far Eastern Economic Review* at *Asiaweek)* can be found through searches.

Newsletters: Although a lot of current news items are posted on the net, some prefer newsletters. *Tibetan Bulletin,* from the government-in-exile, is issued six times a year. *Tibetan Review,* issued monthly in Delhi, acts as a forum for frank discussion (subscription information can be obtained through the site *www.ncinet.de/users/toi/tibetan_review.htm*). The

ICT's hefty newsletter, *Tibet Press Watch*, is published six times a year: payment is via membership dues. In the UK, TIN's *News Review* is a quarterly news round-up (*www.tibetinfo.net*)—this can be e-mailed, faxed or sent in printed form.

Mailing Lists

To join announcement and discussion lists you need an e-mail address. The services are free of charge. Due to potential high e-mail volume you might request digest format. **WTN-L** or World Tibet Network News is an announcement service based in Montreal, Canada: it regularly sends out batches of news items on Tibetan matters culled from global sources. The service reaches more than 40 countries. To subscribe, send an e-mail to *listserv@vm1.mcgill.ca* with only the message: SUB WTN-L [your name and e-mail address]. **TIBET-L** is the Tibet Interest List, an Indiana-based discussion group for Tibetan issues—many of the topics posted verge on the esoteric. To join, send an e-mail to *listserv@listserv.indiana.edu* with only the message: SUB TIBET-L [your name and e-mail address]. **E-mail Alert Network** is a service from ICT—contact their website (*www. savetibet.org*). **The Oriental-List** is Peter Neville-Hadley's discussion list about China and its near neighbours, including Tibet. He's the author of *China: The Silk Routes.* This is a moderated discussion list—applicants are accepted on the basis of ad-free on-topic discussion. Contact *pnh@axion. net* to subscribe.

The Chinese Viewpoint

With links to over a thousand websites on China (some are in Chinese language, so you need special plug-ins) is *www.aweto.com/china,* the website of the Aweto Company. A number of the sites listed are banned in China, including China News Digest (*www.cnd.org*), formed by a group of Chinese scholars in New York. The Chinese government has been slow off the mark when it comes to launching into cyberspace, but give them time. The standard Chinese arguments about the Tibet issue and about human rights are aired at the Chinese Embassy in Washington website at *www.china-embassy.org* (on the main page, click on Issues & Events, and then click on "Tibet", "Human Rights", or "Religious Beliefs in China"). It's useful when travelling in Tibet to familiarise yourself with Chinese jargon and rhetoric. From this site, there are also links for Xinhua News Agency, People's Daily and other Beijing publications.

Activism

At *www.tibet.org/Resources/TSG,* you can locate the Tibet support group closest to you: a number of local chapters have their own websites. In the

US, consult ICT (*www.savetibet.org*); in the UK, consult Free Tibet Campaign (*freetibet.org*). Students for a Free Tibet (SFT) is a grassroots movement in US colleges and schools, initiated by the US Tibet Committee and ICT, and spurred by the Tibetan Freedom Concerts. Affiliated with more than 300 colleges and schools across North America, it has grown fast. Check *www.tibet.org/sft* for chapters in the US. SFT is partly supported by the Milarepa Fund (*www.milarepa.org*), whose website features soundclips and video clips from the Tibetan Freedom Concerts.

Human Rights: Discussion of human rights is a taboo topic in China. Despite the threat of heavy fines or imprisonment, Chinese surfers have found ways past filters to reach some of the following sites. The site *www.un.org/rights* features full text of the Universal Declaration of Human Rights. Out of New York are: Human Rights in China (*www.hrichina.org*), set up by Chinese scientists and scholars; Human Rights Watch (*www.hrw. org*); and Amnesty International (*www.amnesty.org*). From New Jersey comes Digital Freedom Network (*www.dfn.org*), a forum for exiled dissidents to reach their fellow citizens (assuming they have internet access). At the *www.tibet.org* site, click on Barkhor Community Space, then go to the Human Rights update newsletter.

Tibetan Buddhism

Tend to your soul in cyberspace: the internet sangha welcomes you. Lots of sites and links: you can download a blessing or bring up a mandala to contemplate. You can even tap into the Karmapa lineage homepage via the Tsurphu Foundation at *www.maui.net/~tsurphu/karmapa* with material on the 17th Karmapa, installed at Tsurphu Monastery in Tibet. At *www. chron.com/mandala* overhead video cameras capture the creation of a sand mandala at the Museum of Fine Arts in Houston in 1996. For a directory of US and international dharma centres, consult the Tricycle Hub at *www.tricycle.com* and then click on Dharma Center Directory; also go to Dharma Connections section for dharma news and more ideas.

LEXICON

CHINASPEAK

Chinese rhetoric on Tibet is an odd mix of the irrational and the predictable. This quote is taken from the magazine *Beijing Review,* 1983, describing the Lhasa uprising of 1959:

> The imperialists and a small number of reactionary elements in Tibet's upper ruling clique could not reconcile themselves to the peaceful liberation of Tibet and its return to the embrace of the motherland. The reactionary elements were intent upon launching an armed rebellion, negating the agreement and detaching Tibet from China. Abetted by the imperialists, they continued to sabotage and create disturbances. Despite the central government's consistent persuasion and education, they finally launched an armed rebellion on March 10, 1959. But, contrary to their desires, this rebellion accelerated the destruction of Tibet's reactionary forces and brought Tibet onto the bright, democratic, socialist road sooner than expected.

This puts forward the standard Beijing bafflegab on Tibet—unchanged for the last 40 years. For maximum effect, try and listen to this stuff spoken out loud—with a shrill Chinese accent and lots of static.

China's Tibet—to reinforce the idea that Tibet is not a separate country, attach the word "China" to it. Chinese-produced tourist brochures and maps all specify "Tibet, China," or "China-Tibet."

counter-revolutionary—anyone who opposes official policy, an enemy of the state, or "committed with the goal of overthrowing the political power of the dictatorship of the proletariat and the socialist system". Despite an official Beijing repeal of this crime to placate international critics, those previously convicted of it still languish in prison. Now prisoners continue to be convicted—they are just held without charge or trial. Another term is "reactionary".

the Dalai—in June 1998, when President Clinton went on national Chinese television to say he thought the Dalai Lama was "an honest man," this must've been news to a billion Chinese—more used to hearing him cursed as a treasonous demon. In rhetoric, the Chinese often employ the abbreviated form "the Dalai"—which is considered insulting by the Tibetans. Followers of the Dalai Lama are called "the Dalai clique." Chinese news sources call the exiled leader a "splittist" and even "a major hindrance to the development of Tibetan Buddhism."

foreign imperialists—general all-purpose scapegoats. It is never specified which country they're from, but the popular candidates are "bad elements" from Taiwan, the USA, the UK and Germany. After the Dalai Lama received the Nobel Peace Prize, Norway was added to the blacklist.

hot topic—a newish term to denote anything like taxes or price increases that dissidents (reactionaries) supposedly capitalise on to foment unrest and demonstrations. Tibetan independence is, of course, very hot. So is the Dalai Lama—when asked what they think of him, most Chinese squirm and try to drop the subject like a hot potato.

internal affairs—Chinese shorthand for "back off, it's a domestic dispute, it's no concern of yours what we do behind closed doors—don't meddle in our affairs."

minority nationality—the minorities, or non-Hans, are viewed as being part of the big happy Han family, even if they don't speak the same language. A minority theme park outside Beijing presents them spending their time dancing and singing, rather like happy children. Within Tibet, however, the Tibetans are less politely referred to as "barbarians."

the Motherland—as well as referring to mainland China, this term embraces any parts of Asia that China wants to occupy. A number of China's neighbours have had trouble with this concept, including Russia, India, Taiwan, Vietnam and the Philippines. *Love the Motherland*—the name of a campaign for Chinese schoolchildren in 1998. *Splitting the Motherland*—an all-embracing heinous crime in Chinese eyes.

peaceful liberation—a reference to the entry of the People's Liberation Army into Tibet in 1950. Some Chinese sources admit that the invasion was in fact not entirely peaceful—some Tibetans resisted, so the PLA was reluctantly forced to machine-gun the hapless Tibetans to clear them out of the way. Mostly, however, the people loved the PLA, according to official sources.

re-education—mainly for monks, teaching them to see that black is white, and white is black, to say the Dalai Lama is bad, and to say the Chinese-chosen Panchen Lama is good. Sometimes monasteries are closed to tourism while this is in progress. The authorities might as well hang out a sign: Closed For Revision.

serfdom—the pre-1950 state of ordinary Tibetan, locked into exploitation by Tibetan nobility and monastic overseers. The Chinese broke down this class system. How? By replacing the Tibetan masters with harsher Chinese ones.

Soul Boy—the 11th Panchen Lama—a child into whose soul the 10th Panchen was reincarnated. The boy is the most hotly disputed reincarnate in Tibetan history. "Soul Boy" is a translation of the Chinese term applied to reincarnations, "Lingtong" (ling=soul, tong=boy/child). Tibetans find the translation annoying and misleading.

spiritual pollution—an odd term for an atheist nation to develop but this refers to interference from outside sources, such as Westerners, in the form of books, tapes, videos and so on. Some of these are "black" (political pollution), others "yellow" (pornographic pollution).

splittists—favourite Chinese term for those advocating independence for Tibet, or separatist. The idea here is that Motherland must stay whole—anybody that splits off a piece will ruin the symmetry. Other chunks where splittists seem to be hard at work include Xinjiang, Mongolia and Taiwan.

GLOSSARY

For details on popular icons, refer to *The Jokhang* (Lhasa)

ani—nun

Bon—pre-Buddhist religion of Tibet

chang—fermented barley-beer, a potent milky liquid

chorten—inverted bell-shaped shrine containing relics, or the ashes or embalmed body of a high lama (*stupa* in Sanskrit)

dharma—the word of the Buddha and his teachings

dorje—"thunderbolt"—a sceptre-like ritual object, made of brass, used against the powers of darkness

dzong—castle or fort, usually grafted onto a high ridge

gompa—active monastery

gonkhang—protector chapel at a monastery

kata—white greeting scarf, made of cotton or silk, presented on ceremonial occasions or offered at monasteries

kora—clockwise circuit of a sacred temple, lake or mountain

lakhang—chapel or inner sanctuary

lama—master spiritual teacher or guru

Losar—Tibetan New Year, usually celebrated around February

mandala—mystical circle (often enclosing a square) representing the Buddhist cosmos—used as a meditational aid (*chilkor* in Tibetan)

mani stone—stone tablet inscribed with mantra, often included as part of a mani-wall, composed of many such stones

mantra—sacred syllables repeated many times as part of spiritual practice, such as *om mani padme hum* ("hail to the jewel in the lotus heart"—a phrase addressed to the Buddha)

momo—Tibetan meat dumpling

Monlam—the Great Prayer Festival, around the time of Losar

nirvana—release from the cycle of mortal existence and rebirths

potrang—palace

prayer-flag—small flag printed with sacred prayers, activated by the power of the wind

prayer-wheel—large fixed wheel or small hand-held wheel containing mantras, activated by the spinning of the wheel

prostrator—pilgrim who measures the distance to a sacred destination with the length of his or her body, flung prone along the ground

rinpoche—"precious one"—a reincarnate lama, also known when young as a *tulku*

Saka Dawa—day of Buddha's enlightenment, celebrated around June

sutra—sacred text, written or spoken teachings of the Buddha

tanka—painted portable scroll, usually depicting a deity, on fine cotton or silk; can be used as a teaching aid

tantra—the "web of life", or vajrayana, is the form of Buddhism most often associated with Tibet—employs radical steps to seek enlightenment within a single lifetime

torma—ritual "cake" sculpted from tsampa and yak-butter

tsampa—ground barley-flour, a Tibetan staple food

tulku—reincarnate lama

yak—hairy high-altitude cattle, "cow with a skirt"

yabyum—tantric sexual pose of deity and consort, symbolising fusion of opposites—often misconstrued by Westerners